BrightRED Study Guide

CfE HIGHER

MODERN STUDIES

Caleb Marwick, Heidi Stoutjesdyk
and Derek Timpany

BrightRED
PUBLISHING

First published in 2015 by:
Bright Red Publishing Ltd
1 Torphichen Street
Edinburgh
EH3 8HX

A CIP record for this book is available from the British Library

ISBN 978-1-906736-66-8

With thanks to:
PDQ Digital Media Solutions Ltd (layout), Project One Publishing Solutions (editorial).

Cover design and series book design by Caleb Rutherford – e i d e t i c

Acknowledgements
Every effort has been made to seek all copyright holders. If any have been overlooked, then Bright Red Publishing will be delighted to make the necessary arrangements.

Permission has been sought from all relevant copyright holders and Bright Red Publishing is grateful for the use of the following:

Brian McNeil (CC BY-SA 3.0)[1] (p 10); John Lord (CC BY 2.0)[2] (p 11); Catherine Bebbington/UK Parliament Copyright (OPL)[3] (p 14); UK Parliament Copyright (OPL)[3] (p 14); UK Parliament Copyright (OPL)[3] (p 16); UK Parliament Copyright (OPL)[3] (p 17); Cover of the Enterprise and Regulatory Reform Act 2013 © Crown Copyright (OPL)[3] (p 17); sborisov/iStock.com (p 19); Image taken from http://www.number10.gov.uk/meet-the-pm © Crown Copyright (OGL)[4] (p 20); Liberal Democrats (CC BY-ND 2.0)[5] (p 22); Colin/Wikimedia Commons (CC BY-SA 4.0)[6] (p 24); Image taken from www.scottish.parliament.uk/PublicInformationdocuments/Committees-240613.pdf © Scottish Parliamentary Corporate Body – 2012 (Open Scottish Parliament Licence)[7] (p 26); Image taken from http://www.scotland.gov.uk/About/image-gallery/cabinet/cabinetmembers © The Scottish Government (OGL)[4] (p 27); Image taken from http://www.scotland.gov.uk/About/People/14944/Scottish-Cabinet/nicolasturgeonmsp © The Scottish Government (OGL)[4] (p 28); Image taken from https://www.flickr.com/photos/scottishgovernment/15844164455 © The Scottish Government (OGL)[4] (p 30); Image taken from http://www.scotland.gov.uk/About/image-gallery/cabinet/cabinetmembers © The Scottish Government (OGL)[4] (p 30); Image taken from https://www.flickr.com/photos/scottishgovernment/15223472814 © The Scottish Government (OGL)[4] (p 30); Scottish Futures Trust (p 33); Fangz (public domain) (p 41); Brythones (CC BY-SA 4.0)[6] (p 41); Two images by Barryob (CC BY-SA 3.0)[1] (pp 41 & 43); Brythones (public domain) (p 43); Brythones (CC BY-SA 4.0)[6] (p 43); Logo © Twitter, Inc (p 45); Logo © Facebook (p 45); Logo © YouTube, LLC (p 45); Logo © Mumsnet Limited (p 45); claudiodivizia/iStock.com (p 47); Scrap Trident Coalition (p 49); Image licenced by Ingram Image (p 53); gualtiero boffi/Shutterstock.com (p 54); gpointstudio/Shutterstock.com (p 54); Image taken from https://commons.wikimedia.org/wiki/File:Chancellor_of_the_Exchequer_George_Osborne_%286128163568%29.jpg © Foreign and Commonwealth Office (OGL)[4] (p 58); Zep 19 (CC BY 2.0)[2] (p 59); Andy Dean Photography/Shutterstock.com (p 62); wgmbh/iStock.com (p 63); Monkey Business Images/Shutterstock.com (p 65); Giuseppe Milo (CC BY 2.0)[2] (p 67); Image licenced by Ingram Image (p 68); Image licenced by Ingram Image (p 70); John Lord (CC BY 2.0)[2] (p 72); Image licenced by Ingram Image (p 75); George Rex (CC BY-SA 2.0)[8] (p 75); Lydia (CC BY 2.0)[2] (p 77); Ninian Reid (CC BY 2.0)[2] (p 78); Tony Webster (CC BY 2.0)[2] (p 80); Image licenced by Ingram Image (p 82); Caleb Rutherford e i d e t i c (p 83); Paul Birrell (CC BY-SA 2.0)[8] (p 84); rearwindowart/iStock.com (p 85); Front cover of 'Constitution of the People's Republic of China' © Foreign Languages Press (p 90); Chunhai Cao/iStock.com (p 90); VOA (public domain) (p 91); VitalyEdush/iStock.com (p 91); Ministerio de Relaciones Exteriores (CC BY-SA 2.0)[8] (p 91); VOA (public domain) (p 92); Senado Federal (CC BY 2.0)[2] (p 92); Pablo Tupin-Noriega (CC BY-SA 4.0)[6] (p 92); Chairman of the Joint Chiefs of Staff (CC BY 2.0)[2] (p 93); PromesaArtStudio/iStock.com (p 93); Miaow Miaow (CC BY-SA 3.0)[1] (p 94); Pasu Au Yeung (CC BY 2.0)[2] (p 95); David Shankbone/Wikimedia Commons (CC BY 3.0)[9] (p 97); Fu Wah International Group Logo (p 97); Startrooper (CC BY 2.0)[2] (p 97); JESP62/iStock.com (p 98); dmsl/iStock.com (p 102); Harald Groven (CC BY-SA 2.0)[8] (p 103); Image licenced by Ingram Image (p 105); Chensiyuan (CC BY-SA 3.0)[1] (p 106); MONUSCO Photos (CC BY-SA 2.0)[8] (p 107); 123ArtistImages/iStock.com (p 107); U.S. Army (CC BY 2.0)[2] (p 109); U. S. Government (public domain) (p 110); Lew Palm/Ezeu (public domain) (p 110); Lars Plougmann (CC BY-SA 2.0)[8] (p 110); Pumbaa80 (public domain) (p 111); UNMEER/Simon Ruf (CC BY-ND 2.0)[5] (p 113); ArnoldPlaton (CC BY-SA 3.0)[1] (p 115); Michelle Obama, Office of the First Lady (public domain) (p 115); Fabio Rodrigues Pozzebom/Agência Brasil (CC BY 3.0 BR)[10] (p 117); Embassy of Equatorial Guinea (CC BY-ND 2.0)[5] (p 117); Mooddoom/iStock.com (p 117); Simon Fraser University - University Communications (CC BY 2.0)[2] (p 120); Simon Davis/DFID - UK Department for International Development (p 121); Emblem of the African Union/Fair Use (p 123); Image licenced by Ingram Image (p 124); DonkeyHotey (CC BY 2.0)[2] (p 125); Republic of Korea (CC BY-SA 2.0)[8] (p 126); Pete Souza (public domain) (p 127); Mark Fischer (CC BY-SA 2.0)[8] (p 127); Wapcaplet (CC BY-SA 3.0)[1] (p 128); pressureUA/iStock.com (p 129); Keith Allison (CC BY-SA 2.0)[8] (p 131); Niloo138/iStock.com (p 131); Lwp Kommunikáció (CC BY 2.0)[2] (p 131); Fibonacci Blue (CC BY 2.0)[2] (p 131); United States State Department (public domain) (p 139); AdrianHancu/iStock.com (p 140); U.S. Air Force photo by Airman Miranda U. Moorer (public domain) (p 141).

[1] (CC BY-SA 3.0) http://creativecommons.org/licenses/by-sa/3.0/
[2] (CC BY 2.0)[2] http://creativecommons.org/licenses/by/2.0/
[3] (OPL) Contains Parliamentary information licensed under the Open Parliament Licence. http://www.parliament.uk/site-information/copyright/open-parliament-licence/
[4] (OGL) Contains public sector information licensed under the Open Government Licence v3.0. (http://www.nationalarchives.gov.uk/doc/open-government-licence/version/3/)
[5] (CC BY-ND 2.0) http://creativecommons.org/licenses/by-nd/2.0/
[6] (CC BY-SA 4.0) http://creativecommons.org/licenses/by-sa/4.0/
[7] Contains information licensed under the Open Scottish Parliament Licence v2.0 (http://www.scottish.parliament.uk/Fol/OpenScottishParliamentLicence.pdf)
[8] (CC BY-SA 2.0) http://creativecommons.org/licenses/by-sa/2.0/
[9] (CC BY 3.0) http://creativecommons.org/licenses/by/3.0/
[10] (CC BY 3.0 BR) http://creativecommons.org/licenses/by/3.0/br/deed.en

Printed and bound in the UK by Martins the Printers.

CONTENTS

INTRODUCTION

INTRODUCING CfE HIGHER MODERN STUDIES

Higher Modern Studies is one of the most popular subjects in the Scottish curriculum with over 10 000 young people sitting the qualification annually. In undertaking Higher Modern Studies you will have opportunities to work collaboratively with your classmates, while at the same time, you will enjoy the freedom to work independently and explore contemporary areas of personal interest.

Choosing Modern Studies at Higher level will provide you with the opportunity to study, in detail, either *Decision Making in Scotland* or *the United Kingdom*, provide you with an understanding of *Social Inequality* or *Crime and the Law*, and give you an insight into the important role played by a *G20 World Power* or the global impact of a significant *World Issue*.

As well as developing a deeper understanding of international contemporary political and socio-economic issues, you will improve your skills as a critical and reflective thinker. Most importantly, you will have the chance to further your research and information-handling skills, including identifying selectivity from complex sources, analysing a given view against detailed evidence and drawing extended conclusions.

THE BENEFITS OF STUDYING HIGHER MODERN STUDIES

Modern Studies plays a key role in developing political literacy and will help you to develop a number of higher-order thinking skills, such as analysis, synthesis and evaluation. You may also have the opportunity to take part in activities which will help to engage you in your studies, including debates, research projects and field trips/visits. In addition, you may hear from outside speakers such as politicians, people in industry or the public services, or those who work in the voluntary sector. By participating in discussions, delivering presentations, undertaking research activities and collaborating with others, you will develop a range of transferable skills – skills for life, skills for learning and skills for work – which will put you in a strong position to move into college, university or worthwhile employment.

EXTERNAL ASSESSMENT COMPONENT 1: QUESTION PAPER

A strong performance in the final examination (question paper) is important to achieve a top grade in Higher Modern Studies. The question paper is worth **60 marks**. This constitutes two-thirds of the total course assessment, and is graded A–D. The majority of marks within the question paper are allocated to assessing knowledge and understanding, with the remainder awarded for the application of information-handling skills. The question paper will measure the **breadth** and **application** of your learning, and challenge you to demonstrate to the examiner the extent to which you understand the subject. You will have **2 hours 15 minutes** to complete the question paper. Effective time management is crucial if you wish to secure a top grade. Practising assessment questions under timed conditions is excellent exam preparation.

Breadth and application (knowledge and understanding)

The question paper will test **your knowledge and understanding** in all three units of the Higher Modern Studies course:

- Democracy in Scotland and the United Kingdom (20 marks)
- Social Issues in the United Kingdom (20 marks)
- International Issues (20 marks)

You will be required to show the examiner the **breadth** of your knowledge and understanding by **giving detailed descriptions and explanations** and **demonstrating your ability to analyse and evaluate** complex social, political and economic issues. You must include **relevant** examples throughout your answers and aim to make them as **current** as possible.

contd

Challenge (skills)

The question paper will also provide you with the opportunity to **demonstrate higher-order thinking skills**. The **skills questions** require you to **use a range of sources** to:

- detect and explain the degree of objectivity/selectivity
- draw and support complex conclusions.

The question paper will also require you to **demonstrate skills by giving detailed explanations, analysis and evaluation of complex issues**.

EXTERNAL ASSESSMENT COMPONENT 2: ASSIGNMENT

The assignment is worth **30 marks** (⅓ of the total course assessment). It is a report based on your own research on a particular topic. Unlike the question paper, there is more emphasis on the assessment of skills as opposed to knowledge and understanding. After you have completed your research (approximately 8 hours of teaching and learning time), you will have up to **1 hour 30 minutes** to complete the assignment, which will be conducted in accordance with SQA guidelines *'under a high level of supervision and control'* within your school or college. To achieve success, you are required to:

- select an appropriate Modern Studies topic or issue
- research this topic, using a variety of sources/research methods
- synthesise and analyse the information that you have collected
- evaluate the reliability of the sources/research methods employed
- draw a conclusion using your knowledge and understanding
- recognise and show awareness of alternatives to the conclusion reached
- write up your findings in the form of a report.

THE MANDATORY UNITS

To achieve a course award in Modern Studies, you must also pass the mandatory units:

- Democracy in Scotland and the United Kingdom
- Social Issues in the United Kingdom
- International Issues.

These will be assessed internally by your teachers or lecturers. As in the question paper, you will be required to **demonstrate your knowledge and understanding** and **apply your skills**.

You will be required to demonstrate your knowledge and understanding of:

- political issues in Scotland or the United Kingdom
- social issues, focusing on either social inequality or crime and the law
- international issues, through the study of a world power or significant world issue.

Skills will also be assessed in each of the unit assessments, where you will use multiple sources of information to:

- detect and explain the degree of objectivity and selectivity
- make and justify decisions
- draw and support complex conclusions.

HOW THIS STUDY GUIDE WILL HELP YOU

This guide will give you the best possible chance of achieving success in the Higher Modern Studies course. It contains a range of information covering each part of the course and will increase your understanding of key topics and themes through the provision of high quality descriptions and current exemplification. Here you'll find important facts, key points to remember, useful websites and interesting video clips, with an extensive range of questions and activities. This Study Guide will support both your classroom learning and independent study, and put you in a strong position to realise your potential and succeed in the final external examination. Good luck!

ONLINE

This book is supported by the BrightRED Digital Zone - log on at www.brightredbooks.net for a world of tests, activities, videos and more.

EXAM SKILLS

In the Higher Modern Studies exam you will be asked questions drawing on your knowledge and understanding questions, and source-based questions to be answered using particular skills and techniques. The whole exam will last 2 hours and 15 minutes and it is recommended that you limit the amount of time you spend on each question depending on the mark allocation. For example, you should spend more time on a question worth 20 marks than on a question worth 12 marks.

SOURCE-BASED SKILLS QUESTIONS

The source-based skills questions you will meet in the exam are discussed at the end of each relevant chapter in this book:

- Democracy in Scotland and the UK: Objectivity skills (pp50–51)
- International Issues: Conclusions skills (p142)

Source-based skills questions can appear in any section of the exam. For example, 'objectivity' might be assessed in questions in the Social Issues section of the exam paper one year, but in the Political Issues section the following year.

There will only be one source-based skills question in any section of the exam, but you must answer it regardless of the topic. For example, you may have studied Crime and the Law as your Social Issue in class, but the source-based skills question in the exam is based on Social Inequalities. You still answer it. The topic of the question is technically irrelevant since your answer should be based entirely on the information provided in the sources and no other knowledge is required.

It is recommended that you spend no more than around 20 minutes on each source-based skills question, and there will be **two** in the exam. **Both** should be attempted, regardless of the topic.

DON'T FORGET

'Decision-making using sources' questions are only assessed within the Social Issues section of the course as Outcomes and not in the final exam, however, these techniques are useful for the Higher Assignment (see pp88–89).

EXTENDED RESPONSES

Essays are your opportunity to display your knowledge and understanding as well as your analysis and evaluation skills. You are expected to answer **three essay questions** in the exam.

Higher Modern Studies questions can use a variety of question stems; analyse, evaluate, discuss and to what extent. You will be given two options to choose from in each section based on topics you have studied. Only answer one of them in each section.

EXTENDED RESPONSE QUESTIONS (12 MARKS)

There are two question stems that require a 12-mark response: **analyse** and **evaluate**. Each has its own requirements but there are also similarities in how they should be tackled:

- You should have an introduction, a main body and a conclusion.
- Aim to complete at least four paragraphs and provide at least two relevant points of knowledge throughout.
- Each paragraph should describe an issue by making a point, explaining it and providing an example to support it.
- Aim to make an overall balanced argument using terms like 'however' or, 'on the other hand' to identify alternative arguments.
- Include a range of points, at least two relevant aspects of knowledge, detailed description or explanation and a range of relevant examples.
- Compare different views, consider possible consequences or make links between factors.

Marks are allocated based on the following criteria:

Knowledge, explanation and exemplification	up to 8 marks
Analysis/evaluation	up to a notional 4 marks

contd

- Aim to spend no longer than 20–25 minutes answering 12-mark questions in an exam.

Analyse questions

You are required to identify parts of an issue, the relationship between these parts and their relationships with the whole issue.

Example:

Analyse the ways in which citizens' views are represented within the political system of the world power you have studied.

Evaluate questions

You are required to make a judgement based on criteria and determine the value of an idea/statement/opinion. You must make an evaluative comment at the end of each paragraph stating a judgement or conclusion and placing a value on a point.

Example:

Evaluate the effectiveness of parliamentary representation in holding the government to account.

EXTENDED RESPONSE QUESTIONS (20 MARKS)

There are two question stems that require a 20-mark response: **discuss** and **to what extent**. Each has its own requirements but there are also similarities in how they should be tackled.

- Use a clear and consistent line of argument throughout.
- Use a clear and sensible structure, include a range of points with detailed explanation and relevant exemplification as well as extended analysis and evaluation.
- Each paragraph (up to 6) should describe an issue by making a point, explaining it and providing an example to support it.
- Aim to make an overall balanced argument using terms like 'however' or, 'on the other hand' to identify alternative arguments.
- Include an analytical, balanced conclusion.
- Aim to spend no longer than 40–45 minutes answering 20-mark questions in an exam.

Discuss questions

You will be given a statement to analyse and evaluate. You are required to communicate ideas and information on the issue in the statement made and analyse and evaluate different views on the issue.

Example:

International organisations have been successful in resolving a significant world issue. Discuss with reference to a world issue you have studied.

To what extent questions

You should analyse the issue in question and draw a conclusion or conclusions, making an evaluative judgement that you can support with evidence.

Example:

To what extent have UK Government policies tackled social inequalities?

Marks are allocated based on the following criteria:

Knowledge, explanation and exemplification	up to 8 marks
Analysis	up to 6 marks
Structure	up to 2 marks
Conclusions	up to 4 marks

 **ONLINE**

For example answers to the question types mentioned here, head to www. brightredbooks.net

THINGS TO DO AND THINK ABOUT

Head to the digital zone to look at some more examples of extended response questions.

THE ASSIGNMENT

AN OVERVIEW

The assignment is an opportunity to demonstrate the skills and knowledge gained within the context of a Modern Studies issue with minimum support. It is worth 30 marks. The assignment has two stages: **research** and **production of evidence**.

The research stage involves investigating your chosen issue and organising and finding sources. The production of evidence involves writing up your report under controlled conditions within 1 hour 30 minutes. You will be allowed to take a Research Evidence sheet into the write-up consisting of the information gathered during the research stage. This will be submitted to the SQA for marking along with the assignment and should be no more than two single-sided sheets of A4 paper. This should be mostly used for source information and each source used should be referenced at least once in your assignment. You should not simply copy from the Research Evidence but expand and develop the information presented and, most importantly, you must link to your knowledge of the topic. Synthesis is highly creditworthy.

DON'T FORGET

Make sure the evidence is clearly laid out and easy for the marker to see where references to sources have been made. You are not credited for anything which you copy directly from the Research Evidence sheet during the write up.

WHAT IS REQUIRED IN THE RESEARCH STAGE?

- Identify a Modern Studies issue about which there are alternative views, for example, Scottish Independence. Explain, in detail, the possible different courses of action.
- Research the issue using a range of sources of information. You must find these sources yourself.
- Analyse and synthesise information from your chosen sources. Consider at least **two** courses of action related to your chosen issue and provide detailed and synthesised evidence to support your analysis.
- Evaluate the usefulness and reliability of the sources you have chosen. For example, is there evidence of bias in any of them? You must make a clear and comparative judgement of **at least two** of the sources and make a clear statement about reliability.
- Reach a decision about the issue.
- Show detailed knowledge and understanding of the issue to support your decision.
- Show awareness of alternative views and explain why your decision is preferable.
- Organise your information into a report format. Marks are awarded for structure so it is recommended that you use headings to organise your information.

DON'T FORGET

Synthesis means to combine evidence from two or more sources to support a point.

SAMPLE REPORT FORMAT

Subject: State your chosen issue, for example, Membership of the EU

Options: Present possible decisions related to your chosen issue, for example, stay in the EU, leave the EU or renegotiate terms of EU membership

Author: Your name   **Date:**

Recipient: State the government official likely to deal with your report

This format can be expanded upon under each of the following headings to create a report relevant to your chosen issue.

Introduction

Outline the issue you have chosen by describing it and setting it in the context of today's society. You should identify three possible arguments (for, against and an alternative).

Example:

To decide I will evaluate all sides of the argument and come to a balanced conclusion using a range of sources.

contd

Decision

State your decision related to the title or hypothesis of your report.

Example:

Upon reviewing the evidence for each argument I have decided that my original hypothesis .... is the correct decision.

Methodology

Outline **at least two** of the sources used during your research and evaluate their reliability. You must come to a conclusion about which source was the most useful and explain why.

Example:

To investigate my chosen topic I used several different sources to incorporate the best possible evidence. These sources included newspaper articles, website articles, TV programmes and a survey. When conducting my research I found that the ....were useful because they were .... However, they were not entirely reliable because... I also found that ....

Arguments for

Provide **at least three** arguments with detailed explanations in favour of your decision.

Arguments against and rebuttal

Provide **at least three** arguments that may be presented against your decision and rebut (counter argue against) each using evidence from the sources.

Example:

*It has been argued that ...., however,...........................
Furthermore,...........................*

Provide **at least two** arguments that would be in favour of the third option you originally stated and rebut them.

Example:

It has also been suggested that ...., however,.......................................

Conclusion

Finally, summarise the main points in support of your decision in a paragraph.

Example:

*Overall, I reached my decision based on the fact that the evidence shows..............................
The evidence in favour of my decision out-weighs that which supports any alternative views.*

THINGS TO DO AND THINK ABOUT

In preparation for your final SQA-assessed assignment decide on **at least two** possible topics related to each of the three sections of the course. For each of these topics create a research question and gather three sources as per the outline above. For example:

Topic: Prisoners and the right to vote

Question: Should prisoners have the right to vote in the UK?

Sources: In favour: http://www.theguardian.com/politics/2015/feb/12/uk-prisoners-banned-voting-echr

Against: http://www.bbc.co.uk/news/uk-politics-20053244

Alternative: http://www.howardleaguescotland.org.uk/news/2013/december/prisoner-voting-and-independence-referendum

Some further topic examples could be:

- Minimum pricing on alcohol
- UK membership of the EU
- Smoking ban/cigarette packaging
- Minimum wage
- USA in the United Nations
- Changing the voting age
- Abolition of the House of Lords
- Means testing of more benefits
- Police Scotland and guns

THE UK CONSTITUTIONAL ARRANGEMENT

Decision-making for Scotland and the UK takes place at many levels. Developing an understanding of the way the different elements interact is key to developing your knowledge of Scottish and UK decision-making. There are also the National Assembly for Wales, and the Northern Ireland Assembly, each of which has legislative powers in some areas.

While the UK Parliament has evolved over centuries, the Scottish Parliament began in 1999. As such, the UK Parliament is largely run according to convention (tradition), while the Scottish Parliament was able to define its own procedures and structures. It began life with the **founding principles**.

Accountable	Parliament must answer to the public. The government must answer to the parliament.
Open and encourage participation	Parliament should be accessible. Parliament should involve the people of Scotland wherever possible.
Power sharing	Power is shared between the Scottish Government, Parliament, and people.
Equal opportunities	For all.

The founding principles of the Scottish Parliament

THE EUROPEAN UNION AND DECISION-MAKING FOR SCOTLAND

The European Union (EU) makes many policies which all EU member states (including the UK) have to adopt. In addition, there are **reserved matters** – decisions which the UK Parliament makes and which apply to the whole of the UK (including Scotland), and **devolved matters** – decisions which the Scottish Parliament can make for Scotland and which only apply to Scotland.

EU matters	Reserved matters	Devolved matters
Free trade between Member States	Benefits and social security	Agriculture, forestry and fisheries
Common Commercial Policy: trade rules with outside EU	Immigration	Education and training
Competition law: avoiding firms abusing power	Defence	Environment
	Foreign policy	Health and social services
Internal market: freedom to move, live, study and trade	Employment	Housing
	Broadcasting	Law and order (including the licensing of air weapons)
Trans-European networks (e.g. roads and railways)	Trade and industry	
	Nuclear energy, oil, coal, gas and electricity	Local government
Energy (e.g. banning energy-inefficient light bulbs)	Consumer rights	Sport and the arts
	Data protection	Tourism and economic development
Areas of freedom, security and justice (e.g. human rights)	The Constitution	Many aspects of transport
Common Fisheries Policy		Renewable energy

Some policy areas decided at different levels

THE UK'S CONSTITUTIONAL FUTURE

One key area of cooperation between the Scottish and UK Parliaments concerns the constitutional future of the UK. The Independence Referendum of 18th September 2014 was given legal standing by a **Section 30 Order** (an exception to the rules of the **Scotland Act 1998**), agreed by the UK Parliament in January 2013.

After the 'No' vote, the UK Government established the **Smith Commission** headed by Lord Smith of Kelvin, to investigate further powers for the Scottish Parliament.

The Commission's recommendations were adopted into draft proposals (a **Command Paper**) published by the UK Government in January 2015. The Conservatives, Labour and the Liberal Democrats all pledged to make sure that the new Scotland Bill would become law after the 2015 UK General Election, whichever party or parties form the government.

An EU membership referendum by 2017 was a manifesto promise of the Conservative Party before the 2015 UK General Election. However, the leaders of the SNP and Plaid Cymru have both stated their belief that the UK should only leave if all four countries (England, Scotland, Wales and Northern Ireland) each vote to leave.

contd

AREAS OF COOPERATION BETWEEN THE BODIES

In January 2015, it was announced that the power to change the voting age to 16 would be devolved in time for the 2016 Scottish Election, in a 'fast-track' process. This is in advance of the new Scotland Bill being introduced to the UK Parliament.

In May 2014, Nicola Sturgeon (then Deputy First Minister) announced that the power to set the cap (limit) on Discretionary Housing Payments was to be devolved to Scotland, which would allow the Scottish Government to use some of its budget to offset the effects of the UK Government's ending of the spare room subsidy (the so-called **Bedroom Tax**).

Scotland, the UK and the EU all cooperate in fisheries policy. While the UK is the EU Member State, the Scottish Government usually sends its own representatives to EU discussions as fisheries are a **devolved matter**. However, in November 2014, the UK Government sent an English Lord to speak at an EU Council fisheries meeting, 95% of which would affect Scotland: a decision then Scottish First Minister Alex Salmond described as a 'travesty'.

Scottish fishing boats in Fraserburgh

AREAS OF CONFLICT BETWEEN THE BODIES

One key area of debate after the Independence Referendum is what the devolution of further powers for Scotland means for decision-making in the UK Parliament. Having Scottish MPs voting for laws which do not apply in Scotland, such as the English education system or health services (while English MPs have no say over devolved matters), has been controversial for decades – this is the so-called **West Lothian Question**, named by West Lothian MP Tam Dalyell in 1977. After the Independence Referendum, four proposals (three Conservative and one Liberal Democrat) were introduced to the UK Parliament about having only 'English votes for English laws' (EVEL). In January 2015, First Minister Nicola Sturgeon said that any SNP MPs would vote on English health laws – something they don't normally do – if it would have an effect on the Scottish budget.

In 2005, the European Court of Human Rights ruled that prisoners should have the right to vote in elections in the UK. Two UK governments failed to deliver this before the 2015 UK General Election. Scottish prisoners were not allowed to vote in the Independence Referendum after the UK Supreme Court threw out two prisoners' attempt to overturn the ban in July 2014.

In May 2012, the Scottish Parliament passed the Alcohol Minimum Pricing Bill, which would set a minimum price of 50p per unit of alcohol. However, The Scotch Whisky Association (which represents 90% of the production industry) successfully brought a case against this legislation, believing the law would break EU free trade law, and the case was referred to the Court of Justice of the European Union in April 2014. This could mean that the implementation of the law could be delayed until as late as 2016, or indeed deemed to break EU law and stopped altogether.

🗨 THINGS TO DO AND THINK ABOUT

1 Examine the passage of the Scotland Bill 2015 closely.
   a Did the Bill get passed as introduced?
   b Who (if anyone) raised concerns or proposes amendments?
   c Do you feel it meets the Smith Commission proposals?
2 Keep track of the Scottish Minimum Alcohol Pricing Bill. Does the EU block it?
3 Does the UK Parliament adopt similar legislation to the Scottish Parliament?
4 Essay practice: Evaluate the view that the Scottish Parliament has the power to make the most important decisions for Scotland.

THE ROLE OF REPRESENTATIVES

In a representative democracy the electorate give decision-makers the right to speak and act on their behalf. This section details the responsibilities and roles of elected representatives.

As it is a **representative democracy**, the UK's public trusts those they elect to speak and act on their behalf in parliament (UK, Scottish, Welsh or Northern Irish).

PRESSURE ON REPRESENTATIVES

Views of constituents

M(S)Ps are elected to represent their constituents – the people who live in their constituency. If they do not vote and behave in a way in which their constituents are happy with, they may not win re-election. This can conflict with their party's wishes, or indeed their governmental role. Iain Duncan Smith, Work and Pensions Secretary, signed a petition to maintain services at a hospital in his constituency. In cases such as this, M(S)Ps (and government ministers) need to state clearly that they are acting on behalf of their constituents, not the department they are minister of. As M(S)Ps have to represent all of their constituents – even those who did not vote for them – it can be very tricky to keep everyone happy.

Party whips

In the UK Parliament, party whips are MPs or Lords appointed to make sure that enough members of their party vote the way that the leadership wants them to. Every week, whips send out a mailing ('The Whip') to all of their party's members, which contains details of all upcoming parliamentary activities. When the whips require MPs to vote a certain way, they underline the whip with one, two or three lines.

Three-line whips are the most important, and are usually used for significant votes. The closer the vote is likely to be, the more important the job of the whips. If MPs vote against a three-line whip they may be expected to resign from a government position. In some cases, they may be suspended or expelled from the party and have to sit officially as an independent MP until the whip is restored. Expulsion from the party may also mean they can only stand as an independent in the next general election, so parties have a lot of power over the MPs divisions.

Pairing is a convention whereby MPs from opposing parties agree not to vote in agreed **divisions** (votes). This is an informal arrangement, but must be agreed to by the whips (who check that the deal is followed). Whips rarely allow this for important vote.

Personal views

Representatives must balance party pressures against their own beliefs and values. Their own point of view may be very different from that of their constituents, and/or their party's. In 2014, Baroness Warsi, Foreign Office minister and former Conservative Party chairman, resigned from the government as she felt their policy on the crisis in Gaza was morally indefensible.

MPs and ministers can also be moved from their government position because of their beliefs. Justine Greening was moved from Transport Secretary to International Development Secretary in David Cameron's September 2012 Cabinet reshuffle because of her vocal opposition to government policy on the expansion of Heathrow Airport.

FACT

Conservative MP Stewart Jackson resigned his position as Private Parliamentary Secretary for the Northern Ireland Secretary in October 2011, after defying a three-line whip and voting for a referendum of UK membership of the EU (with 80 other Conservative MPs). He said: "Some things are more important than party preferment. The bond of trust with my constituents"

VIDEO LINK

Head to www. brightredbooks.net to watch Baroness Warsi's resignation speech.

PRIVATE MEMBER'S BILLS

One way in which MPs and MSPs can represent their constituents', personal, or party's views is by introducing a **Private Member's Bill** (called a **Member's Bill** in the Scottish Parliament). This allows MPs a chance to limit the government's dominance of the laws made by parliament. In March 2010 the Offences Aggravated by Prejudice (Scotland) Act, which classifies hate crimes against disabled, lesbian, gay, bisexual and transgender people as being as serious as racist crimes, came into force in Scotland. Introduced by Green MSP Patrick Harvie in 2008, it received votes from MSPs from all parties. In March 2014 the Citizenship (Armed Forces) Act, introduced as a Private Member's Bill by MP Jonathan Lord (Conservative, Woking), received Royal Assent. This altered the rules for applying for British citizenship for members or former members of the armed forces.

However, Private Member's Bills often fall (are not enacted), or are adopted by the government (such as Neil Findlay's bill on lobbying, discussed later).

BEHAVE APPROPRIATELY

One of the basic characteristics which people look for in M(S)Ps is that they behave in a way appropriate for public figures. This responsibility has not always been fulfilled. Eric Joyce MP was elected to serve Falkirk as a Labour Candidate in 2005 and 2010. However, in February 2012, he was stripped of the **party whip**, after being charged with three counts of common assault after allegedly striking at least four MPs in the House of Parliament's Strangers' Bar. He resigned from the Labour Party in March 2012, and began sitting as an Independent. Since then, he has been involved in a number of other incidents, including being found guilty of assaulting two teenagers in a shop in London. He stood down in the 2015 election.

In Scotland, Bill Walker was elected as SNP MSP for Dunfermline in the 2011 Scottish Parliament Election. In March 2012, he was suspended by the SNP after allegations that he had subjected his three former wives to domestic abuse. He was jailed for 12 months in September 2013, after being found guilty of all 23 charges of assault and one of breach of the peace (all of which he denied). He had resigned as an (Independent) MSP on 7th September 2013, after what he called a 'media onslaught', and 94 MSPs had backed a motion introduced by Willie Rennie (Liberal Democrat) on 23rd August 2013: 'That the parliament believes that Bill Walker MSP should vacate his seat in the parliament immediately.'

The UK Government introduced the Recall of MPs Bill 2014–15, which would trigger a recall petition if an MP is sentenced to prison, or is suspended from the House of Commons for at least 21 sitting days. If 10% of party members eligible to appoint candidates sign the petition, a **by-election** would be held.

CHECKS AND BALANCES IN THE POLITICAL SYSTEM

Within the UK and Scottish Parliaments, there are a number of checks and balances to prevent excessive dominance by one person or party. You may be aware of a similar system in US politics. Representatives, whether in government or opposition, must play their part in this process. Full discussion of the checks and balances is given elsewhere in the book.

DON'T FORGET

In order to be an effective representative, there must be an element of trust and respect from the constituents.

ONLINE TEST

Head to www. brightredbooks.net and test yourself on the role of representatives.

ONLINE

The 'Checks and balances in the UK and Scottish political systems' table on www.brightredbooks.net gives an overview of all the checks and balances in each system.

THINGS TO DO AND THINK ABOUT

1   As you work through this chapter, note down examples of the checks and balances in the Scottish and/or UK systems.

ROLE OF THE UK LEGISLATURE: THE PARLIAMENT CHAMBER

MPs are elected to represent their constituents in the House of Commons. Nowhere is this more visible than in the chamber of the House of Commons.

ONLINE

Read about Nigel Dodds being expelled from Commons chamber at www. brightredbooks.net

DEBATES

Debates in the House of Commons give MPs the chance to formally discuss bills and deliberate issues brought forward by an MP from the government or opposition. Firstly, the MP in question moves a motion (introduces the subject) in the **First Reading**, and the Speaker repeats this.

The motion is then debated by all the MPs who are present. MPs can raise their constituents' concerns during this discussion. MPs take it in turns to speak, and there are strict rules (**Standing Orders**) which the Speaker enforces.

This discussion is often heated, so the Speaker must take charge. MPs who use **unparliamentary language** (not speaking in a manner that the Speaker deems to be appropriate) may be disciplined by the Speaker and/or their party. In July 2013 Nigel Dodds of the Democratic Unionist Party was expelled from the House of Commons for describing the Northern Ireland Secretary's answer to a question as 'deliberately deceptive'.

ONLINE

Read 'Hillsborough papers: David Cameron "profoundly sorry"' at www. brightredbooks.net

MPs can hold the government to account during these debates, and these can be an occasion when ministers apologise for their earlier actions. In September 2012 Prime Minister David Cameron apologised to the families of the 96 people killed in the Hillsborough Disaster as 'these families have suffered a double injustice': not just their deaths, but allegations that the victims had in some way contributed to their own deaths.

Divisions

Debates may or may not be concluded by holding a **division** (vote). Because the government usually has a majority of seats in the House of Commons, it is expected that the government will win most divisions.

Divisions, however, give MPs from opposition parties, and indeed from within the government, the chance to strongly express their own or their constituents' opposing view. A defeat in a Commons vote can be embarrassing for, and undermine, a Prime Minister. In August 2013, the Conservative–Liberal Democrat Coalition Government lost a Commons vote on taking military action against the Syrian Government 285–272, after 30 Conservative and 9 Liberal Democrat MPs **rebelled** (voted against the government's motion).

Divisions do not only affect the government, however. Labour MP Jim Fitzpatrick resigned from the **Shadow Cabinet** the day before this division, as he did not support Ed Miliband's policy on Syria, as he was 'opposed to military intervention in Syria, full stop'.

Other types of debate

Adjournment Debates are general debates which allow MPs to hold general debates on a topic without the need to hold a **division**. These can allow MPs to debate government

contd

policy without reaching a decision on it, or allow backbench MPs to raise a constituency issue. There is a 30-minute Adjournment Debate held at the end of each day's sitting.

MPs can request that the House of Commons consider an issue urgently by applying to the **Speaker** for an **Emergency Debate**. However, these are rarely granted. Between May 2012 and September 2014 only 1 out of 6 requests was granted, and that was a debate on 'Royal Charter on Press Conduct' applied for by Prime Minister David Cameron.

QUESTION TIME

Question Time is an opportunity for MPs to question government ministers about decisions they have made or matters which are under their department's remit. This takes place for one hour, Monday to Thursday, as the first part of parliament's working day. Question Time allows MPs to keep a close check on the government, and the work they are doing. In June 2014, Ian Murray (Labour, Edinburgh South) asked Jenny Willott, Parliamentary Under-Secretary of State for Business, Innovation and Skills, about the government's track record of punishing companies which had broken minimum wage law: 'Just like the Chancellor's hollow promise to increase the national minimum wage to £7, is this not just another example of the government failing to stand up for the lowest paid against rogue employers?'

The minister always has the chance to respond, though, and will usually be very well prepared to answer any question, as they must be submitted three days in advance. In this case, Ms Willott replied fully, mentioning the government was 'increasing fourfold the penalty that employers have to pay'.

Prime Minister's Question Time (PMQs)

For half an hour from midday every Wednesday, it is the turn of the Prime Minister to be questioned by MPs from the opposition and government. The Leader of the Opposition can ask six questions in total, while other MPs may only ask one question (which must be submitted in advance), plus a **supplementary question** on any subject. These supplementary questions in particular give opposition MPs the chance to ask questions which the PM has not seen.

In March 2014, Labour MP Ian Murray asked: 'Are we really all in this together when the Prime Minister thinks that some public sector workers do not even deserve a 1% pay rise while he signs off on bumper pay rises of up to 40% for his own government's special advisers?'

However, the Prime Minister has the benefit of extensive research carried out by government departments, who try to ensure that he has a good grounding on any topic which is likely to come up. In the above example, the PM replied: 'Let me answer the honourable Gentleman very directly: under our plans, everyone in the NHS will get at least a 1% pay rise, and this is something I was told was supported by the Labour party. This is what the leader of the Labour party said…'

Occasionally, an MP simply seeks to undermine or humiliate the Prime Minister and their government. In February 2013, during the horsemeat scandal, Labour MP Anas Sarwar used PMQs to suggest that the Prime Minister's answers may be '100% bull', much to the other MPs' (and PM's) amusement.

THINGS TO DO AND THINK ABOUT

1 Watch a recent edition of Prime Minister's Question Time.
   a Note down the topics they are quizzed upon.
   b Do they seem to respond successfully?
2 Find a recent example of your MP contributing in the Commons chamber in the ways described above.
3 Essay practice: Evaluate the view that parliamentary representatives have little influence in decision-making. You should refer to parliamentary representatives in Scotland, the UK or both in your answer.

ONLINE

Read more about this by clicking the link 'PMQs: Cameron teased on horsemeat and "100% bull"' at www.brightredbooks.net

DON'T FORGET

Debates and divisions are two of the most high-profile ways in which MPs can represent their constituents.

ONLINE TEST

Want to revise the parliament chamber? Test yourself at www.brightredbooks.net

ROLE OF THE UK LEGISLATURE: COMMITTEES

SELECT COMMITTEES

Select Committees are responsible for **scrutinising** (examining closely) the work of the government. There are Select Committees in both the Commons and the Lords. Commons Select Committees are usually responsible for a government department, while the Lords' Committees concentrate on four main areas: Europe, science, economics and the UK constitution.

Select Committees have a minimum of 11 members and their Chairs, who are elected by MPs in a secret ballot. The membership of committees (when taken together) is designed to reflect the share of seats in the Commons. The membership of each committee is agreed after each election through negotiations between party whips (sometimes called the **usual channels**). Select Committee membership can, however, be changed between elections. The government would like to have control of all committees in key policy areas, but these negotiations mean it is difficult for any party to have the say it would like to.

A Select Committee

MPs join committees either because they are experienced in that policy area, or it covers an area their constituents have an interest in. Ian Murray MP (Labour, Edinburgh South) has been a member of the Business, Innovation and Skills Committee, Environmental Audit Committee and the Committees on Arms Export Controls.

Commons Select Committees hold **inquiries** into the spending, policies and administration within their policy area. They gather written evidence, and can call for oral evidence. Written evidence can be submitted by anyone, while witnesses are always called by the committee.

Select Committees can summon government ministers to appear and justify actions in their department or indeed their government. This can be a very difficult meeting for the minister, as the issues on which they are questioned are often of high public interest. In September 2012, Home Secretary Theresa May was summoned to appear before the Home Affairs Select Committee in the wake of the Rotherham sexual abuse scandal. She said: 'National government must also, and will, assist. That is why I will chair meetings with other ministers... to look at what happened in Rotherham.'

Even the Prime Minister can be called to appear, if the committee deems it necessary. PM David Cameron was called to appear before the Liaison Select Committee in May 2014, and was quizzed by Labour MP Keith Vaz about his plans for migration to the UK. He stated: 'Getting migration figures down is much harder work, because there are a lot of different elements to migration.'

Committees publish their findings on the UK Parliament website, and the government usually has 60 days to reply to the committee's recommendations, either in a self-published report (**Command Paper**), or a memo to the committee.

Committees give the legislature the power to demand answers and responses from the government. However, the government responses are not always to the committee's liking (as in the case study below).

Joint Committees

Joint Committees are made up of MPs and members of the House of Lords. They work in a very similar way to Select Committees. Two Joint Committees – Human Rights, and Statutory Instruments (which examines legislation) – meet regularly.

FACT ✓

After the 2015 Election, SNP MPs Pete Wishart and Angus MacNeil were appointed as chairs of the Scottish Affairs Committee and Energy and Climate Change Committee respectively.

contd

Case Study: Home Affairs Select Committee and Drugs Policy

In 2012, the Home Affairs Committee decided to investigate UK drugs policy.

22 April: Comedian and former drug addict Russell Brand called as one of many witnesses. He states: 'what I think we need to do is address the social, mental and spiritual problems that are leading young people, or people of all ages, into taking drugs.'

3 July: Right Hon Kenneth Clarke QC MP, Lord Chancellor and Secretary of State for Justice, gives evidence.

3 December: Committee findings are published, including a recommendation for a 'fundamental review of all UK drugs policy', including exploring the idea of decriminalisation, through the establishment of a Royal Commission.

10 December: Prime Minister David Cameron rejected this proposal, stating:

'I don't support decriminalisation. We have a policy which actually is working in Britain. Drugs use is coming down, the emphasis on treatment is absolutely right, and we need to continue with that to make sure we can really make a difference. Also, we need to do more to keep drugs out of our prisons.

'These are the government's priorities and I think we should continue with that rather than have some very, very long-term Royal Commission.'

VIDEO LINK

Watch Russell Brand giving evidence at www.brightredbooks.net

ONLINE

Read more about Cameron rejecting calls for a Royal Commission on drugs at www.brightredbooks.net

LEGISLATIVE COMMITTEES

After a bill has had its First and Second Reading, the bill is normally passed to a specially-formed legislative committee for consideration. These may be Public Bill Committees, Private Bill Committees, or general legislative committees. These committees take written evidence (which anyone may submit), and may call for written and/or oral evidence from witnesses. The first witness is usually the government minister of the relevant department.

Legislative Committees have between 16 and 50 members, and membership is shared between the parties in proportion to the number of MPs each party has. This means that overall there is always a government majority of committee members.

MPs can seek to limit the government's power by amending bills which the government puts forward in parliament. These may or may not be accepted by the committee. In June 2012, Ian Murray (Labour, Edinburgh South) proposed an amendment to the government's Enterprise and Regulatory Reform Bill:

'The purpose of our amendments is to make employment tribunals less complicated... Business is demanding that, the trade unions are demanding a simpler and more effective procedure, employers are demanding that, and employees are also demanding it.'

Because the government usually dominates the membership of a committee, it is often difficult for opposition MPs to have their amendments passed. In the above example, Ian Murray's amendment was defeated 13–7, by a Committee chaired by a Conservative MP and attended by 11 Conservative MPs and one Liberal Democrat.

Enterprise and Regulatory Reform Act 2013

DON'T FORGET

While both Select and Legislative Committees can call witnesses and summon government ministers to testify, only Legislative Committees can directly amend legislation.

THINGS TO DO AND THINK ABOUT

1 Find an up-to-date example of a minister being called as a witness in a Select Committee inquiry.
   a Was the committee supportive of their recent actions?
   b How did the minister cope with the questions?
2 Find examples of your constituency MP acting in committees:
   a asking a question in a select committee
   b proposing an amendment in a legislative committee.
3 Essay practice: Analyse the role of committees in influencing decision-making. You should refer to committees in Scotland or the UK or both in your answer.

ONLINE TEST

How well have you learned about this topic? Head to www.brightredbooks.net and take the test.

ROLE OF THE UK LEGISLATURE: THE HOUSE OF LORDS

Unlike the Scottish Parliament, the UK Parliament has two houses: the House of Commons and the House of Lords. This type of system is called a **bicameral** legislature.

MEMBERSHIP OF THE HOUSE OF LORDS

There are around 800 Members of the House of Lords. There are three types of members, or **peers**, all of whom are unelected.

Most members of the Lords are **life peers**, officially appointed by the Queen. They are either recommended by the Prime Minister, or the independent Appointments Commission. Those recommended by the Prime Minister have been called **working peers**, and are expected to frequently attend the House or Lords. Experienced MPs are often appointed as working peers after leaving the House of Commons. The Appointments Commission is an independent body which recommends people based on their expertise, knowledge and experience in a specific area: like health or business. The Commission tries to 'ensure that the House of Lords represents the diversity of the people of the UK.'

Before 1999, most peers inherited their title from a parent, and this title was passed down through the generations. Since 1999, these titles – **excepted hereditary peers** – became life peerages, and upon leaving the house (or dying) each peer's place is filled by an election. Only previous life peers are eligible for election, and those from within the leaving peer's party can vote.

The final 26 peers are **bishops** from the Church of England – the only religion officially represented on the basis of their religion. The bishops (such as the Archbishop of Canterbury) maintain their peerage as long as they stay in their position, and their peerage passes on when they retire or leave the church.

Hereditary peers and working peers will be party-affiliated (either government or **opposition**), while those recommended by the Appointments Commission and bishops will be non-party affiliated: **crossbenchers**.

Party/group	Peers	
Conservative	224	Government 224
Labour	213	Opposition 328
Liberal Democrat	101	
Other Parties	14	
Crossbench	178	Neutral 226
Non-affiliated	22	
Bishops	26	
Total	778	Non-government 554

House of Lords membership (May 2015)

Lords Reform

Labour, the Conservatives, and the Liberal Democrats all included **reform** of (change to) the House of Lords in their 2010 UK General Election manifestos. The SNP wanted to scrap the House of Lords completely.

In June 2012, the Coalition Government introduced the House of Lords Reform Bill, with the intention of reducing the numbers of peers and introducing an element of election to the appointment of peers. This would have given a House of Lords consisting of 360 elected members (elected to serve one 15-year term in batches of 120, every five years); 90 appointed members; up to 12 Church of England Bishops; and any ministerial members (of the government).

However, in August 2012, Deputy Prime Minister Nick Clegg (Liberal Democrat) announced the Bill would be abandoned, as he saw that it would not pass without the Conservatives guaranteeing it time in the House of Commons in a **programme motion**.

THE WORK OF THE HOUSE OF LORDS

The House of Lords exists to work in partnership with the House of Commons, but is independent of it. It assists in making laws, scrutinising bills, and scrutinising the actions of the government.

contd

Making laws

Members of the House of Lords can introduce Private Members' Bills, in the same way that MPs can. If a Private Members' Bill in the Lords is supported by an MP, it can continue in the Commons. Similarly to MP's Members' Bills, it is highly unlikely that Private Member's Bills from the Lords will be granted much time in the Commons. Instead, introducing a Private Members' Bill is used to ensure the topic is debated in the Lords.

Scrutinising bills

The biggest single part of the work of the House of Lords is scrutinising bills, or proposed laws. Around half of the time in the House of Lords is spent doing this. As the UK Parliament is a **bicameral** legislature, and the House of Commons is usually governed by a majority government, the House of Lords performs a crucial role in limiting the power of the UK Government. As peers don't have to face re-election, they can give a long-term, expert opinion on legislation, without worrying about the short-term whim of the electorate.

Peers may also join Select Committees, and help investigate proposed new laws.

In January 2014, the House of Lords voted 180–130 to end the debate on the government's EU (Referendum) Bill at committee stage. This meant the bill failed, and David Cameron was forced to threaten to use the Parliament Act to force the bill through parliament (which would allow for an in-out EU membership referendum before 2017).

Since the Parliament Act 1949, the Lords cannot amend or delay Money Bills (bills about taxes or public money). Money Bills will receive Royal Assent even if the Lords doesn't pass them. It also allows for parliament to reintroduce a bill in the next parliamentary session, where it can pass unopposed.

Under the **Salisbury Convention**, the House of Lords does not vote against **manifesto** policies of the government, as this would be seem to directly undermine the wishes of the electorate.

Questions

Peers can keep a close eye on the work of the government by questioning a government spokesperson at Question Time, usually at the start of business on Mondays to Thursday. Peers can either ask questions in person (up to four each, plus supplementary questions), or submit them in writing.

In December 2014, Baroness Jones of Whitchurch (Labour) asked the question: 'To ask Her Majesty's Government what assessment they have made of the impact of child poverty on children's early years educational development.' Lord Nash (Conservative), Parliamentary Under-Secretary of State for Schools, replied: 'This government is improving children's outcomes through key reforms including additional funding for disadvantaged children...'

Debates

In debates, peers add their considerable experience to the discussion of government proposals. In December 2014, Lord Alan Sugar spoke in the debate during the Second Reading of the government's Small Business, Enterprise and Employment Bill, stating: 'This Bill does not go far enough in offering practical, common-sense solutions for small businesses.' Famous from his TV show *The Apprentice*, Lord Sugar was appointed as an expert on business. His criticism made the government re-examine the details of the bill.

Motions of no confidence

The House of Lords can also debate a **motion of no confidence** in the government. This has only happened once in the modern era. In December 1993, an opposition **motion of no confidence** was defeated 95–282.

THINGS TO DO AND THINK ABOUT

1 Find a recent example of the House of Lords:
  a introducing a bill
  b voting on a bill
  c asking a government minister a question.
2 Essay practice: Evaluate the importance of the House of Lords in decision-making in the UK.

FACT

Members of the Lords submit about 10 000 written questions to the government annually.

VIDEO LINK

What is the House of Lords? Watch the clip at www.brightredbooks.net

DON'T FORGET

Peers are there to add a long-term, experienced opinion to bills, policies and decisions.

ONLINE TEST

Head to www.brightredbooks.net and test yourself on this topic

ROLE OF THE UK EXECUTIVE: THE PRIME MINISTER

The Prime Minister is the person asked by the monarch (Queen) to form the government after a UK General Election. By **convention** (what normally or traditionally has happened), the Queen will ask the leader of the party which wins most seats to form the government. David Cameron became UK Prime Minister on 12 May 2010, after Gordon Brown resigned when it became clear that the Conservatives and Liberal Democrats had agreed to form a **coalition** government. In the 2015 Election, the Conservatives won a majority and he was asked by the Queen to remain as Prime Minister, and form a government.

ONLINE

Check out the Queen's Speech from 2015 at www.brightredbooks.net

FACT

When David Cameron announced his final coalition **Cabinet** in July 2014, he appointed Liberal Democrats to 5 of the 22 roles, including Alistair Carmichael (Liberal Democrat, Orkney and Shetland) as Scottish Secretary.

FACT

Margaret Thatcher appointed an average of 18 peers per year; Tony Blair an average of 37; David Cameron (by August 2014) an average of 43.

POWERS OF THE PRIME MINISTER

Once appointed into the position, the Prime Minister has a range of powers.

Leader of government

The Prime Minister is responsible for the overall direction of the UK Government. At the start of each parliamentary session, or after each election, the Queen delivers the **Queen's Speech** at the State Opening of parliament. This speech is actually written by the government, and outlines their proposed policies and legislation. On 27 May 2015, the Queen's Speech outlined the government's programme of 26 new bills, including an EU referendum by the end of 2017, an income tax freeze, and a right-to-buy for housing association tenants.

However, these bills must pass through full parliamentary **scrutiny**, including the committee system, before becoming law. In July 2012, the House of Lords Reform Bill was dropped after the government had removed a programme motion (giving it parliamentary time), and then Deputy Prime Minister Nick Clegg (Liberal Democrat) realised it was not going to make it through the legislative process.

Appointment

The Prime Minster has the power to choose whom they wish to appoint as members of the Cabinet. Usually, the winning party has a majority of seats, and the Cabinet will all be appointed from one party. However, when appointing a **coalition** government (e.g. 2010-2015), the Prime Minister has to negotiate with the leader of the coalition party about who should be appointed, and to which roles.

The Prime Minister can also appoint **life peers** to the House of Lords. This allows the Prime Minister to alter the balance of power to a certain extent. There are often allegations of **cronyism** (appointing friends or allies), such as when David Cameron appointed Michael Farmer a life peer in August 2014. Farmer has donated nearly £6.5m to the Conservatives, and is the party treasurer.

Representing the UK

The Prime Minister is responsible for representing the UK to the rest of the world. This can be in official or unofficial roles.

It was David Cameron as Prime Minister who signed the Edinburgh Agreement: the agreement with the Scottish Government which allowed for the 2014 Scottish Independence Referendum.

In January 2015, David Cameron, in a joint press conference with German Chancellor Angela Merkel, stated that he was 'convinced' he would be able to 'fix the problems' in the UK's relationship with the European Union (EU).

LIMITS TO THE PRIME MINISTER'S POWERS

The Prime Minister's powers rely on them maintaining an image as a strong and competent leader. There are a number of ways this can be called into question.

Prime Minister David Cameron

Prime Minister's Questions (PMQs)

For half an hour from noon every Wednesday, the Prime Minister is quizzed by MPs from the opposition and their own government's party or parties. This is seen as the most confrontational aspect of the UK Parliament's work, home to heated debates mainly between the leader of the opposition and the Prime Minister.

Questions for PMQs can be submitted by any MP up until three days before PMQs. The session usually starts with the **open question**, a routine question about the Prime Minister's plans for that day. The MP who asked this question is then allowed to ask a **supplementary question**: their real question. Many MPs will submit the open question each week, so if their name is drawn they can ask a question on any topic.

The **Leader of the Opposition** is permitted to ask six questions in total in each session and is the only MP allowed to ask further questions on different topics. The Leader of the Opposition and MPs use PMQs as an opportunity to undermine or humiliate the Prime Minister and their government.

In theory, the Prime Minister will not know the topic of any supplementary question, or any question the Leader of the Opposition will ask. However, the Prime Minister has the benefit of extensive research carried out by government departments (within the Civil Service), who try to ensure that he has a good grounding on any topics likely to come up.

Motion of no confidence

To effectively lead the government and the country, the Prime Minister must be trusted to do the job in the proper fashion. While parliament obviously contains many opponents of the Prime Minister and government, they rarely officially question their position.

Under the Fixed Term Parliaments Act 2011, the wording of a **motion of no confidence** is set as 'That this House has no confidence in Her Majesty's Government'. If this is passed by a majority of voting MPs, the Prime Minister has 14 days to form a new government, or an early General Election is called.

The most recent example of a **motion of no confidence** having an impact was the ending of the Labour Government of 1979 by one vote (and subsequent Conservative victory).

Leadership challenges

One limit to the power of the Prime Minister is challenges to their leadership from within their party or government. In the run-up to the Rochester by-election in October 2014, an unnamed Cabinet minister was quoted as saying 'if [Mark] Reckless wins Rochester, there'll be 46 names', meaning that the required number of Conservative MPs would be in favour of holding a leadership contest. Adam Afriyie (Conservative, Windsor) was rumoured to be prepared to stand against Cameron, although Afriyie denied this. Mark Reckless did win the Rochester and Strood by-election in November 2014, but the leadership challenge never materialised.

DON'T FORGET

A Prime Minister's success depends on them being seen as competent in the eyes of parliament, their government and party, and the British public.

 THINGS TO DO AND THINK ABOUT

1 Review the progress of the bills in the 2015 Queen's Speech: http://www.bbc.co.uk/news/uk-politics-32894214.
   a Do they all pass?   **b** Do any face difficulties?
2 Essay practice: Evaluate the importance of the Prime Minister in decision-making in the UK.

ONLINE TEST

Test your knowledge of the Prime Minister's role at www.brightredbooks.net

ROLE OF THE UK EXECUTIVE: THE UK GOVERNMENT

The UK Government is responsible for making and carrying out policies on the reserved powers. Depending on the share of seats after each election, the government will either be a **coalition** (made up of members from more than one party), **minority** (made up of one party which has less than half the seats in parliament) or **majority** (where the winning party has more than half the seats in parliament).

ONLINE

Who's who in David Cameron's cabinet? Follow the link at www.brightredbooks.net to find out.

Vince Cable

THE CABINET

The Cabinet is the central decision-making body of the UK Government. It is made up of the Prime Minister and other senior ministers (usually called **Secretaries of State**), who are each responsible for the work of a government department. Cabinet members are usually MPs. Cabinet meetings take place once a week, usually in 10 Downing Street but occasionally elsewhere.

The Prime Minister can appoint whomever they like to be in their Cabinet, based on their expertise in that subject area. If the government is a majority government, the ministers will all be members of the same party. After the 2015 UK General Election, David Cameron appointed the Rt Hon Sajid Javid as Secretary of State for Business, Innovation and Skills. Before being elected, Mr Javid was a senior Managing Director with Deutsche Bank AG, having worked at a bank in New York since 1991.

If the government is in coalition (like the Conservative–Liberal Democrat government of 2010–2015), then the Cabinet will be made up of members of both parties. The Rt Hon Vince Cable MP (Liberal Democrat, Twickenham) held Mr Javid's position from 2010 to 2015. His outspoken views caused Prime Minister David Cameron a number of problems.

Junior ministers

The Prime Minister also appoints junior ministers, who assist the Secretaries of State by taking responsibility for a particular area within a department. In May 2015, Andrew Dunlop was appointed Parliamentary Under-Secretary of State for Scotland.

POWERS OF THE UK GOVERNMENT

The main power of the UK Government is to propose legislation, called **Government Bills**. Usually, the UK Government is elected with a majority, and so can pass the majority of its manifesto policies. The Conservative Government elected in 2015 should be able to pass their policies with little meaningful opposition in the House of Commons.

Under a coalition, both (or all) parties in government have to agree to policy before it can be introduced. This may be problematic as it may involve compromises to be made between the coalition partners' differing manifestos policies on the area, or trade-offs to be made as regards a different policy area. David Cameron was aware of the difficulties of coalition government, and stated in 2013: 'I prefer a more decisive form of government.'

In coming up with policy, Secretaries of State and junior ministers are each supported by staff in the **Civil Service**. The Civil Service is divided into departments, agencies, and non-departmental government bodies (NDPBs). Civil servants (those who work for the Civil Service) are not party-affiliated and so their expertise is not lost if one party loses a General Election. There are more than 410 000 civil servants who work for the UK Government overall.

contd

Collective responsibility

Most decisions regarding government departments are agreed either in Cabinet committees, discussions and negotiations between departments, or in meetings between the Prime Minister and the relevant minister. Cabinet, therefore, is somewhat of a rubberstamp of pre-arranged decisions. If two (or more) ministers disagree about a decision, they may take it to Cabinet, but only in exceptional circumstances.

The UK Government operates on the basis of **collective responsibility**. This means that once a decision has been made by the government, all members of the government have to support this decision. To protect this, the minutes (written record) of Cabinet meetings are kept secret on a 'need to know' basis.

However, the 2010–2015 Conservative–Liberal Democrat Coalition Government had some challenges to **collective responsibility**. For example, the Liberal Democrats spoke out against coalition policy, such as in June 2014, when Nick Clegg announced that the Liberal Democrats would abandon the coalition policy of free schools if elected in the 2015 election. In addition, rebellions, in which government MPs voted against the government, became more common. The 2010–2012 session of parliament had the highest rate of rebellion since 1945, with coalition MPs voting against government policy in 44% of divisions. In October 2011, 81 Conservative rebels voted for an immediate referendum on EU membership.

Outspoken members of government can undermine the principle of confidentiality of collective responsibility. Vince Cable (Liberal Democrat, Twickenham) was caught out by two undercover reporters from *The Telegraph*, and said: 'I have a nuclear option... If they push me too far then I can walk out of the government and bring the government down and they know that.'

VIDEO LINK

Vince Cable tells Lib Dem conference Tories have reverted to 'nasty party' (2013): www.brightredbooks.net

CHECKS ON THE GOVERNMENT

There are many ways in which the legislature (parliament) can scrutinise the UK Government, limiting its power.

Motions of no confidence

MPs who are not satisfied with the actions in, or abilities to perform, their role, they can put forward a **motion of no confidence** in a government minister or junior minister. In October 2014, there was a **motion of no confidence** in Lord Freud, Parliamentary Under-Secretary for Welfare Reform, after he suggested that disabled workers could be paid less than the minimum wage. The **motion of no confidence** was defeated by 302–243 votes.

VIDEO LINK

Watch the Urgent Question on government action following the election of Sepp Blatter as president of FIFA: www.brightredbooks.net

Question Time

Question Time is an opportunity for MPs to question government and Parliamentary Under-Secretaries probing questions about the areas they are responsible for. This takes place at the start of each day's sitting, Monday to Thursday. Which government department answers questions is decided by a rota called the Order of Oral Questions.

Urgent Questions can also be asked to a minister when the Speaker agrees it is in the public interest. In June 2015, the Secretary of State for Culture, Media and Sport, John Whittingdale, was asked about the re-election of Sepp Blatter as FIFA President after the corruption scandal which emerged in the same week as the re-election.

DON'T FORGET

The success of a government depends on its effective delivery of policy, and unity.

ONLINE TEST

Test your knowledge of the role of the UK Government at www.brightredbooks.net

THINGS TO DO AND THINK ABOUT

1 Keep an eye on any Cabinet reshuffles. Who keeps their job, and who is moved on?
2 Find an edition of Ministerial Question Time on **Hansard**.
   a What are the ministers asked?   **b** How well do they answer the questions?
3 Essay practice: Evaluate the effectiveness of parliamentary representation in holding the government to account. You should refer to parliamentary representatives in Scotland or the United Kingdom or both in your answer

ROLE OF THE SCOTTISH LEGISLATURE: THE PARLIAMENT CHAMBER

MSPs are elected to represent their constituents in the Scottish Parliament. The most high-profile way they can do this is in the Scottish Parliament Chamber.

DEBATES

Debates in the Scottish Parliament give MSPs the chance to formally discuss bills and consider issues brought forward by an MSP from the government or opposition, or from a committee.

Firstly, the Presiding Officer introduces the topic of the debate, and requests that MSPs press their 'request-to-speak' buttons. The Presiding Officer decides who will speak in a debate, and for how long, based on the number of MSPs who wish to contribute. By contributing to a debate, MSPs can raise their constituents' concerns during this discussion.

If the discussion becomes heated, the Presiding Officer will enforce the rules of parliament. In November 2012, Michael McMahon (Labour, Uddingston and Bellshill) was suspended for telling Presiding Officer Tricia Marwick 'You are out of order' during a debate, something the Presiding Officer described as a 'gross discourtesy'.

MSPs can hold the government to account during these debates, raising issues which seek to highlight the government's failings, or undermine their achievements. In March 2014, Gavin Brown MSP (Conservative, Lothian) introduced motion S4M-09462 on Scotland's Finances, raising questions about what he saw as a lack of financial predictions in the White Paper on Scottish Independence.

Parliamentary votes

Decisions in the Scottish Parliament, in a debate or on a bill, are made by a vote. Unlike the UK Parliament, MSPs vote using digital consoles. Almost all votes are held at **Decision Time**, held at 5pm when parliament meets on Mondays to Thursdays, or noon when it meets on a Friday. Votes are held on most of the issues discussed that day.

Because the Scottish Government is usually a coalition or minority government, it usually has to rely on the support of other parties and other MSPs to allow it to win votes at Decision Time. Despite gaining the support of the Scottish Conservatives and the late Independent MSP Margo MacDonald, the minority SNP Government's Budget for 2009–10 lost a parliamentary vote in January 2009.

The majority government formed by the SNP after the 2011 General Election allowed unprecedented opportunities for one-party dominance.

Parliamentary votes do allow MSPs from opposition parties, and indeed from within the government, to strongly express their or their constituents' opposing view.

In September 2013, three SNP MSPs (Christine Grahame, chair of the Justice Committee, Sandra White and Stewart Maxwell) rebelled and voted against a government motion to deduct any imprisoned MSP's pay by 90% for the time of their imprisonment.

Members' business debates

Business debates take place on a motion proposed by an MSP who is not a minister or a Cabinet secretary. These usually highlight local issues which may not otherwise gain national attention, or highlight successes or events which matter to the MSP's constituents. These are given 45 minutes at the end of each day's sitting, and no votes are taken. In April 2014, Alison Johnstone (Green, Lothian) used a Members' Business Debate to support the fan ownership of football clubs.

ONLINE

Find out about Michael McMahon MSP being suspended from the Scottish Parliament at www. brightredbooks.net

QUESTION TIME

General Question Time and Portfolio Question Time are opportunities for MSPs to question Cabinet secretaries and government ministers about decisions they have made or matters which are under their department's remit. These usually take place weekly on a Wednesday and Thursday afternoon. The MSPs who get to ask a question are selected randomly by computer from all those who have submitted their names by noon on the Monday. The MSP must submit their question by noon on the Wednesday.

Question Time allows MPs to keep a close check on the government, and the work they are doing. In October 2014, Jim Eadie (SNP, Edinburgh Southern), Alison Johnstone (Green, Lothian) and Cameron Buchanan (Conservative, Lothian) asked then Minister for Local Government and Planning, Derek Mackay (SNP), about a controversial planning application in Craighouse in Edinburgh and the Scottish Government's failure to **call in** the decision (take control of the decision from the local council) based on opposition.

The minister always has the chance to respond, though, and will usually be very well prepared to answer any question, as they must be submitted in advance. In this case, Mr Mackay responded by stating: 'Those who have objected might not be happy with the local authority's decision, but I emphasise again that I do not have adequate grounds for believing that it would be appropriate to call the application in.'

First Minister's Question Time (FMQs)

For half an hour from 12 noon every Thursday, it is the turn of the First Minister to be questioned by MSPs from the opposition and government. This is seen as the most confrontational aspect of the Scottish Parliament's work, and can lead to fiery debates primarily between the opposition party leaders and the First Minister.

Questions for FMQs that week can be submitted by any MSP at any point between the end of the previous FMQs and noon on the Monday. The Presiding Officer selects the questions based on a number of criteria, including that 'a reasonable political balance between the parties is maintained over time', and how often an MSP has asked questions before. MSPs are permitted to ask follow-on questions, which the First Minister will not have read in advance.

However, the First Minister has the benefit of extensive research carried out by government departments, who try to ensure that they have a good grounding on any topic which is likely to come up.

Opposition party leaders and MSPs often seek to undermine or humiliate the First Minister and their government. In October 2014, Liberal Democrat leader Willie Rennie asked: 'When the First Minister goes, will he please take Kenny MacAskill with him?... Surely the First Minister has had enough of defending the Cabinet Secretary for Justice.' Alex Salmond replied: 'I will give just one of the many reasons why I will not do what Willie Rennie suggests... crime in Scotland is at a 39-year low. That is why the justice secretary is on a high.'

DON'T FORGET

Debates and votes are two of the most high-profile ways in which MSPs can represent their constituents.

ONLINE TEST

Test yourself on this topic at www.brightredbooks.net

THINGS TO DO AND THINK ABOUT

1   Watch a recent edition of First Minister's Question Time.
    a   Note the topics they are quizzed upon.
    b   Do they seem to respond successfully?
2   Find a recent example of your MSP contributing in the chamber in the ways described above.
3   Essay practice: Evaluate the view that parliamentary representatives have little influence in decision making. You should refer to parliamentary representatives in Scotland or the UK or both in your answer.

ROLE OF THE SCOTTISH LEGISLATURE: COMMITTEES

Who sits where?

Typical seating arrangements at a committee meeting

Committees play a vital role in the work of the Scottish Parliament. The Scottish Parliament is **unicameral** (has only one house) so the committees are even more important than they are in the UK Parliament.

Committees are heavily involved in scrutinising the laws that government or MSPs want to make, and do this to make sure that the decisions made are the best possible for Scotland.

Mandatory	Subject
Standards, Procedures and Public Appointments Committee	Economy, Energy and Tourism Committee
Finance Committee	Education and Culture Committee
Public Audit Committee	Health and Sport Committee
European and External Relations Committee	Infrastructure and Capital Investment Committee
Equal Opportunities Committee	Justice Committee
Public Petitions Committee	Justice Sub-Committee on Policing
Delegated Powers and Law Reform Committee	Local Government and Regeneration Committee
	Rural Affairs, Climate Change and Environment Committee
	Welfare Reform Committee

Scottish Parliament Committees
[14th October 2014]

TYPES OF COMMITTEE

Committees are formed after each Scottish General Election. **Mandatory committees** must be formed to cover the same policy area after every election. **Subject committees** may be slightly different after each election, according to government priorities. For example, education fell under the remit of the Education, Lifelong Learning and Culture Committee in the 3rd Session of the Scottish Parliament (2007–2011), but fell under the remit of the Education and Culture Committee in the 4th Session (2011–2016)

There can also be **Bill Committees**, formed when a specific bill does not fit clearly within the remit of one of the other committees. The Referendum (Scotland) Bill Committee was formed in October 2012, with a remit to consider matters relating to the referendum. In October 2014 (after the referendum), it became the 'Devolution (Further Powers) Committee'.

MEMBERSHIP OF COMMITTEES

Each committee in the Scottish Parliament is made up of between five and fifteen MSPs, although in practice, most have between seven and nine members. The membership of committees (when taken together) is designed to reflect the share of seats in the Scottish Parliament. The membership of each committee is proposed by the **Parliamentary Bureau** (the Presiding Officer and a representative from each party with five or more MSPs), but must be approved by a parliamentary vote.

2007–11	2011–2016
	Delegated Powers and Law Reform
Finance	Finance
	Justice
Health and Sport	Education and Culture
Standards, Procedures and Public Appointments	European and External Relations
	Local Government and Regeneration
Rural Affairs and Environment	Rural Affairs, Climate Change and Environment
	Infrastructure and Capital Investment
4 out of 14	8 out of 15

SNP Committees conveners

Each committee also has a **convenor** who leads each meeting. The committee members choose the convener from a party recommended by the Parliamentary Bureau and approved by the parliament. The allocation of convenerships is also designed to reflect the share of seats in parliament. There is also a **Conveners Group**, chaired by the Presiding Officer. In September 2013, the Conveners Group called First Minister Alex Salmond for questioning on the government's legislative programme.

MSPs join committees either because they are experienced in that policy area, or it covers an area their constituents have an interest in. Michael Russell MSP (SNP, Argyll and Bute) is a member of the Rural Affairs, Climate Change and Environment Committee, as its decisions affect his rural constituency in the Highlands and Islands.

As the Additional Member System makes it very likely that coalition or minority governments will be formed after each election, committees can provide a very effective check on government. In such cases, the government will have a minority of committee members (overall) and conveners.

contd

However, the majority SNP Government (2011–2016) is able to dominate committees in terms of membership of key committees (like Economy, Energy and Tourism), and convenerships. This could mean that the Scottish Government is not under as much scrutiny as previous governments have been.

COMMITTEE INQUIRIES

Committees hold **inquiries** into the spending, policies and administration within their policy area. They may go on a fact-finding mission, or hold a hearing away from the Scottish Parliament if they feel it will benefit their work. Committees gather written evidence, and can call for oral evidence from witnesses. Written evidence can be submitted by anyone, while witnesses are always called by the committee.

Committees can summon a government minister to appear and justify actions in their department or indeed their government. This can be a very difficult meeting for the minister, as the issues they may be questioned on are often of high public interest. In October 2014, the then Cabinet Secretary for Education and Lifelong Learning, Michael Russell, was called to give evidence on the first year of N4 and N5 qualifications under the Curriculum for Excellence.

Michael Russell MSP

Case Study – Scottish Government renewable energy targets

In 2012, the Economy, Energy and Tourism Committee decided to investigate the Scottish Government's 2020 renewable energy targets.

25 April: Donald Trump, American business tycoon and star of the American TV show *The Apprentice* was called as one of many witnesses. He claims that the placing of offshore wind turbines around Scotland's coast (including near his multi-million pound Aberdeenshire golf resort) will damage tourism.

20 June: Fergus Ewing, Minister for Energy, Enterprise and Tourism, gives evidence.

23 November: Committee findings are published. The report raised a concern that 'from the evidence we received, there is a risk that the 2020 target may not be met'.

In its formal response to the Committee report, the Scottish Government states that its updated figures, in particular as regards renewable heating, show that greater progress towards the targets had been made: 'This puts us firmly on course to achieve our 2020 target.'

VIDEO LINK

Watch highlights of Michael Russell giving evidence on N4 and N5 to committee at www.brightredbooks.net

VIDEO LINK

Watch Donald Trump giving evidence at www.brightredbooks.net

COMMITTEES AND LEGISLATION

Committees in the Scottish Parliament have an absolutely crucial role to play in the legislative process. As the Scottish Parliament is a unicameral legislature, committees have a great responsibility over the validity of legislation. Besides the committee responsible for the bill, only the parliament sitting together will review the details of each bill, and they only have a limited time to do this.

As soon as a bill is introduced, it is referred to the committee which will examine it, called the **lead committee**. They may also consult with other committees with an interest in the bill's subject. At this early stage, the committee will take preliminary evidence and recommend whether or not parliament should agree to the **general principles** of the bill, which determines whether it should be given any parliamentary consideration. For example, under Stage 1 of the Marriage and Civil Partnership (Scotland) Bill, which legalised same-sex marriage in Scotland, the committee heard from witnesses including the director of Stonewall Scotland (a gay rights charity) and the Church of Scotland.

If parliament agrees to the general principles of the bill, the lead committee will begin to examine every aspect of the bill in minute detail.

DON'T FORGET

Committees in Scotland are particularly important, as there is no second chamber (like the UK House of Lords) which reviews bills.

THINGS TO DO AND THINK ABOUT

1 Find examples of your constituency MSP, or one of your list MSPs, acting in committees:
a Asking a committee witness a question.
b Proposing an amendment in a committee.
2 Essay practice: Analyse the role of committees in influencing decision-making. You should refer to committees in Scotland or the UK or both in your answer.

ONLINE TEST

How well have you learned about this topic? Head to www.brightredbooks.net and take the test.

ROLE OF THE SCOTTISH EXECUTIVE: THE FIRST MINISTER

FACT

Election of Nicola Sturgeon as First Minister:
19 November 2014

Candidate	Party	Votes
Nicola Sturgeon	SNP	66
Ruth Davidson	Conservative	15
Abstain		39

Name	Party	Term	Reason for leaving
Donald Dewar	Labour	May 1999 – October 2000	Died in office
Henry McLeish	Labour	October 2000 – November 2001	Resigned over Officegate (controversial office expenses)
Jack McConnell	Labour	November 2001 – May 2007	Party came second in 2007 Election
Alex Salmond	SNP	May 2007 – November 2014	Resigned after referendum defeat
Nicola Sturgeon	SNP	November 2014 -	

Scotland's First Ministers

OVERVIEW

The First Minister is elected by MSPs after each Scottish Election (or if the First Minister leaves office) but is officially appointed by the Queen. Nicola Sturgeon was elected First Minister of Scotland in November 2014 after Alex Salmond stood down following the independence referendum. All Labour, Liberal Democrat and Green MSPs in attendance chose to **abstain** (not vote).

All five full-time First Ministers so far have been the leader of the largest party in parliament.

POWERS OF THE FIRST MINISTER

Once elected (and appointed) to their position, the First Minister has a range of powers.

Leader of government

The First Minister is responsible for the overall direction of the Scottish Government. After each election, being appointed to the role, or at another key point in the parliament session, the First Minister will publicly announce the overall plans of their government. A week after being elected First Minister, Nicola Sturgeon announced her government's first legislative programme of 12 bills, including a Land Reform Bill and a Higher Education Governance Bill.

However, these bills must pass through full parliamentary scrutiny, including the committee system, before becoming law. In September 2010, the minority SNP Government led by Alex Salmond dropped plans for an independence referendum before the 2011 election (a 2007-election manifesto pledge), realising it would not make it through a parliamentary vote.

Cabinet appointment

The First Minister has the power to appoint members of the Cabinet. These nominations must be approved by a parliamentary vote before they are appointed in the role. Nicola Sturgeon announced her first Cabinet on 21 November 2014, but these appointments only became official when parliament approved of the nominations some days later.

In appointing a **coalition** government (for example, 1999–2003 and 2007), the First Minister has to negotiate with the leader(s) of their junior coalition partner(s) about whom should be appointed, and to which roles.

If the First Minister presides over a minority government, there can be a risk of their nominations to Cabinet being outvoted. At the parliamentary sitting where appointments are debated, all other party leaders are given the opportunity to voice their opposition to their appointments. When Alex Salmond's first government appointments were debated in May 2007, opposition leaders moved amendments calling for the removal of John Swinney and Richard Lochhead. However, there is little chance of opposition parties agreeing on alternative candidates for these roles, who they could then persuade the First Minister to nominate for appointment. The opposition is largely symbolic, and opposition parties rarely vote against appointments; choosing instead to **abstain** (not vote).

First Minister
Nicola Sturgeon

contd

Alex Salmond's 2007 Cabinet and junior ministerial team were each appointed with a vote of For 49, Against 0, Abstentions 75.

Representing Scotland

The First Minister of Scotland is responsible for representing Scotland to the rest of the world. This can be in official or unofficial roles.

In August 2014, Alex Salmond attended a special service to commemorate the start of WWI at Glasgow Cathedral with Prince Charles, UK Prime Minister David Cameron, and Commonwealth heads of government, as well as UK and Irish politicians.

On the other hand, any international criticism of the Scottish Government lands squarely with the First Minister. When Kenny MacAskill (then Justice Secretary) decided to release the Lockerbie bomber Abdelbaset Ali al-Megrahi, the decision was criticised publicly in a 2010 joint press conference by US President Barack Obama (who called the decision a 'mistake'), and Prime Minister David Cameron (who called it a 'bad decision').

LIMITS TO THE FIRST MINISTER'S POWERS

The First Minister's powers rely on them maintaining an image as a strong and competent leader. There are a number of ways this can be called into question.

First Minister's Questions (FMQs)

The First Minister must face tough questions from opposing MSPs at First Minister's Questions every Thursday in the parliament chamber. An unsuccessful showing at FMQs, in the full light of the media, would make the First Minister seem incapable of doing their job well.

Motion of no confidence

In order to effectively lead the government and the country, the First Minister must be trusted to do their job in the proper fashion. While the Scottish Parliament obviously contains many opponents of the First Minister, they rarely officially question their position.

If the First Minister is seen to have seriously stepped out of line, the Scottish Parliament can debate and vote on a motion of no confidence. Any MSP can propose a motion of no confidence if they have the support of 25 MSPs, and the Cabinet secretary or minister in question is usually given 2 days' notice. In November 2001, First Minister Henry McLeish (Labour) resigned before a motion of no confidence was going to be debated: 'This parliament must now turn its energies once more to its real and pressing business: the concerns of the people of Scotland. I want us to be allowed to do that with a minimum of distraction. That is why I am resigning.'

Leadership challenges

One possible limit to the power of the First Minister would be challenges to their leadership from within their party or government. The potential for this is much greater when there is a coalition government, as the government and Cabinet will not be united by party loyalty to one leader. However, even in the case of Henry McLeish's resignation as First Minister in a Lab–Lib coalition government, the Liberal Democrats supported him throughout the scandal.

VIDEO LINK

Watch Henry McLeish's resignation at www. brightredbooks.net

DON'T FORGET

A First Minister's success depends on them being seen as competent in the eyes of parliament, their government and party, and the Scottish public.

ONLINE TEST

Head to www. brightredbooks.net and test yourself on your knowledge of the role of the First Minister.

THINGS TO DO AND THINK ABOUT

1. Keep a close eye on the bills in Nicola Sturgeon's first legislative programme: http://www.bbc.co.uk/news/uk-scotland-30225203.
    a   Do they all pass?   b   Do any face difficulties?
2. Find out why the Conservatives proposed a motion of no confidence in Henry McLeish.
3. Essay practice: Evaluate the importance of the First Minister in decision-making in Scotland.

ROLE OF THE SCOTTISH EXECUTIVE: THE SCOTTISH GOVERNMENT

The Scottish Government is responsible for making and carrying out policies on the devolved powers. Depending on the share of seats after each election, it can either be a **coalition**, **minority** or **majority**.

First Minister Nicola Sturgeon's first Cabinet (21 November 2014)

DON'T FORGET

The nature of the Scottish electoral system is such that a coalition is more likely in Scotland than it is the UK Parliament.

THE CABINET

The Cabinet is the central decision-making body of the Scottish Government. It is made up of the First Minister and other senior ministers, called **Cabinet Secretaries**, who are each responsible for the work of a government department. It usually meets weekly, while parliament is in session, at Bute House, Charlotte Square, Edinburgh.

The First Minister can propose whomever they like to be in their Cabinet, based on their expertise in that subject area. These members must be approved by a vote of the Scottish Parliament. If the Scottish Government is a majority government (like the SNP government from 2011–2016), then the ministers will all be members of the same party. For example, John Swinney (SNP, Perthshire North) was appointed Deputy First Minister and Cabinet Secretary for Finance, Constitution and Economy in First Minister Nicola Sturgeon's first cabinet in November 2014. He has been Cabinet Secretary for Finance since the SNP came into power in 2007. Before being elected for the first time, Mr Swinney worked for five years as a business and economic development consultant.

If the government is a coalition government (like the Labour–Liberal Democrat governments of 1999–2003 and 2003–2007), then the Cabinet will be made up of members of both parties. In 2005, Tavish Scott (Liberal Democrat, Shetland) was appointed Minister for Transport under Labour First Minister Jack McConnell.

Junior ministers

The First Minister also appoints junior ministers, who are responsible for specific policy areas. For example, Aileen Campbell MSP (SNP, Clydesdale), was appointed Minister for Children and Young People in 2011.

John Swinney MSP

POWERS OF THE SCOTTISH GOVERNMENT

The main power of the Scottish Government is to propose legislation, called **Executive Bills**. Under a coalition, both (or all) parties in government have to agree to policy before it can be introduced. This may be problematic as it may involve compromises to be made between the coalition partners' differing manifestos policies on the area, or trade-offs to be made as regards a different policy area. For example, the Liberal Democrats agreed to join a coalition with Labour in 2003 only if a proportional representation (PR) system was adopted for local council elections, and so we now use the Single Transferable Vote (STV) for local elections.

In a minority government, the government must rely on the power of persuasion to convince other parties to vote with it. The abolition of the £2 289 Graduate Endowment Fee in 2008 was passed with the support of the Liberal Democrats, Greens, the late Margo MacDonald (Independent, Lothian), and one Labour MSP, Elaine Smith.

When elected with a majority in 2011, the SNP did not have these restrictions.

In coming up with policy, Cabinet Secretaries and junior ministers are each supported by staff in the relevant Scottish Government **directorate** (department in charge of a

Aileen Campbell MSP

contd

particular policy area). The members of these **directorates** are not party-affiliated; and so their expertise is not lost if one party loses a Scottish General Election. There are more than 5 000 civil servants who work for the Scottish Government overall.

Collective responsibility

Cabinet may be invited to consider a matter which the Cabinet Secretary wishes to have advice on. If two (or more) Cabinet Secretaries disagree about a decision, they must not bring the issue to Cabinet until all other options (including meetings between those who disagree) have been tried. The Scottish Government operates on the basis of **collective responsibility**. This means that once a decision has been made by the government (either meeting together or by the Cabinet Secretary on their own), all members of the government have to support this decision. To protect this, the minutes (written record) of Cabinet meetings are kept secret on a 'need to know' basis.

ONLINE

Check out Alex Salmond's 2011 victory speech at www.brightredbooks.net

Acts of the Scottish Parliament by Session

Session/Type of Government	Executive Bills	Member's Bills	Private Bills	Committee Bills	Total
2003–2007 (Coalition)	53 (80%)	3 (5%)	9 (14%)	1 (2%)	66
2007–2011 (Minority)	42 (80%)	7 (13%)	2 (4%)	2 (4%)	53
2011–2014 (Majority) (Incomplete Session)	38 (84%)	3 (7%)	4 (9%)	0 (0%)	45

CHECKS ON THE GOVERNMENT

There are many ways in which parliament can scrutinise the Scottish Government.

Motions of no confidence

Any MSP can let the Presiding Officer know that the Scottish Government (as a group) or an individual Cabinet Secretary or junior minister is no longer trusted to carry out their role and can call for a **motion of no confidence**. If this is supported by at least 25 MSPs, the motion is given time in the parliament chamber, usually at least two days later. However, provided the government (which is bound by collective responsibility) has a majority in parliament, or can convince other members, it is likely that the vote will not pass. In May 2014, the Labour group of MSPs called for a vote of no confidence in Health Secretary Alex Neil, over his role in controversial changes to mental health services in his constituency. The vote was defeated 57–67, but Mr Neil was moved from Health to Social Justice, Communities and Pensioner's Rights in Nicola Sturgeon's first Cabinet.

Question Time

General Question Time and Portfolio Question Time are opportunities for MSPs to question Cabinet Secretaries and junior ministers about decisions they have made or matters which are under their department's remit.

MSPs can scrutinise the performance of the Cabinet Secretary or minister's department (or the official themselves) by asking probing questions. In November 2014, Alex Johnstone (Conservative, North East Scotland) asked Fiona Hyslop, Cabinet Secretary for Culture, Europe and External Affairs, about what he saw as 'a central belt bias at the expense of the north-east' in music funding from the Scottish Government-funded organisation Creative Scotland. Due to the extensive research carried out by the directorate, Ms Hyslop was able to quickly give a list of festivals funded by Creative Scotland, before adding: 'The member might want to reflect not only on his cultural experience but on his geography.'

MSPs can also highlight perceived failings of (members of) the Cabinet during First Minister's Question Time. In Alex Salmond's last FMQs as First Minister, Jackie Baillie (Labour, Dumbarton) asked: 'Given their record of failure, which members of the First Minister's Cabinet would he recommend should keep their jobs when his deputy takes over?'

DON'T FORGET

The success of a government depends on its effective delivery of policy, and unity.

ONLINE TEST

Head to www. brightredbooks.net and test yourself on your knowledge of the role of the Scottish Government.

THINGS TO DO AND THINK ABOUT

1 Using the quote from Jackie Baillie as an internet search term, find out:
   a which members of Alex Salmond's Cabinet she criticised directly.
   b what happened to each of these when Nicola Sturgeon announced her first Cabinet.
2 Keep an eye on any Cabinet reshuffles: who keeps their job, and who is moved on?
3 Essay practice: Evaluate the effectiveness of parliamentary representation in holding the government to account. You should refer to parliamentary representatives in Scotland or the United Kingdom or both in your answer.

LOCAL GOVERNMENT IN SCOTLAND

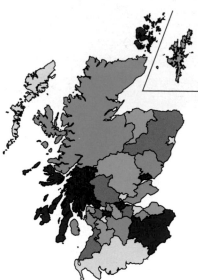

Scottish local authorities
Each local authority is governed by a local council, elected using the Single Transferable Vote system. There are 1 223 local councillors in Scotland.

Local government in Scotland provides a range of services in a local area. Scotland is divided into 32 local authorities, ranging in size from 26 square miles in Dundee to 12 437 square miles in the Highlands, and from about 20 000 people in the Orkney Islands to over 600 000 in Glasgow.

LOCAL COUNCIL FUNDING

Most local councils get the majority (around 85%) of their money in a **General Revenue Grant** from the Scottish Government. The rest of their money comes from:

- Grants are sometimes given by the Scottish Government for **capital expenditure** (for expensive projects, like new schools or bridges).

- **Non-domestic rates** are local taxes on businesses. Local authorities with large industries tend to get a higher share from this.

- **Council Tax** is paid on each residential property (house or flat), roughly based on its value.

Comparison of council funding (2014–15 Budgets)

Funding source	City of Edinburgh	Highland Council
General revenue grant	£373m (38%)	£451m (80%)
Non-domestic rates	£366m (38%)	£0m (0%)
Council Tax	£232m (24%)	£112m (20%)

As the Scottish Government provides so much of local authorities' budgets, the Scottish Government can often effectively force its will onto local councils.

COSLA

The Convention of Scottish Local Authorities (COSLA) is an organisation which local councils can join in order to allow efficient cooperation, and to gain representation in discussions with the Scottish Government, and for nation-wide pay agreements with trade unions.

The **Concordat** was an agreement between the Scottish Government and COSLA made in 2007, 'based on mutual respect and partnership', covering a range of funding and servicing issues.

Aberdeen, Glasgow, Renfrewshire and South Lanarkshire Councils have all informed COSLA that they will leave in 2015, due to complaints about funding allocation,

decision-making, and what they see as its powerlessness in negotiations with the Scottish Government.

In February 2014, Inverclyde – a small local authority – announced its intention to leave COSLA in 2015, but reversed its decision in October 2014 after COSLA altered its constitution to highlight the fact that there is no hierarchy between members. COSLA funding is divided up according to an area's wealth, its population demographics, and how rural or urban the population is: a very complicated formula. Some Labour councils (like Inverclyde) felt this was unfair. Inverclyde's annual membership fees are £60 000.

COOPERATION WITH THE SCOTTISH GOVERNMENT

Scottish Futures Trust

The SNP Government set up the Scottish Futures Trust (SFT) in 2008 in order to oversee capital spending (big building projects) by the government, government agencies, and councils. By finding ways of avoiding some of the high costs of private development, including

expensive consultants' fees, these organisations have been able to save considerably more money than the £4m per year it costs to run SFT. The new Boroughmuir High School in Edinburgh (opening in 2016) is partly funded through the Scottish Government's £1.25bn 'Scotland's Schools for the Future' Programme, managed by SFT.

contd

There has, however, been criticism of some of the delays some SFT projects have had. The new Royal Hospital for Sick Children in Edinburgh was supposed to be open by the end of 2012, but now it is estimated to be ready in 2017.

Tackling the 'Bedroom Tax'

When the UK Government announced it was to scrap the spare room subsidy in 2013, a moved dubbed the **'bedroom tax'** by critics, COSLA was quick to raise concerns. COSLA President David O'Neill (Labour, North Ayrshire) said: 'The huge damage it will do to our communities is not something that COSLA can support, and nor should others.'

The Scottish Government fought very hard to limit the damaging effects of this policy. In May 2014, then Deputy First Minister Nicola Sturgeon announced that due to Scottish Government action, 'there will be no need for anyone to fall into rent arrears, or face eviction, as a result of the "bedroom tax"'. After negotiations between the Scottish and UK Governments, the power to set the cap on Discretionary Housing Payments was devolved to Scotland. Jackie Baillie (Labour, Dumbarton) had previously introduced a bill on the matter, and criticised the Scottish Government for what she saw as a delayed response.

CONFLICT WITH THE SCOTTISH GOVERNMENT

Council Tax

Under the Concordat, Council Tax levels have been frozen at 2007–08 levels. In December 2014, Finance Secretary John Swinney pledged to give local authorities almost £10.85bn to run services for the next year, in exchange for maintaining the Council Tax freeze (amongst other commitments).

SFT benefits to infrastructure investment in Scotland

However, stopping councils from generating extra funding by raising Council Tax has meant that councils have had to make more cuts than they might have done otherwise. The SNP's electoral popularity came at the expense of the money available for local councils to provide frontline services. Sarah Boyack (Labour, Lothian) in 2013 said it has caused 35 000 jobs to be lost. Aberdeen City Council finance convener Willie Young said: 'There must also be respect for local government because people voted us in to look after local services and make our own decisions on Council Tax. This policy represents centralisation at its worst.'

Edinburgh trams

In 2002, *Transport Initiatives Edinburgh* (**Tie**) was formed to look at long-term transport for the city. The SNP minority government wanted to scrap the proposed tram system, in favour of other national transport targets, but was defeated 81 to 47 in a Scottish Parliament vote in June 2007.

In August 2011, after the budget had spiralled, The City of Edinburgh Council held a vote on whether to stop the trams at Haymarket, rather than continuing to St Andrew Square. The council vote passed after the SNP abstained. Later in August 2011, the now-majority SNP government decided that this change was not acceptable, and refused to pay its final payment of £72m to The City of Edinburgh Council.

This government intervention forced The City of Edinburgh Council to have a second vote, and it was decided on a 28–15 vote that the trams would continue to St. Andrews Square. In September 2011, the Scottish Government sent in a team of officials to take up senior transport positions at the Council. The trams were completed in May 2014, and in December 2014 The City of Edinburgh Council was asked to commission a £400 000 report into extending the trams to Leith.

DON'T FORGET

Local councils are **accountable** for the money they spend and the quality of services they provide.

ONLINE

Learn more about local government in Scotland by following the link at www.brightredbooks.net

THINGS TO DO AND THINK ABOUT

1 Look for details of any interaction between your local council and the Scottish Government.
2 Find an example of an SFT project in your local council.
3 Essay practice: In carrying out its functions, local government in Scotland has come into conflict with the Scottish Government. Discuss this view.

ONLINE TEST

Head to www.brightredbooks.net and test your knowledge of Scottish local councils.

VOTING SYSTEMS: FIRST PAST THE POST (FPTP)

England	533
Scotland	59
Wales	40
Northern Ireland	18

Constituencies in the
UK Parliament

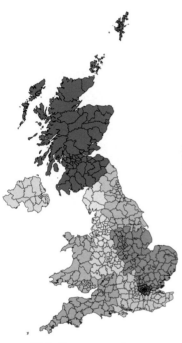

UK Parliament constituency map

Candidate	Party	Votes	% vote
Ian Murray	Labour	19,293	39.1
Neil Hay	SNP	16,656	33.8
Miles Briggs	Conservative	8,626	17.5
Phyl Meyer	Green	2,090	4.2
Pramod Subbaraman	Liberal Democrat	1,823	3.7
Paul Marshall	UKIP	601	1.2
Colin Fox	SSP	197	0.4
Majority		**2,637**	**5.4**
Turnout		**49,286**	**74.9**

2015 General Election Result,
Edinburgh South

OVERVIEW

The **First Past The Post (FPTP)** voting system is used to elect Members of the UK Parliament.

There are 650 seats in the UK Parliament (**constituencies**) which each elects one MP. Constituencies are roughly based on population size, with an average number of voters (**electorate**) of approximately 71 000.

The winning candidate in each seat requires only a **plurality** (more than any other, but not a majority) to win the seat. The party which wins more seats than any other is invited by the Queen to form the government.

Every constituency must hold an election in the UK General Election, which were set to take place every five years (under normal circumstances) under the Fixed-term Parliaments Act 2011.

BY-ELECTIONS

If a seat becomes vacant between general elections, a **by-election** must be held. The seat may become vacant due to the MP dying in office, resigning, becoming a member of the House of Lords, or in some other way becoming ineligible as an MP. By-elections can often be seen as a **protest vote**, when the electorate have a chance to voice their discontent with the government, without actually questioning the balance of power in the country.

In October 2014, the United Kingdom Independence Party (UKIP) gained its first elected MP, when Douglas Carswell won the Clacton by-election. The by-election was called when Mr Carswell, who previously held the seat for the Conservative Party, resigned as an MP after **defecting** to UKIP.

ADVANTAGES OF FIRST PAST THE POST

Simplicity

In order to vote, voters simply mark the candidate they would like to win in the box next to their name, ideally with a cross (X). This is simpler than some other voting systems, such as those used in Scottish elections.

Additionally, each party will only put forward one candidate per seat, so voters need not do a great deal of research into the viewpoints of individual candidates; they can vote to express their party preference. An SNP supporter in Edinburgh South in 2015 would know that Neil Hay was likely to share most of their main political beliefs, without having to know about him specifically.

Constituency link

It is the job of each MP to represent all their **constituents**, including those who do not vote for them. That means that each MP is directly accountable to their constituents, so constituents must clearly know who to contact with their concerns. In Edinburgh South, supporters of any party know that if they want an issue raised in the UK Parliament, it is Ian Murray MP whom they need to contact.

Strong, stable government

As each seat is winner-takes-all, the UK General Election almost always ends up with either a Conservative or Labour Party majority. The 7-month minority Labour

contd

Government of February–October 1974 was the only time there was not a majority government between 1945 and 2010.

Majority government means that the winning party has a clear **mandate** (authority to govern), and the other parties and the public could feel they are entitled to carry out their **manifesto** promises. Even the House of Lords will not vote against manifesto promises from a majority government, under the **Salisbury Convention**. Such parliaments are likely to pass a lot of legislation, and have clear policies and direction.

However, as parties almost always win a majority of seats on a minority of votes, it may be seen as undemocratic as these policies, which are essentially unopposed in the parliament, were voted for by less than half of all voters.

Party	Seats	Votes	% of seats	% of votes
Conservative	331	11,334,576	50.9%	36.9%
Labour	232	9,347,304	35.7%	30.4%
SNP	56	1,454,436	8.6%	4.7%
Liberal Democrat	8	2,415,862	1.2%	7.9%
UKIP	1	3,881,099	0.2%	12.6%
Green Party	1	1,157,613	0.2%	3.8%

UK General Election results 2015 (selected parties)

DISADVANTAGES OF FIRST PAST THE POST

Safe seats

Most of the UK General Election seats are described as **safe** (the seat is usually won by the same party in most elections). Some are so predictable that the Electoral Reform Society was able to predict the winner correctly in 363 of 368 seats. Orkney and Shetland is arguably the safest constituency in Scotland. It has elected a Liberal/Liberal Democrat MP in every election since 1950, and Alistair Carmichael (Liberal Democrat, Orkney and Shetland) won the Liberal Democrats' only Scottish constituency in the 2015 election, albeit with a hugely reduced majority (3.6%, down from 51.3% in 2010).

This causes parties to focus their campaign efforts on seats they have a chance of gaining, or risk of losing; and the others can be ignored. The British Electoral Study found that approximately 70% of people in marginal seats were contacted by political parties before the 2010 election, compared to 54% of those in safe seats.

However, this may allow for the very best politicians to be in parliament. Political parties can put their very best candidates (like their leaders and leadership teams) in their party's safest seats, so that their government is staffed by the best people for the jobs. David Cameron's seat, Witney in Oxfordshire, has been won by the Conservatives in every UK General Election since 1974, and he won it with a 43% majority in 2015.

Disproportionality

As FPTP rewards the winning of seats, and not overall votes, there can be a huge disparity between the overall share of votes a party wins across the country, and the share of seats won. This could be seen as limiting the **mandate** of the government and their carrying out of manifesto policies. In the 2015 UK General Election, the Conservatives won a majority of 50.9% of seats in the House of Commons, with 36.9% of the votes.

Disproportionality also punishes smaller parties, by rewarding the concentration of votes in fewer constituencies. This is because smaller parties tend to finish second in a lot of constituencies, while the Conservatives and Labour tend to win the seat, or receive few votes.

Wasted votes

As a **plurality** of votes is required to win a seat, the vast majority of votes in each constituency do not contribute to the result. This could either be votes for losing candidates, or votes for the winning candidate over the number of votes required to win. Across the UK, the figure for wasted votes in 2015 has been calculated as 74%.

 FACT

If votes for UKIP translated into seats in the same way that they did for the Conservatives, UKIP would have won 113 seats in the 2015 UK General Election.

 ONLINE

Follow the link to the Electoral Reform Society at www.brightredbooks.net

 VIDEO LINK

For more on this, check out the clip at www.brightredbooks.net

 **ONLINE TEST**

Head to www.brightredbooks.net and test yourself on the FPTP voting system.

 THINGS TO DO AND THINK ABOUT

1 Find examples of the advantages and disadvantages of FPTP from your constituency's, and nearby constituencies', election results.

VOTING SYSTEMS: THE ADDITIONAL MEMBER SYSTEM (AMS)

The Additional Member System (AMS) is used to elect Members of the Scottish Parliament (MSPs). It is a **hybrid** or **mixed system**, because it uses a mixture of First Past The Post (FPTP) and a type of Proportional Representation (PR) list.

SCOTTISH PARLIAMENT CONSTITUENCIES

There are 73 Scottish Parliament constituencies, which each elect one MSP using FPTP. This means that to win each seat, the winning candidate only needs to receive one more vote than the person coming second. Just as in UK General Elections, FPTP elections in each constituency result in a **disproportional** share of seats nationally.

Scottish Parliament constituencies

SCOTTISH PARLIAMENT REGIONS

Under AMS, Scotland is also divided up into eight electoral regions, and each region elects seven MSPs, giving a total of 56 regional, or list, MSPs. Parties who wish to stand in a region decide on a list of candidates, and the party name will appear on the ballot paper.

To vote, voters mark their **preferred party** (not candidate) on the ballot paper. The order of the candidates on the list is decided by the parties themselves, and so voters have no choice in the order they are placed. Parties usually place their most important or influential candidates high up a regional list, as well as having them stand as a constituency candidate, in order to maximise their chances of being elected.

The party list element of AMS uses the **d'Hondt** formula to distribute the 56 regional seats between the parties, to give as **proportional** an overall result as possible. This works by running various rounds of counting, in which the votes for each party in that region are divided by the number of elected MSPs the party has already had elected, plus one.

Scottish Parliament regions

$$\frac{\text{votes}}{\text{seats} + 1}$$

The d'Hondt Formula

As you can see from the 2011 results, the Labour Party's **under-representation** in the constituency seats was counteracted by **over-representation** in the regional seats, giving almost perfect proportionality overall.

Party	Constituencies		Regions		Overall			
	% vote	% seats	% vote	% seats	Votes	Seats	% vote	% seats
SNP	45.5	73	44.0	29	1 779 336	69	44.7%	53.5%
Labour	31.7	21	26.3	39	1 154 020	37	29.0%	28.7%
Conservative	13.9	4	12.4	21	522 619	15	13.1%	11.6%
Liberal Democrat	7.9	1.5	5.2	5	399 346	5	10.0%	3.9%
Others	1.1	0	12.1	5	124 952	3	3.1%	2.3%

Scottish Parliament Election results 2011

BY-ELECTIONS

When a constituency seat becomes vacant between Scottish Parliament Elections, a by-election must be held. In October 2013, Labour's Cara Hilton won the Dunfermline by-election, after SNP MSP Bill Walker was thrown out of the party and jailed.

There is no such system in place for a regional MSP resigning from their party. In October 2012, Highlands and Islands MSPs Jean Urquhart and John Finnie resigned from the SNP when the party dropped its long-standing opposition to NATO. They continued to sit as independent MSPs, but vote for SNP manifesto policies.

contd

ADVANTAGES OF THE ADDITIONAL MEMBER SYSTEM

Proportionality

Using AMS means that all parties feel they have a realistic chance of gaining MSPs and that their vote share is represented in parliament. However, the system was disproportional enough to allow the SNP a majority of MSPs on a minority of the vote in 2011.

Constituency link

Constituency MSPs, elected by FPTP, ensure that each constituent knows that they have one specific MSP whose job it is to represent their area, including those who did not vote for them. Furthermore, it could be argued that the list MSPs, who are likely to be from a range of parties, allow constituents a greatly increased chance of being able to contact someone who represents both their area and the party they support, and a choice of people to contact after each election.

On the other hand, as list MSPs have not been voted in as individual candidates, some people believe they are 'second-class' MSPs, who nobody knows enough about to turn to anyway, and are therefore not as accountable as constituency MSPs.

Coalition/minority government

As AMS is broadly proportional, it is likely that the result of each election will be a coalition or minority government. In the Scottish Parliament there were Labour–Liberal Democrat coalition governments from 1999–2003 and 2003–2007, and an SNP minority government from 2007–2011. This means that government decisions and Acts passed must be the result of consultation between at least two parties, and so will reflect more of the country's views than those of a majority government elected on a minority of votes.

However, while mathematically unlikely, the SNP managed to gain a majority government in 2011, despite getting a plurality of the vote (45%). This means that the SNP can carry forward their policies largely unopposed with a strong **mandate**, having been elected under a broadly proportional system. Others also argue that coalitions and minority governments are slow and inefficient ways of running a country.

Constituency	
Marco Biagi	SNP
Lothian Region	
Sarah Boyack	Labour
Kezia Dugdale	Labour
Neil Findlay	Labour
Gavin Brown	Conservative
Cameron Buchanan	Conservative
Alison Johnstone	Green
Vacant seat	

MSPs representing Edinburgh Central [October 2015]

DISADVANTAGES OF THE ADDITIONAL MEMBER SYSTEM

Parties are more powerful than voters

It could be argued that parties are placed in a very powerful position, as the order of candidates is decided by political parties, and voters have no way of deciding between them. This means that candidates may campaign with their main priority being keeping the party leadership happy, rather than appealing to the voters' wishes.

Some may argue that parties perform a useful function by choosing the party lists. It could be argued that this allows them to put forward the best people for election, so voters don't have to get to know up to seven candidates from each party, before each election.

List MSPs

A number of questions have been raised about the legitimacy and importance of the regional list MSPs. Firstly, parties can place candidates as FPTP candidates and first on a region's list. Voters could feel like an unpopular candidate for a popular party should not have the right to be elected at the second chance. Secondly, they may be spread so thinly across a geographically huge area (like Highlands and Islands) that they cannot hope to effectively represent their diverse region. Finally, the lack of by-elections questions the legitimacy of some list MSPs.

 DON'T FORGET

The newly-formed Scottish Parliament chose AMS, above all other systems, when setting up the first elections in 1999.

ONLINE

Follow the link at www.brightredbooks.net for more information.

 **ONLINE TEST**

Head to www.brightredbooks.net and test yourself on the AMS voting system.

 THINGS TO DO AND THINK ABOUT

1   Essay practice: Evaluate the view that the Additional Member System (AMS) leads to better representation than First Past the Post (FPTP).

VOTING SYSTEMS: SINGLE TRANSFERABLE VOTE AND THE PARTY LIST

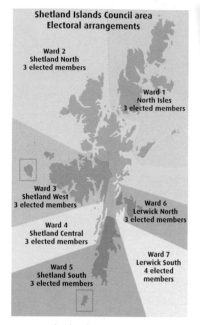

Shetland Council Wards

City of Edinburgh Council Wards

Name of Candidate	Party	Result
William Bonnar	Scottish Socialist Party	*Excluded (Stage 6)*
Thomas Muirhead Connor	Conservative	*Excluded (Stage 7)*
Moira Ann Crawford	Scottish Green Party	*Excluded (Stage 8)*
Jean Douglas	Britannica	*Excluded (Stage 4)*
Jahangir Hanif	SNP	Elected (Stage 3)
Mhairi Hunter	SNP	Elected (Stage 9)
David Mansfield Jago	Liberal Democrats	*Excluded (Stage 5)*
Anne-Marie Millar	Independent	*Unsuccessful (Stage 9)*
James Scanlon	Labour Party	Elected (Stage 1)
Soryia Siddique	Labour Party	Elected (Stage 2)

Glasgow City Council Election results 2012: Ward 8 Southside Central

Year	2003	2012
Voting system	FPTP	STV
Candidates	27.7%	23.4%
Councillors	21.8%	24.3%

Female candidates in Scottish local elections

SINGLE TRANSFERABLE VOTE

The Single Transferable Vote (STV) has been used for Scottish local council elections since the 2007 elections. It was a 2003 Scottish Election manifesto policy of the Liberal Democrats, and the Lib Dems were not prepared to enter into a coalition government with Labour unless it was implemented: a deal-breaker. Up until this point, Labour had dominated Scottish local councils through the First Past the Post system.

STV is a form of proportional representation. This means that the share of representatives for each party elected in an election should closely reflect the share of votes for that party.

Scotland's 32 local authorities elect 1 223 councillors, who are elected in electoral areas called **multi-member wards**. Each **ward** elects three or four councillors. Urban, densely-populated areas have more wards than rural areas.

Voting

To vote, voters rank-order candidates in order of preference by numbering them ('1' being the first choice, '2' being next favourite, and so on). Parties often put forward multiple candidates, as they may well win more than one seat in each ward.

In order to be elected, a candidate must meet a **quota** (specific share) of votes. Once all the votes have been counted and a candidate is elected (has met the quota), any votes that candidate receives over the amount required are called **surplus votes**, and are '**re-allocated**' (redistributed) to the next preference candidates.

If the seats are not filled by the re-allocation of surplus votes, then the candidate with the fewest votes by that stage is eliminated, and their next-preference votes are re-allocated. This means nearly all votes will contribute to the result at some stage.

STV Quota formula

$$\text{Quota} = \frac{\text{Share of votes}}{\text{Number of seats available} + 1}$$

Advantages of Single Transferable Vote

STV gives voters far more choice than FPTP or AMS. Voters can choose not just between candidates from different parties, but in many wards can choose between candidates within a party. In 2012, there was an average of 7.1 candidates standing in each ward, compared to 3.4 in the 2003 local council election, when FPTP was used. It can be time-consuming, however, and voters may not know many candidates or have many strong preferences. In 2012, only 23% of ballot papers contained a fourth preference vote.

STV gives voters a real chance to have a say in the result of the election. As three or four candidates are elected in each ward, there is a strong possibility that most people's first preference candidate is elected at some stage. In 2012, 76.7% of voters gave their first preference vote to a successful candidate. In the 2003 FPTP election, only 52.3% of voters voted for a successful candidate.

STV, in theory, should benefit ethnic minority and female candidates. As parties can nominate more than one candidate per ward, there is a potential electoral advantage in presenting a diverse range of candidates, as different candidates may appeal to different sections of the electorate. In the 2012 election for Glasgow's Southside Central Ward, Labour had one white male and one female ethnic minority candidate elected, and the SNP had one male ethnic minority candidate and one white female candidate elected.

contd

Disadvantages of STV

Critics of STV claim that it is a confusing system. In 2012, 1.7% of votes were rejected, compared to 0.77% in the 1999 FPTP local council election. The most common reason for ballots being rejected (50%) is this is that voters indicated more than one first preference.

As each ward must elect at least three councillors, there can be extremely large wards in rural areas with a low population. In wards like Highland Council's Ward 6: Wester Ross, Strathpeffer and Lochalsh, constituents may rarely see their councillors at all.

Party	% 1st Preferences	% Seats	Councils controlled
Conservative	13.3%	9.4%	0
Green	2.3%	1.1%	0
Labour	31.4%	32.2%	4
Liberal Democrat	6.6%	5.8%	0
SNP	32.3%	34.8%	2
Independent	12.1%	16.4%	3
Others	1.9%	0.33%	0

2012 Scottish Local Council Election Results Summary

THE PARTY LIST SYSTEM

The Party List system is a proportional representation voting system, used to elect the UK's 73 Members of the European Parliament (MEPs). Under this system, the UK is divided up into 12 electoral regions, one of which is Scotland. It is called the Party List system as political parties, not candidates, appear on the ballot paper.

Voting

In Party List elections, voters simply place an 'X' next to their preferred party. Seats are allocated to the parties using the d'Hondt formula (just like the regional list used in AMS), resulting in a broadly proportional result overall.

Advantages of the Party List

The Party List's biggest advantage is its proportionality. The share of seats each party wins is very close to the share of votes it receives nationally. However, in each region the result may be quite disproportional, such as UKIP (compared to the Greens) in Scotland.

The second advantage of the Party List system is that large, multi-member regions allow parties the opportunity to promote under-represented groups (like ethnic minorities or women). In the 2014 elections, almost 40% of the UK's MEPs elected were women (compared to 29% of MPs), and 10% of MEPs elected were from an ethnic minority (compared to 6.6% of MPs).

Another advantage of the Party List system is that there are relatively few wasted votes. As seats are allocated through the d'Hondt system, people can vote for their preferred party knowing that party has a realistic chance of being elected.

Finally, the Party Lists system, with its large multi-member regions sees that the vast majority of voters will be represented by at least one MEP from the party they voted for. In Scotland in the 2014 election, supporters of the SNP, Labour, the Conservatives and UKIP (82% of Scottish voters) are represented by at least one MEP.

Disadvantages of the Party List

As the order of the candidates on each party's list is chosen by the party, not by voter preference, the voters have a very limited choice in who represents them. UKIP voters may have preferred Kevin Newton, who was second on their party list, but instead their votes elected David Coburn.

Secondly, in such large multi-member regions, the electorate may feel that there is a very weak **constituency link**; that their MEP is too far-removed to represent them and their interests. Scotland's five million citizens have only six MEPs to represent them.

THINGS TO DO AND THINK ABOUT

1   Essay practice: Evaluate the effectiveness of proportional representation (PR) systems in providing fair representation.

Party	% Votes	MEPs (%)
UKIP	27%	24 (33%)
Labour	25%	20 (27%)
Conservative	24%	19 (26%)
Green	8%	3 (4%)
SNP	2%	2 (3%)
Liberal Democrat	7%	1 (1%)
Sinn Fein*	-	1 (1%)
DUP*	-	1 (1%)
Plaid Cymru	1%	1 (1%)
Ulster Unionists*	-	1 (1%)
Others	6%	0

2014 European Parliament Elections: UK (*Northern Irish parties, elected using STV)

VOTING INFLUENCES: SOCIOLOGICAL FACTORS

There are a number of factors which seem to affect a person's likelihood of supporting one party over another. Factors about that person's characteristics, such as social class or age, are called **sociological** influences.

	Voting (%)				
	Con.	Lab.	Lib Dem	UKIP	Other
All	38	31	8	13	10
Gender					
Male	38	30	8	14	10
Female	37	33	8	12	10
Age					
18-24	27	43	5	8	17
25-34	33	36	7	10	14
35-44	35	35	10	10	10
45-54	36	33	8	14	9
55-64	37	31	9	14	9
65+	47	23	8	17	5
Social class					
AB	45	26	12	8	9
C1	41	29	8	11	11
C2	32	32	6	19	11
DE	27	41	5	17	10
Men by class					
AB	46	25	11	10	8
C1	42	27	8	12	11
C2	30	32	5	21	12
DE	26	40	4	18	12
Women by class					
AB	44	28	12	6	10
C1	41	31	8	10	10
C2	34	33	7	17	9
DE	28	42	5	16	9
Ethnicity					
White	39	28	8	14	11
Non-white	23	65	4	2	6

2015 UK General Election: Voting by Group (Ipsos-MORI)

	Voting (%)					
	Con.	Lab.	Lib Dem	SNP	Green	Other
All	13	29	10	45	5	7
Gender						
Male	12	24	4	46	6	8
Female	12	29	6	43	4	6
Age						
18-34	7	24	8	43	10	8
35-54	10	28	4	47	6	5
55+	17	26	5	42	2	8
Social class						
AB	14	25	5	41	8	7
C1	17	25	8	41	6	3
C2DE	9	28	4	47	4	8

2011 Scottish Parliament Election: Voting by Group (Scottish Election Study)

SOCIAL CLASS

Social class refers to the socio-economic section of society a person belongs to. There are a number of ways of measuring this, but the most commonly used in voting behaviour is the Social Grade System, based on the National Readership Survey (NRS).

Social class and voting

One would expect that people vote for the political party which represents their personal economic interests. This is called **class partisanship**.

As its name suggests, Labour could be expected to speak up for the interests of normal working people, those in the working class (social classes D and E). One would therefore expect their vote among the lower social classes to be high. Similarly, as the party more associated with private education and wealth, one would expect the Conservative vote among the upper and middle classes (social classes A and B) to be high. In Scottish Parliament Elections, the SNP's collectivist policies (like free prescriptions and university tuition) have been popular with those in the working class.

Class dealignment

The link between social class and voting has been on the decline in the last few decades. As working and industrial patterns have changed in the UK, the traditional split between middle and working classes (ABC1 and C2DE) have been blurred. Party policies from both Labour and the Conservatives have reflected this, with policies from both designed to appeal to a wider range of voters. As such, between the October 1974 and 2015 UK General Elections, the Conservative vote in social classes ABC1 has decreased from 56% to 45%, and the Labour vote in DE has decreased from 57% to 41%.

GEOGRAPHICAL VOTING PATTERNS

Clearly linked to social class are geographical patterns of voting. Wealthy constituencies tend to vote Conservative, while working class areas tend to vote Labour. Conservative seats are concentrated in the wealthy south-east of England and in rural constituencies, while Labour votes are in the less affluent large cities in the north of England and (traditionally) in the central belt of Scotland.

However, there are some more affluent constituencies which elect Labour MPs. Dulwich and West Norwood, a diverse London constituency with an average income of £32 695, elected Helen Hayes with 54.1% of the vote.

In Scottish Parliamentary Elections, there are similar geographical patterns of voting. Most of Labour's constituency seats in 2011 came from urban areas of relative deprivation, such as the seats around Glasgow (like Glasgow Maryhill and Springburn), or Edinburgh Northern and Leith. Two of the three seats won by the Conservatives are along the border with England.

GENDER

There is a noticeable difference in votes between the genders in UK General Elections. More women vote Labour or Liberal Democrat, and they're less likely to vote Conservative.

contd

One reason for this is the fact that women are much more likely to be employed in the public sector than men. This means that Conservative policies of public spending cuts, and encouraging private business, are not as popular with women.

Secondly, cuts to family benefits, such as child tax credits for middle-class families and child benefit, are unlikely to encourage middle-class women to vote Conservative.

Thirdly, Labour's female-friendly policies, such as the use of all-women shortlists for UK General Election candidates, which resulted in 101 women Labour MPs being elected in 1997, may make women feel that Labour work more in their interest.

Different voting patterns between the genders become more pronounced when examined with social class. In Scottish elections, women are more likely to vote for Labour or the Liberal Democrats, while men are more likely to vote for the SNP or the Greens.

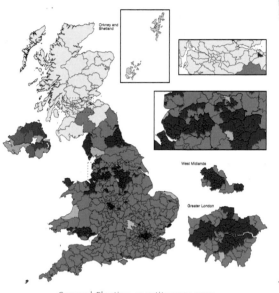

General Election constituency map

AGE

Younger voters tend to vote for more collectivist parties, which favour government providing for people through welfare and social provision. In UK General Elections, Labour and the Liberal Democrats achieve a higher share of the youth vote, and see their vote decline as the age of voter increases.

Conversely, the Conservatives see their vote increase considerably as the age of voter increases. This is likely because of a combination of its focus on traditional values on issues like family, and low-tax policies (such as raising the threshold for inheritance tax) being attractive to more elderly voters who are more likely to have savings.

In Scottish Parliamentary Elections, the Conservatives' vote share also increases with voter age. The Liberal Democrats, and particularly the Scottish Green Party, see their vote decline as voters age.

ETHNICITY

In the UK, ethnic minority groups are more likely to be in poverty than white people. Voting among ethnic minorities, therefore, tends to favour the Labour Party, with its tradition of collectivist policies to help those in need. The Conservatives, on the other hand, tend to do much worse among ethnic minorities than among white voters.

Scottish Parliament Election 2011: Constituency results

Party	All ethnic minorities	Mixed/ multiple	Asian	Black	Other
Labour	54%	41%	53%	70%	32%
Conservative	25%	22%	29%	16%	31%
Lib Dem	7%	12%	7%	5%	9%
Other	10%	19%	8%	7%	18%

UK General Election 2015: Ethnic Minority Voting (YouGov)

THINGS TO DO AND THINK ABOUT

1 Examine your constituency's results at the last UK and/or Scottish Parliament Election.
   a Do they suggest sociological factors are a strong indicator of voter choice?
   b Which factors seem to be most important in your constituency?

VOTING INFLUENCES: RATIONAL CHOICE

DON'T FORGET

Rational choice theories of voting suggest that voters are swayed by not just one, but a range of factors.

ONLINE

Check out the link at www. brightredbooks.net to see which party's policies you agree with.

FLOATING VOTERS

While many believe that the key voting influences are sociological, there are others who believe that modern voters are more discerning than that and that the political parties have to work harder to convince individuals to vote for them. People who are not clearly aligned to one party are called **floating voters**.

When asked halfway through the 2015 UK General Election campaign, 34% of voters said that they may change their vote before election day. This was a huge increase on the 18% who said the same during the 1992 Election campaign. On the day before the 2015 UK General Election, 21% of voters said they might change their vote.

For floating voters, it is conscious decisions about which party best represents a voter's interests or wishes which are the main determinant of voting outcomes. These are called **rational choice** theories of voting.

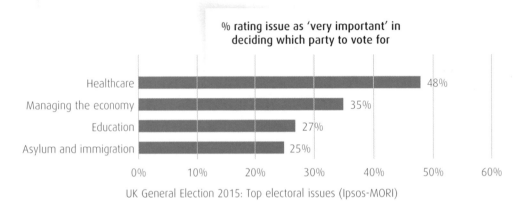

% rating issue as 'very important' in deciding which party to vote for

Healthcare	48%
Managing the economy	35%
Education	27%
Asylum and immigration	25%

UK General Election 2015: Top electoral issues (Ipsos-MORI)

	% thinking party had best policies on issue			
Issue	Conservative	Labour	Lib Dem	Other/don't know
Healthcare	23%	36%	6%	35%
Economy	41%	23%	6%	30%
Education	23%	31%	7%	39%
Asylum and immigration	17%	21%	6%	56%

UK General Election 2015: Voters views of party policies on selected issues (Ipsos-MORI)

WHICH ISSUES MATTER?

Before the 2015 UK General Election, a great deal of research was done into which issues mattered to the UK public.

Before the 2011 Scottish Parliament Election, voters were asked to compare how good a job had been done by the minority SNP Government (2007–2011), compared to if Labour had been in government. SNP had a score of +36, meaning that 36% more people thought they had done a good job than a bad one, whereas Labour had a score of -12.

FACT

In the 2010 UK General Election, voters ranked party leaders as having equal electoral importance to party policies.

Factor	2015	2010	1992
Policies	4.3	3.8	4.7
Leaders	2.6	3.8	3.3
Party	3.0	2.2	2.0

Electoral importance (out of a total of 10) in UK General Elections

LEADERSHIP

One factor which certainly affects the electoral success of a party is the public's perceptions of its leader. In both the UK and Scottish Parliament elections, voters know that their vote should have some sort of impact on who becomes Prime Minister or First Minister. In fact, in the 2011 Scottish Parliament Election, the SNP used 'Alex Salmond for First Minister: SNP' on the regional ballot.

The Scotsman newspaper backed the SNP in the 2011 election, but its coverage seemed more in favour of Alex Salmond than the SNP itself: 'So, the SNP's record is mixed. It failed on some big-ticket items but delivered in other areas. What has been more important, however, has been the style of government, and particularly of Mr Salmond as First Minister... In contrast to the statesman-like presence of Mr Salmond, Labour's Iain Gray, though clearly a sincere and decent man, often looked ill at ease as a front-line politician.'

TV leaders' debates

Televised TV debates were held before the 2010 and 2015 UK General and 2011 Scottish Parliament elections. In the 2010 election, 60% of voters surveyed said that the

 contd

performance of the leaders in the debates will help them decide who to vote for. However, Nick Clegg failed to significantly improve the Liberal Democrats' electoral performance, despite a very strong performance in these debates.

Leader competency

There are a number of characteristics people look for in a Prime Minister as leader of the country. Despite favourable public perceptions of some characteristics, Ed Miliband was always behind David Cameron in one crucial statistic: 27% thought Miliband would make the most capable Prime Minister, compared to Cameron's 42%.

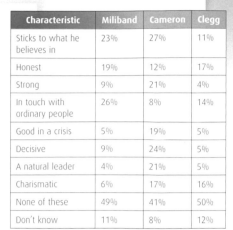

Characteristic	Miliband	Cameron	Clegg
Sticks to what he believes in	23%	27%	11%
Honest	19%	12%	17%
Strong	9%	21%	4%
In touch with ordinary people	26%	8%	14%
Good in a crisis	5%	19%	5%
Decisive	9%	24%	5%
A natural leader	4%	21%	5%
Charismatic	6%	17%	16%
None of these	49%	41%	50%
Don't know	11%	8%	12%

UK General Election 2015:
Survey of Leader Characteristics
(May 2015, YouGov)

TACTICAL VOTING

The two-party system in UK General Elections encourages opponents of one of the big two parties, Labour and Conservative, to vote for another party to keep their most disliked party out. Instead of voting for their favourite party, they vote for another party who will defeat their least favourite.

In the 1997 UK General Election, it has been estimated that as many as 20 seats for Labour and 12 for the Liberal Democrats were won by the other party's supporters voting tactically to get rid of the Conservatives. Before the 2010 UK General Election, the Green Party candidate for the Weston-super-Mare seat decided not to stand, stating that FPTP 'forces people to vote tactically, and in my case, to stand tactically'.

In the run-up to the 2015 election, a number of newspapers ran tactical voting guides, telling party supporters which other party to vote for to tactically use their vote. The *Daily Mirror* (a pro-Labour paper) ran a front page two days before the 2010 General Election, listing the 71 marginal constituencies where Labour–Lib Dem tactical voting could cost the Conservatives the election.

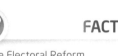

FACT

The Electoral Reform Society estimates that 9% of voters (2.8m) in the 2015 UK General Elections voted tactically.

TWIN-TRACK OR SPLIT-TICKET VOTING

For decades, UK General Elections have been a contest between the Conservatives and Labour. As it only stands in Scottish constituencies, the SNP can only ever achieve a maximum of 59 seats in a UK General Election. This seemed to lead SNP supporters (such as those in social classes DE) to vote for Labour in UK General Elections.

The evidence would suggest this is the case: in elections between the formation of the Scottish Parliament in 1999 and the 2010 General Election, Labour had an average vote in Scotland of 32%, and 42% of the Scottish vote in the UK General Elections. The SNP had a Scottish Election average vote of 32%, compared to only 18% of the Scottish vote in UK General Elections. The SNP's results in 2015 may demonstrate the end of this, however.

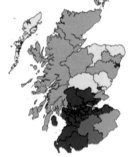

2010 UK General
Election: Scotland

2011 Scottish Election
Constituencies

2015 UK General
Election: Scotland

THINGS TO DO AND THINK ABOUT

1 Why do you think the number of floating voters has increased in the last 20 years? Note down your ideas, and add to this as you continue working through the unit.
2 56% of the public surveyed thought that 'Other/don't know' had the best policies on asylum and immigration; much higher than other policy areas. How might you explain this?

ONLINE TEST

Head to www. brightredbooks.net and test yourself on voting influences.

VOTING INFLUENCES: THE MEDIA

The media in all its forms is a huge part of everyday life in Scotland and the UK. It helps to keep us informed about what is happening in terms of laws and decisions being made, and also the actions of those in power.

In the run-up to elections, there are a number of ways in which this may have an influence on the way people vote.

VIDEO LINK

Check out the Party Election Broadcasts at www.brightredbooks.net

VIDEO LINK

Watch the highlights of the 2015 Leaders' Debate: http://www.bbc.co.uk/news/election-2015-32171042

ONLINE

Follow the link 'PMQs (14/01/15): Miliband and Cameron clash over 2015 leaders' debates' at www.brightredbooks.net

FACT

'Can I vote for the SNP?' was the sixth most googled question on the night of the 2015 Leaders' TV Debate

PARTY POLITICAL BROADCASTS AND PARTY ELECTION BROADCASTS (PEBS)

Party Political Broadcasts (PPBs) are TV (or radio) broadcasts produced by political parties, in which they put forward their point of view, or criticise opposition parties. Party broadcasts allow political parties to portray their messages to the public. Their message is not altered or interpreted by journalists or outside influences.

TV LEADERS' DEBATES

For the first time in the 2010 UK General Election, and the 2011 Scottish Parliamentary Election, the leaders of the main parties in each country participated in televised debates. Before the 2015 General Election, David Cameron (Conservative) and Ed Miliband (Labour) only shared a stage in one televised debate: a seven-party debate also involving the leaders of the Liberal Democrats, SNP, UKIP, Plaid Cymru and Greens.

While Cameron and Miliband were tied in first place for the number of people who had thought they had won the debate, arguably the biggest winner was Nicola Sturgeon of the SNP. She was only 2% behind Cameron and Miliband, and 1% behind Nigel Farage (UKIP). This is a remarkable achievement given that no members of a YouGov panel of 11 ordinary voters could name her in the week running up to the debate.

A strong performance in televised debates is not a guarantee of electoral success, however. In 2010, Nick Clegg was seen to have won the first debate by 51% of the public surveyed, and the second with a plurality of 33%, but the Liberal Democrats only increased their vote share by 1% in the election, and actually won three fewer seats.

NEWSPAPERS

Unlike the broadcast media (TV and radio), newspapers can be (and are) very open about their support for a party. Owners and editors of newspapers hope that through their support, voters can be persuaded to vote for the newspaper's preferred candidate or party.

Newspapers and election campaigns

In the run-up to elections, newspapers often dedicate a considerable amount of space to their preferred party or candidate. In the UK in 2010, *The Sun* changed to support the Conservative Party, 13 years after changing from the Conservatives to the Labour Party. Before the 2011 Scottish Election, *The Scottish Sun* performed a similar U-turn, supporting the SNP: 'Play it again, Salm', after warning voters in 2007 that 'vote SNP today and you put Scotland's head in a noose'.

Newspaper	Party support (2015)	Circulation June 2014	Change since June 2013
The Sun (English edition)	Conservative	2 033 606 (UK)	-9.37% (UK)
The Scottish Sun	SNP		
Daily Mail	Conservative	1 673 579	-7.36%
Daily Mirror	Labour	958 674	-7.71%
Daily Telegraph	Conservative	514 592	-5.94%
Daily Express	UKIP	479 704	-8.15%
The Times	Conservative–Lib Dem coalition	393 530	0.66%
Financial Times	Conservative–Lib Dem coalition	220 532	-14.68%
Daily Record	Labour	213 896	-15.33%
The Guardian	Labour	185 313	-0.90%
The Independent	Conservative–Lib Dem coalition	63 505	-13.08%

Selected newspapers' party support and circulation

OPINION POLLS

Opinion polls are surveys in which members of the public are asked to state who they will vote for in an upcoming election. It could be argued that seeing a very clear predicted result in opinion polls could put off voters, who think their vote won't matter to the overall outcome.

However, opinion polls are sometimes very inaccurate. Every opinion poll in the run-up to the 2015 UK General Election predicted a very close result between the Conservative and Labour parties, with a coalition very likely. However, the BBC exit poll, published when the polling stations closed on Election night, suggested the possibility of a large Conservative win, but still did not accurately predict a Conservative majority.

Party	May2015.com (New Statesman) 7 May 2015	BBC Exit Poll 7 May 2015	Result 7 May 2015
Conservative	273	316	331
Labour	201	239	232
SNP	56	58	56
Liberal Democrat	28	10	8
UKIP	2	2	1
Green	1	2	1

Opinion Polls and the 2015 UK General Election: Seats predicted/won per party

NEWSPAPERS: MAJOR INFLUENCE OR NOT?

Evidence suggests that newspaper support is important to electoral success.

However, there has been a decline in the share of people voting in line with their newspaper's preference. Only half of voters (51%) in 2010 voted in line with their newspaper's preference, a drop from the 62% who did in 1992.

It may also be the case that rather than the voters following the newspapers, the reverse is true, and newspapers decide which side to support when they see which way their readership is likely to vote. *The Sun* announced its support for the Conservative Party on 30 September 2009, with the headline: 'Labour's lost it'. By that point, the Conservatives already had a lead over Labour in the opinion polls of between 7% and 15%.

ONLINE

Check out the link 'Election 2015: the front pages – in pictures' at www. brightredbooks.net

THE INTERNET AND SOCIAL MEDIA

All the major parties, and almost all candidates, take to Twitter and Facebook to publicise their activities on the campaign trail.

In the 2011 Scottish Parliament Election Campaign, the SNP clearly had the most successful social media campaign.

Party	Avg. mentions per day	% sentiment of mentions (Twitter and Facebook)		
		Positive	Neutral	Negative
SNP	613	47%	36%	18%
Scottish Labour	518	16%	35%	49%
Scottish Conservatives	290	34%	26%	40%
Scottish Liberal Democrats	215	38%	40%	23%

Social Media and the 2011 Scottish Parliament Election (Ipsos-MORI)

David Cameron, Ed Miliband, and Alex Salmond have all taken part in live webchats with the popular website for parents Mumsnet.

Improvements in technology now allow parties to target specific groups of voters more accurately, so it was suggested that social media would be more important in 2015 and beyond.

However, there is little evidence via parties which achieved a large amount of social media traffic (for example, UKIP) that it significantly impacted the outcome of the 2015 General Election. On the other hand, the Conservatives did win a majority after apparently spending £100 000 a month on Facebook advertising.

ONLINE

Learn more about how social media might have had an effect on the 2015 UK General Election at www. brightredbooks.net

ONLINE TEST

Head to www. brightredbooks.net and test yourself on voting influences.

THINGS TO DO AND THINK ABOUT

1 Essay practice: Evaluate the importance of social class as a factor influencing voting behaviour.

POLITICAL INFORMATION AND PARTICIPATION: THE MEDIA

News source	%
Television	75
Tabloid newspapers	27
Radio	26
News websites	20
Broadsheet newspapers	16
Friends and/or family	10
Social media	6
Political party leaflets and magazines	4
Charity and pressure group leaflets and magazines	3
Others	5
Not applicable, I don't follow political news	8
Don't know	3

Main sources of political news and information (up to 3 selected each): Hansard Society (2011)

Type of media	%
Broadsheet newspapers	34
Tabloid newspapers	29
TV news programmes	38
Radio news programmes	19

Hansard Survey (2011): 'They do a good job keeping politicians accountable for their conduct.'

VIDEO LINK

Watch David Cameron's interview with BBC *Newsnight* (30/09/14) at www.brightredbooks.net

VIDEO LINK

Watch Russell Brand face Nigel Farage on Question Time (11/12/14) at www.brightredbooks.net

ONLINE

Check out the Independence Referendum Day newspaper front pages at www.brightredbooks.net

The media performs two key functions in a democracy: providing the public with political information, and giving people an opportunity to participate in politics by having their say. In order to make informed choices about political opinions, many people rely on a free press to give them the information they desire.

During election campaigns, the media really come to the fore, but the media still have a role to play at other points in the electoral cycle.

HIGHLIGHTING FAILINGS OF POLITICIANS

The media keeps a very close eye on representatives. Through investigative reporting in particular, failings or misdemeanours of those in positions of power can be highlighted to the general public. From May 2009, *The Daily Telegraph* began publishing details of MPs expenses, showing the things that MPs were claiming money for from the taxpayer. Former Home Secretary Jacqui Smith (Labour) lost her seat in the 2010 election after embarrassing details of her expenses, including two pornographic movies bought by her husband, were revealed by the media.

POLITICAL TV PROGRAMMES

Political TV programmes, from the serious to the satirical, are an important part of the public's political education. 55% of people surveyed in 2011 said that TV news programmes 'help the public learn about what is happening in politics', and 38% stated that they 'do a good job keeping politicians accountable for their conduct'.

In September 2014, Prime Minister David Cameron was rigorously questioned by the BBC *Newsnight* team on a range of issues to consider which sort of Conservative he is: a moderniser or a more socially conservative person.

The BBC's *Question Time* allows members of the public to ask topical questions to a panel designed to offer a range of responses. However, there has been criticism of how fairly guest spots are allocated. As of June 2015, Nigel Farage had appeared on *Question Time* 13 times since May 2010, joint-first in terms of appearances with Caroline Flint MP (Labour, Don Valley). For most of this time, UKIP had no elected representatives in the UK or Scottish Parliaments, and yet Caroline Lucas MP (Green, Brighton Pavillion), elected an MP in 2010, has only appeared 9 times. The Scottish Greens have only appeared twice (despite having two MSPS since the 2011 Scottish Parliament Election): the same number of times as Russell Brand.

COVERAGE OF ISSUES AND PARTY POLICIES

Newspapers are permitted to display bias, in a way that the broadcast media are not allowed to. In the reporting of political policies and legislation, newspapers' bias will be evident. For example, Conservative policies are likely to be well-received by the *Daily Express*, but opposed by the *Daily Mirror*. In September 2013, Conservative Chancellor George Osborne unveiled a new 'Help To Work' scheme for the long-term unemployed. The *Daily Express* ran with the headline: 'End of Benefits Britain: Now jobless must "work to get dole"'. The *Daily Mirror* ran with 'Forced labour: Conservative party to force the jobless to work for nothing or lose their dole … in the meanest welfare shake-up ever.'

VOICE OF THE PEOPLE?

It could be argued that the media provides an opportunity for the public to present their opinions to the government, one of relatively few ways of doing so between elections. The *Daily Mail* believed it was speaking for the British public when it began campaigns to have veterans of the 'Arctic convoys' (which supplied Russian troops during World War II) rewarded with medals, and to have internet providers put a default block on online access to pornography, to protect children. In December 2012, the *Daily Mail* celebrated success in these areas under the headline: 'Great day for decency': 'This was a hugely cheering day for the Daily Mail, bringing victory for two of our long-fought campaigns'.

DON'T FORGET

A free press is an important part of a democracy.

INCREASING ROLE OF THE MEDIA IN THE POLITICAL SYSTEM?

One reason why many people think the role of the media is becoming increasingly important in the political process is the increase in floating voters. As people are becoming less likely to closely associate themselves with one political party, and more likely to change their votes during an election campaign, the media can provide them with the up-to-the-minute information which will allow them to form political opinions.

Coupled with this is the now round-the-clock availability of news media. For example, 89% of people aged 18–24 see online news sites as 'important' or 'very important' sources of political information, and these are constantly updated. Also, 57% of those aged 18-24 see social media in the same way, and 16% of the UK population share at least one news story via email or social media each week.

Finally, the sheer amount of money spent by political parties on media engagement illustrates how important the media is to them. In the 2010 UK General Election, parties spent £1.5m on party political broadcasts, and £800 000 on press conferences and media: spending £2.3m on media engagement shows it must be useful!

DECREASING ROLE OF THE MEDIA IN THE POLITICAL SYSTEM

Despite the prominent role played by the media, there is some distrust of the media. In 2012, 13% of Hansard Society survey respondents were 'very dissatisfied' with the way the media reports politics in the UK, with a further 6% 'fairly dissatisfied'. A further 36% didn't know, or were 'neither satisfied nor dissatisfied'.

47% of dissatisfied respondents gave the reason that the media often 'don't present the full facts', with a further 40% saying they often 'make little or no attempt to present a story in a balanced way'. This hardly suggests a vibrant and free press, keeping a just eye on decision-makers. However, the public's perceptions of the media seem to be improving: in 2010, 24% were 'very dissatisfied', and 14% 'fairly dissatisfied'.

A second reason why the media may not be very important in the political system is the fact that media is consumed much more selectively now than ever. There are many newspapers, TV channels, and online media to choose from, so people are able to shop around until they find a paper, TV show or social media page which reaffirms political beliefs they also have. This suggests that instead of 70% of readers of *The Telegraph* voting Conservative, the reverse is true – a significant number of Conservative voters choose to buy *The Telegraph* because it mirrors their view.

ONLINE TEST

Head to www.brightredbooks.net and test yourself on political information and participation.

THINGS TO DO AND THINK ABOUT

1 Watch David Cameron's Newsnight interview.
  a Which issues are he asked about?
  b Do you think David Cameron performs well under this scrutiny? Why (not)?
2 Keep an eye on BBC News: The Papers: http://www.bbc.co.uk/news/blogs/the_papers, for different papers' coverage of party policies. How do the different parties' actions get portrayed?

POLITICAL INFORMATION AND PARTICIPATION: PRESSURE GROUPS

Pressure groups are organisations of like-minded individuals who share concerns about a certain issue. By joining together, pressure groups are much more likely to influence the decisions which the government makes than individuals would be alone.

Pressure groups give individuals the chance to regularly participate in politics, between elections. While membership of political parties was decreasing before the Scottish Independence Referendum, the membership of pressure groups has been growing steadily for a number of years.

Party / Pressure Group	2014
Conservatives	134 000
Labour	190 000
Liberal Democrat	44 000
SNP	75 000
RSPB	1 200 000

Membership of selected political parties and pressure groups

INSIDER PRESSURE GROUPS

Insider pressure groups are organisations which work closely and formally with political parties and governments. Governments often rely on them for their expertise and advice in policy discussions. They will hold meetings and negotiations with government ministers and their departments, and provide expert witnesses for committee inquiries.

In November 2013, BMA Scotland wrote to the Scottish Government, and lobbied then Health Secretary Alex Neil MSP, about a continued block on bonuses, called 'Distinction Awards', paid to top doctors. BMA Scotland said: 'Scotland is becoming a less attractive place to work and the decision to renew the freeze on higher awards is directly impacting on recruitment and retention, particularly in the intensely competitive market for high-achieving medical academics.'

However, the government does not always heed their advice, and their demands can draw criticism from other parties. This wish has not (as of December 2014) been granted, and the then Shadow Health Secretary Neil Findlay (Labour, Lothian) said: 'With spending on health being squeezed every year, it's hard to make a case for those scarce resources being directed to staff who are paid the highest, especially at a time when lowest-paid staff are to receive only a 1% increase in their pay.'

OUTSIDER PRESSURE GROUPS

Outsider pressure groups do not usually have the same privileged access to decision-makers as insider pressure groups. Without this access, they have to resort to more direct or extreme measures to get their point of view across.

Lobbying is the process of gaining access to government ministers, to try to convince them of a particular point of view. Any group which receives a pass from a member of the House of Lords, in exchange for doing research or administrative support, can move around the UK parliamentary estate unsupervised. Many are concerned about how democratic it is to allow groups access to government in this manner, and David Cameron called lobbying 'the next big scandal waiting to happen' when he was in opposition. However, the UK Government has failed to introduce a statutory register for lobbyists. In the aftermath of these UK concerns, Neil Findlay (Labour, Lothian) promoted a bill on a statutory register in the Scottish Parliament. The Scottish Government decided to propose a bill on this before the 2016 election, with parliament minister Joe Fitzpatrick saying it needed the 'full weight and resources of the government.'

Denied a formal meeting, pressure groups often petition the government. The Scottish Parliament's Public Petitions Committee considers every petition it receives, while the UK Government considers every petition receiving 100 000+ signatures. In December 2014, residents of the New Era Estate in the east end of London, supported by comedian Russell Brand, marched past the offices of Westbrook Partners, the New York investment

contd

VIDEO LINK

Check out the clip 'Russell Brand and Reporter: New Era Estate Rent Row' at www.brightredbooks.net

company which has bought their estate, and which they fear will treble their rents, and presented a 300 000 signature petition to the Prime Minister at Downing Street. There was a great deal of social media and media interest. Westbrook Partners sold the estate to the Dolphin Square Foundation on 19th December 2014.

In order to gain media attention and therefore highlight their cause to as many people as possible, pressure groups can organise marches, demonstrations and protests. In August 2014, the Stop The War coalition of pressure groups arranged marches and rallies around the UK in protest at Israeli military action in Gaza. 20 000 people took part in London, as did several hundred in Edinburgh.

An even more extreme measure which pressure groups can take is **direct action**. This is any action which directly impedes or stops the protested action being carried out. In April 2013, as part of a 250-member protest, about 20 people chained themselves together to block the gate of the Faslane naval base, where Trident (the UK's nuclear submarines) are based. This protest, organised by the Scrap Trident Coalition, resulted in 47 people who were blocking the road being arrested.

PRESSURE GROUP SUCCESS

There are a number of factors which affect whether a pressure group can be seen as successful. The first factor of pressure group success is whether or not their aim is achievable and politically supported. Patrick Harvie MSP was at the Faslane blockade, and urged for a 'Yes' vote in the referendum in order to remove Trident from Scotland: 'If Scotland decides next year to take control of its own defence and foreign affairs policy, we will be able to consign Trident to history and make Scotland a force for peace in the world.' In a May 2013 opinion poll, 50% of respondents thought that if Scotland became independent, Trident should not continue to be based in Scotland, compared to 35% who thought it should.

After the 'No' vote and a very strong predicted result for the SNP in the 2015 UK General Election, *The Telegraph* reported that the SNP included the removal of Trident from Scotland as a policy they would demand in the event of being asked to form a UK coalition government. This would be a huge success for the Scrap Trident Coalition, but it is arguable that this result would not be a result of their actions.

Secondly, the resources that a pressure group has available is a key factor in their success. Pressure groups with large memberships are likely to be able to influence the government as they can claim to speak to a large proportion of the UK population. Many pressure groups have many more members than political parties.

Thirdly, pressure groups with wealthy donors, celebrity endorsements or volunteers who are particularly skilled in things like social media or PR (public relations) are likely to be able to get their message out to a wide audience. It is unlikely if the New Era Estate campaign would be in the news if it wasn't for the support of Russell Brand.

Of course, insider status often greatly increases a pressure group's likelihood of having an influence in the political system.

DON'T FORGET

Pressure groups give members of the public an opportunity to have their opinions represented between elections.

ONLINE TEST

Head to www.brightredbooks.net and test yourself on political information and participation.

THINGS TO DO AND THINK ABOUT

1   Find up-to-date examples of insider and outsider pressure group action.
2   Essay practice: To what extent are groups outside parliament effective in influencing decision-making in government? You may refer to groups in Scotland, the United Kingdom or both in your answer.

UNIT ASSESSMENT: OBJECTIVITY

In order to pass this unit, you must achieve the Assessment Outcomes. Your teacher may choose a range of ways for you to demonstrate that you have done this.

Objectivity:

the evidence supports their point of view; a lack of bias or exaggeration; impartiality

ASSESSMENT OUTCOMES

Outcome 1

1   Use a range of sources of information to detect and explain the degree of objectivity in contexts relating to democracy in the Scottish and United Kingdom political systems by:

1.1   detecting the degree of objectivity, using between two and four sources of information

1.2   synthesising and evaluating evidence in order to explain the degree of objectivity about a political issue, using between two and four sources of information.

Outcome 2

2   Draw on factual and theoretical knowledge and understanding of democracy in the Scottish and United Kingdom political systems by:

2.1   giving detailed descriptions and detailed explanations of a complex political issue which draw on a factual and theoretical knowledge and understanding of democracy in Scotland or the United Kingdom

2.2   analysing a complex political issue in Scotland or the United Kingdom.

OUTCOME 1 SAMPLE ASSESSMENT

Study Source A, B and C then answer the question which follows.

Source A - Viewpoints on Nuclear Submarines at Faslane

Her Majesty's Naval Base Clyde, commonly known as Faslane, is the Royal Navy's main submarine port in Scotland. It is home to the UK's nuclear deterrent, the Trident nuclear submarine system. It is also the home base of a new generation of Astute Class attack submarines. More than 6 500 civilians and service personnel were employed on the site in 2013.

In 2013, the Westminster Coalition Government (Conservatives and Liberal Democrats) were divided over the options for renewing Trident submarines. Conservative Prime Minister David Cameron supported a like-for-like replacement of the nuclear fleet of four submarines, while Liberal Democrat Deputy Prime Minister Nick Clegg supported replacing Trident with just three nuclear submarines to save money.

Elsewhere in the UK there has been a mixed reaction to the Westminster government's proposals to replace Trident. The SNP's Bill Kidd said that the UK Government may think it is acceptable to dump their supply of nuclear weapons in Scotland but the message from Scotland's government,

Scotland's parliament and Scotland's people is that weapons of mass destruction have no place in Scotland. 'Nuclear weapons are an obscenity' he said.

The Campaign for Nuclear Disarmament claimed that 'The UK currently faces no nuclear threat, and no other security threat that can be resolved through the possession or use of nuclear weapons. Possession of nuclear weapons does not deter terrorist attacks and the continued possession of them is more likely to lead to nuclear proliferation than to counter it.'

Taking a different line, the Trident Commission of senior political figures from the Conservative, Labour, Liberal Democrats and the UK's diplomatic services stated: 'If there is more than even a slight chance that the possession of nuclear weapons might play a decisive future role in the defence of the UK and its allies in preventing nuclear blackmail, or in affecting the wider security context within which the UK sits, then they should be retained.'

Adapted from various sources

Source B: Survey of opinions on the UK keeping Trident nuclear weapons

		Total	Should Scotland be an independent country?			Gender		Age			
			Yes	No	Don't know	Male	Female	18–24	25–39	40–59	60+
		%	%	%	%	%	%	%	%	%	%
In principle, do you support or oppose the United Kingdom having nuclear weapons?	Support	37	17	52	20	45	30	26	38	36	43
	Oppose	48	72	33	54	47	49	53	46	52	43
	Don't know	15	10	15	25	8	21	21	16	13	14

Source: adapted from Lord Ashcroft polls: 1236 adults in Scotland, 29th April – 2nd May 2013

contd

> There is little support for retaining the UK's Trident nuclear weapons system.
>
> **View of Phil Davison, anti-nuclear campaigner**

Using only the information from Sources A, B and C:

- State to what extent Phil Davison's view is objective.
- Link and evaluate evidence from the sources to explain the extent of objectivity in the view of Phil Davison.

Source C: Survey – Views on the UK's nuclear weapons future

Which of the following statements comes closest to your view?					
Possible options	**Party supporters**				
	Con	**Lab**	**Lib Dem**	**UKIP**	**Total**
The UK should order new Trident nuclear submarines to maintain our weapons system	49%	25%	12%	48%	32%
The UK should try to find a cheaper system while keeping Trident nuclear weapons	35%	34%	47%	35%	34%
The UK should give up the Trident nuclear weapons system altogether (disarmament)	8%	26%	33%	12%	20%
Don't know	8%	14%	8%	5%	14%

Adapted from YouGov Survey conducted in April 2013

HOW TO PASS OUTCOME 1

When setting out your response, make it very clear how objective this point of view is. Have a look at all the evidence in the sources. Does the evidence seem to support their point of view (show they are being objective), or oppose it (show they are not being objective)?

You are being assessed on your interpretation of the evidence, so even if it seems clear the way the evidence is pointing, you could still pass these outcomes by choosing the other option.

The next section of your answer is crucial. In order to pass Outcome 1.2, you must:

- make at least two developed points which clearly show how objective the statement is
- use at least two sources to explain why you made your judgement on how objective it is.

To explain your judgement on objectivity, you can look to evidence of objectivity (for example, 'Source 1 shows this is not true, as...'), or reasons why the source/view might be objective (or not) (for example, 'The view of the SNP member is likely to be biased, as removal of Trident is a key electoral policy of the SNP...').

"mostly selective", "very selective", "partially true", "very selective in the use of facts", "very objective", "mostly true"

Some possible responses for Outcome 1.1

Sample answer

One possible answer which would pass Outcomes 1.1 and 1.2 is the following:

Phil Davison's view - 'There is little support for retaining the UK's Trident nuclear weapons system' is partially true.	Clear judgement on the level of objectivity	Outcome 1.1
The evidence in the sources supports the statement that there is a large amount of support for removing Trident, as a large share of the public, and pressure groups, are opposed to Scotland having nuclear weapons.	Evaluative overall judgement of the evidence.	Outcome 1.2
The Lord Ashcroft survey (Source B) shows that a plurality of 48% of the public oppose, in principal, the UK having nuclear weapons, and this rises to a large majority of 72% of those in favour of Scottish Independence. The Campaign for Nuclear Disarmament also state that "Possession of nuclear weapons does not deter terrorist attacks and the continued possession of them is more likely to lead to nuclear proliferation than to counter it." (Source A)	Synthesised (linked) evidence from two sources	
However, Phil Davison is exaggerating as a wide range of political parties (and voters for these parties) support retaining Trident.	Evaluative overall judgement of the evidence.	Outcome 1.2
The UK Parliament's Trident Commission, which has Conservative, Labour and Liberal Democrat MPs as members, believes that Trident should be retained (Source A). 49% of Conservative voters want to upgrade Trident, while 35% want to use Trident while looking for a cheaper alternative (Source C).	Synthesised (linked) evidence from two sources	

THINGS TO DO AND THINK ABOUT

1 Using the sample answer as a guide, try to write alternative responses to the Sample Assessment, using different pieces of evidence.

DON'T FORGET

You are being marked for your evaluation of evidence provided, so be sure to fully develop your answers.

SOCIAL INEQUALITY IN THE UK

WHAT IS POVERTY?

ONLINE

For more data on poverty in the UK, head to www.brightredbooks.net

FACT

The poverty line is measured at 60% of the average income but in the last two years, average incomes have fallen significantly meaning the poverty threshold itself is lower and gives rise to a situation where a family in poverty one year can be lifted out the next without their income rising at all.

POVERTY: AN OVERVIEW.

UK official poverty levels are measured by the Department of Work and Pensions using their **Households Below the Average Income** (HBAI) annual report. This information is based on the 20 000 UK households that take part in the Family Resources Survey. The most recent HBAI figures were released in July 2014 based on statistics relating to 2012–13.

- **Household** – One person living alone or a group of people (not necessarily related) living at the same address who share cooking facilities and share a living room, sitting room, or dining area. A household will consist of one or more benefit units/families.

- **Family or Benefit Unit** – A single adult or a couple living as married and any dependent children.

RELATIVE POVERTY

Professor Peter Townsend, the leading authority of the last fifty years on UK poverty, defines poverty as when someone's 'resources are so seriously below those commanded by the average individual or family that they are, in effect, excluded from ordinary living patterns, customs and activities'. Therefore, income poverty thresholds depend on the social norms of the society in which someone lives and on the incomes of the ordinary people in that society. Social norms change over time and as society becomes richer, the levels of income and resources that are considered to be adequate rise. Unless the poorest can keep up with growth in average incomes, they will become more excluded from the opportunities that the rest of society enjoys.

Poverty is measured by net household income, adjusted for size and after housing costs have been deducted. The gap between the cost of essentials to live and real wages continues to widen, meaning less expendable income.

The poverty threshold in 2011/12 per week – Joseph Rowntree Foundation

	Single adult	Couple, no children	Single parent, one young child	Couple, two children aged 6–14
Before housing costs	£172	£256	£223	£392
After housing costs	£128	£220	£172	£357

The latest published poverty statistics are from 2011/12, but for many children and working-age adults with low household incomes, the ongoing tightening of incomes in the last few years can only have increased both the numbers affected by poverty and how far their household incomes are below the poverty line.

FACT

13 million people were in poverty in 2011/12 and average incomes fell by 8% between 2008 and 2011.

The delay in collating and publishing poverty statistics makes it difficult to fully assess the impact of the **welfare reforms** introduced by the UK Government progressively since 2011. These welfare reforms will be discussed in more detail later in this chapter, but most have affected those with low or near-low incomes. Almost all of the welfare reforms have affected both working and non-working families, but the scale and depth of the impacts vary greatly. Many families have been affected by more than one benefit change so the reality is that current poverty levels may be different.

SOCIAL EXCLUSION

The term **social exclusion** refers to the alienation or disenfranchisement of certain people within society. It highlights the fact that the issue of social exclusion relates to low income and to other factors relating to severe and chronic disadvantage, and that these are closely connected. Participation in society can be measured in terms of social relationships, membership of organisations, trust in other people, ownership of possessions and purchase of services. All are lower among people with low incomes.

In today's society, people can be socially excluded in a variety of ways, such as **digital exclusion**, meaning a lack of access to ICT and the internet. Statistics have shown that people in poverty are less likely to have access to ICT and the internet either at home or on a portable electronic device, which has proven to have a **negative impact** on **educational attainment** and **self-esteem**.

DON'T FORGET

Material deprivation, social exclusion and poverty are all very closely linked. It is important to have a wider definition of poverty than one simply based on income alone, particularly when referring to children. For example, living standards can also provide a measurement of poverty.

GROUPS AT RISK OF POVERTY AND SOCIAL EXCLUSION

There are certain groups in society that are more at risk of poverty and social exclusion than others such as women and ethnic minorities. The reasons for this are discussed later.

Children and young people

Children are often born into poverty, which is outwith their control, but they are often the ones hit hardest by the impact of poverty and social exclusion. Children can find themselves stuck in a **poverty cycle** that can impact the rest of their lives. Studies have found that less than 50% of children from the poorest households have home internet access, compared to almost all from the richest families and that there are links between high levels of internet use and higher educational attainment. Childhood economic deprivation increases the likelihood of being socially excluded as an adult and is the strongest predictor of emotional problems, poor educational attainment and engagement in deviant behaviour in adolescence.

The UK and Scottish Governments have tried to tackle child poverty in a variety of ways which will be discussed in more detail later in this chapter, but the Child Poverty Act 2010 has set clear targets for dealing with the significant problem of child poverty to be met by 2020.

Example:

1 Relative low income: The proportion of children living in households where the income is less than 60% of the median household income is to be less than 10%.

2 Combined low income and material deprivation: The proportion of children who are in material deprivation and live in households where the income is less than 70% of the median household income is to be less than 5%.

The elderly

According to 2010 statistics, around 22% of people aged 65 and over in the UK were living in poverty, compared with around 13% of those aged 24–49. There are many factors involved in elderly poverty, but it is likely that those who found themselves on a low income throughout their lives may become entirely reliant on government support in their retirement. This may be in the form of a **state pension**. In 2015, the basic state pension was £115.95 per week.

VIDEO LINK

Foodbanks are becoming more important for working families, struggling to meet their basic needs. Learn more at www. brightredbooks.net

ONLINE TEST

Test yourself on this topic online at www. brightredbooks.net

THINGS TO DO AND THINK ABOUT

1 To get an idea of what some young people who are socially excluded or living in poverty may experience think about your daily routine and create a table of Needs and Wants. Needs are things that you use almost daily that you think you couldn't survive without. Wants are luxuries or items which you could manage without. Are all your 'needs' really needs? Would a young person in poverty be likely to make the same lists? If not, why not?
2 Explain the poverty cycle and why it continues.
3 Why do you think the need for foodbanks is on the rise for working families?

ECONOMIC INEQUALITIES

According to the Equality Trust, people in more equal societies live longer, have better mental health and have better chances for a good education regardless of their background. Community life is stronger where the income gap is narrower, children do better at school and they are less likely to become teenage parents. When inequality is reduced people trust each other more, there is less violence and rates of imprisonment are lower.

There is evidence to show that British society is economically very unequal and that the gap between rich and poor continues to grow.

SOCIAL CLASS

Traditionally, social class has been defined by the Office of National Statistics (ONS) based on employment conditions and pay.

Social class	Category	Type of employment
Higher managerial occupations	1	**1.1** Company directors, police Inspectors, bank managers, senior civil servants, military officers **1.2** Doctor, barrister, solicitor, clergy, librarian, teacher
Lower managerial	2	Nurses and midwives, journalists, actors, prison officers, police and soldiers
Intermediate	3	Clerks, secretaries, driving instructors, computer operators
Small employers	4	Publicans, farmers, play group leaders, window cleaners, painter and decorators
Lower supervisory and craft	5	Printers, plumbers, butchers, bus inspectors, TV engineers, train drivers
Semi-routine occupations	6	Shop assistants, traffic wardens, cooks, bus drivers, hairdressers, postal workers
Routine occupations	7	Waiters, road sweepers, cleaners, couriers, building labourers, refuse collectors
Never worked	8	Long-term unemployed and non-workers.

Terms like upper, middle and working class are rarely used in official statistics as they are so difficult to define. However, category 1.1 in the ONS classifications could be described as **upper middle class**, 1.2, and 2 could be described as **middle class** and 3–7 as **working class**. Category 8 has also been referred to as an **underclass**. This group are difficult to measure as they may work but are not officially registered as doing so. They may not pay taxes and/or National Insurance and could be uneducated and unskilled, relying heavily on the state as a source of income. The UK Government terms families within this category as 'troubled' and the children within this group are often neglected and tend to adopt the behaviours of their parents, meaning the underclass perpetuates itself.

FACT ✓

According to the UK Government, troubled families cost the taxpayer £9 billion every year.

THE GREAT BRITISH CLASS SURVEY 2013

In 2013, 161 000 people participated in the Great British Class Survey. The results showed that people in the UK could now fit into seven social classes. This reflects a shift in the traditional view of social class as no longer can class be measured simply on the basis of occupation, wealth and education. This survey took into account three measures of capital:

- economic capital (income, savings, house value)
- social capital (the number and status of people they know)
- cultural capital (the extent and nature of their cultural interests and activities).

contd

Category	Definition
Elite	The most privileged group in the UK with the highest levels of all three capitals.
Established middle class	They make up around 25% of the UK population and score highly on all three capitals.
Technical middle class	A small group which is prosperous but scores low for social and cultural capital. They are distinguished by their social isolation and cultural apathy.
New affluent workers	A young class group which is socially and culturally active, with middling levels of economic capital.
Traditional working class	Its members have reasonably high house values and make up around 14% of the UK population.
Emergent service workers	A new, young, urban group which is relatively poor but has high social and cultural capital.
Precariat	The poorest, most deprived class, scoring low for social and cultural capital.

The British Social Attitudes Survey 2013 showed that 66% of people polled believed that a person's social class affects their opportunities.

MEASURING ECONOMIC INEQUALITIES

There are three main types of economic inequality:

- income
- pay
- wealth.

Income inequality

Income is all the money received on an individual or household basis from employment (wages, salaries, bonuses etc.), investments, interest on savings, stocks and shares, state benefits, pensions and rent. Income inequality, therefore, refers to the unequal distribution of income within a group.

Pay inequality

Pay refers to payment from employment only. Pay inequality describes the difference between people's pay within one company or across the UK. Issues such as gender and race can affect pay inequality.

Wealth inequality

Wealth refers to the total amount of assets of an individual or household, so wealth inequality refers to the unequal distribution of assets in a group of people.

UK Government **austerity** measures since 2010 have been accused of increasing inequality in Britain. ONS figures from 2011/12 to 2012/13 show that Britain's top earners have pulled away from all other income groups, with the top 20% of households increasing their disposable incomes last year while all others fell. The top fifth of earners saw their annual disposable income rise by £940, while the bottom fifth lost £381 and all other groups lost around £250.

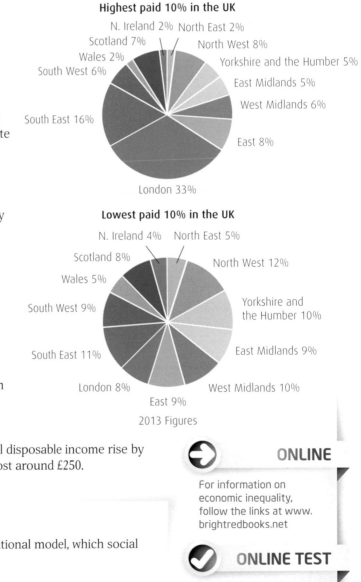

Highest paid 10% in the UK

- N. Ireland 2%
- North East 2%
- Scotland 7%
- North West 8%
- Wales 2%
- Yorkshire and the Humber 5%
- South West 6%
- East Midlands 5%
- South East 16%
- West Midlands 6%
- East 8%
- London 33%

Lowest paid 10% in the UK

- N. Ireland 4%
- North East 5%
- Scotland 8%
- North West 12%
- Wales 5%
- South West 9%
- Yorkshire and the Humber 10%
- South East 11%
- East Midlands 9%
- London 8%
- West Midlands 10%
- East 9%

2013 Figures

 ONLINE

Work out which bracket you fall into by following the link to 'The Great British Class calculator' at www.brightredbooks.net

DON'T FORGET

The fact that several methods of categorising social class exist reflects how difficult it is to measure and people may move among different categories throughout their lifetimes.

 ONLINE

For information on economic inequality, follow the links at www.brightredbooks.net

ONLINE TEST

Take the 'economic inequalities' test at www.brightredbooks.net to revise your knowledge of this.

THINGS TO DO AND THINK ABOUT

1 Think about your own household. According to the traditional model, which social class category do you think your household falls in to?
Explain why you came to this conclusion.
Now use the link to the Great British Class Calculator and answer the questions to determine your new social class. Analyse your result and compare it to your chosen category using the traditional model.

2 Create a spider diagram to reflect as many different factors as you can that may explain why there are economic inequalities in the UK.

CAUSES OF ECONOMIC INEQUALITIES

UNEMPLOYMENT AND WORKLESSNESS

A person is classed as **unemployed** if they are out of work, but are actively looking for work and available to start work within a fortnight. **Worklessness** is when an individual cannot work due to commitments such as looking after children or being a carer, or perhaps due to health reasons. Therefore they are out of work, but not actively seeking employment.

Most people rely on employment as a source of income, but not everyone who wants to work is in employment. **Unemployment figures** are based on a survey carried out by the Office for National Statistics using information from the Department of Work and Pensions (DWP). They show the average number of people unemployed over a three-month period and a new survey is done every month. A separate survey measures the numbers claiming Jobseekers Allowance (JSA), known as the **claimant count**. Unemployment figures and claimant count are different as not everyone who is unemployed is entitled to or claims JSA. Employment figures vary across the UK which is known as the North-South divide.

ZERO-HOURS CONTRACTS

Zero-hours contracts allow employers to hire staff with no guarantee of work, which means employees work only when they are needed by employers, often at short notice. Their pay depends on how often they work. Some zero-hours contracts oblige workers to take the shifts they are offered, but others do not. As of April 2014 there were 583 000 people in the UK on zero-hours contracts, which represented about 2% of the UK workforce. One in five zero-hours workers say they are penalised if they are not available for work and almost half of zero-hours workers say they receive no notice at all or find out at the beginning of an expected shift that work has been cancelled.

High street examples of employers who use zero-hours contracts include Sports Direct, which employs 20 000 of its 23 000 workforce on zero-hours contracts. Pub chain JD Wetherspoon has 80% of its staff on zero-hours contracts. Cinema chain Cineworld and Buckingham Palace also use zero-hour contracts.

Zero-hours contracts can make planning and the management of finances very difficult and can lead to people falling into poverty despite being in employment. Employers say zero-hours contracts allow them to take on staff in response to fluctuating demand for their services, in sectors such as tourism and hospitality.

Employers also say that many workers appreciate the flexibility a zero-hours contract gives them. The CIPD (Chartered Institute of Personnel and Development) carried out research and found some 385 of workers described themselves as employed full-time, working 30 hours or more a week, despite being on zero-hours contracts.

How are people employed?

 = 20,000

22·2m
full-time workers

8·2m
part-time workers

1·4m
zero-hours contracts (based on survey of businesses)*

0·6m
zero-hours workers(based on survey of employees)*

*Figures for zero hours contracts may be higher than zero hours workers because workers can have more than one contract

Source: Labour Force Survey, April 2014/ONS business survey, April 2014

LOW PAY: THE WORKING POOR

Despite the National Minimum Wage, which was increased in October 2014, many employees still find themselves struggling to make ends meet as wages do not keep up with prices. Three million families don't earn enough and 1 in 10 workers earn less than £7 per hour.

contd

Some employment can be low paid and cyclical where some workers may find themselves experiencing periods of unemployment rather than long-term unemployment. This is often referred to as **low pay, no pay**.

As of April 2016, the Minimum Wage will be 'topped up' for people over 25 by a new **compulsory National Living Wage**. This will start at £7.20 per hour and aims to reach £9 per hour by 2020.

The majority of people in poverty are from working households. A record five million UK workers were in low-paid jobs.

Most new jobs are in low paid industries and often provide little prospects for progression or incentives to work more hours. Some workers will actually have to pay back some of the benefits they may have received due to their low pay if they work overtime. This can be as much as 76p deducted from every £1 of overtime earnings and is known as **claw back**.

The cost of childcare has increased 77% in the last ten years. This is not in line with earnings, and some families may find they end up paying more in childcare than they earn due to the type of work available to them.

RECESSION, AUSTERITY AND GOVERNMENT POLICY

Irresponsible lending by many banks led to a global recession in 2008 and governments cut back on public spending. Many businesses were forced to cease trading and unemployment started to rise sharply. When the global financial crisis hit, the UK unemployment rate was a little over 5% or 1.6 million. Towards the end of 2009, with the UK coming out of its severest recession since the 1950s, it was 2.5 million, or 8%.

The impact on welfare has been significant as the government tries to cut back on public spending to cover debts and losses and there has been an increase in means testing.

UK Government Policy	Description
Welfare Reform Act 2013: The Welfare Benefit Cap	A limit on the total amount of certain benefits that most people aged 16 to 64 can get. The level of the cap is: £500 a week for couples (with or without children living with them) £500 a week for single parents whose children live with them £350 a week for single adults who don't have children, or whose children don't live with them. The state retirement age will rise to 66, although this will not happen before 2016 for men and 2020 for women.
Welfare Reform Act 2013 (The 'Bedroom Tax')	The amount of benefit claimants can receive is reduced if they are deemed to have too much living space in the property they are renting from local government.
The Welfare Reform Bill 2015	New Living Wage by 2016. Benefits cap reduced from £26,000 per household to £23,000 in London and £20,000 in the rest of the country. Four year freeze on working age benefits.

Other recent changes include the introduction of the Personal Independence Payment, which replaced Disability Living Allowance for those with long-term disabilities and/ or illnesses and the introduction of the Work Capability Assessment (WCA). The WCA applies to those claiming Incapacity Benefit, Severe Disablement Allowance and Income Support. Individuals are assessed and require a doctor's certificate from ATOS Healthcare to receive state support. ATOS assessments have resulted in many people with serious illnesses and/or disabilities being classed as being fit for work.

THINGS TO DO AND THINK ABOUT

1 Explain why some people may choose not to work due to current government policy.
2 Analyse the factors that can affect access to wealth, e.g. well-connected internships.
3 Describe how the postcode lottery can impact wealth.

FACT

Many companies that offer low-skilled work, such as Tesco, actually pay their workers more than the minimum wage.

VIDEO LINK

Social mobility has been scrutinised recently due to suggestions that a minority of people get access to jobs and internships by being well connected and wealthy. Read more at www. brightredbooks.net

FACT

According to the British Attitudes Survey 2014, 56% of those polled believe that unemployment benefits are not enough to live on.

ONLINE

Read the article on austerity at www. brightredbooks.net

VIDEO LINK

Watch the clips at www. brightredbooks.net for more information on this topic.

DON'T FORGET

Workers in Britain are more likely to be low paid than workers in comparable economies like Germany and Australia.

ONLINE TEST

Test your knowledge of the causes of economic inequalities at www. brightredbooks.net

TACKLING ECONOMIC INEQUALITIES

COLLECTIVIST AND INDIVIDUALIST APPROACHES

The **collectivist approach** means that society is responsible for all its citizens. The state (government, local authorities) has an obligation to provide services such as health and education for all. **Individualists** on the other hand, argue that it is up to each person to look after their own health and welfare and that of their family, and believe that when the state provides too much, some people give up on their own responsibilities. Individualists say collectivism leads to an expensive, inefficient **nanny state** and may prefer private providers of health, education and insurance, believing that competition between service providers saves money and is more efficient. They believe collectivism creates a **dependency culture**, but collectivists disagree stating that the founding principles of the **welfare state** are collectivist, and believing that the state should provide for its citizens through taxation.

Traditionally, Labour has been viewed as collectivist with the Conservatives as individualist. The current government has its own version of an individualist approach and Chancellor George Osborne claims that: 'for too long we've had a system where people who did the right thing – who get up in the morning and work hard – felt penalised for it, while people who did the wrong thing got rewarded for it – that's wrong. There is a question for government and for society about the welfare state, and the taxpayers subsidising lifestyles like that.'

They are not alone in this thinking. The 2013 British Social Attitudes Survey found that 77% of people think that 'large numbers of people' falsely claim benefits and 49% believed that the Government should spend less on unemployment benefits.

THE SCOTTISH PERSPECTIVE

The SNP Government supports universal benefits and a collectivist approach to the welfare state, including policies such as free university tuition fees. But with cuts being imposed on the Scottish budget, opposition parties question the longevity of these policies. Decision-making in Scotland can influence the rest of the UK too.

THE WELFARE STATE AND THE BIG SOCIETY

In 1942, the Beveridge Report was published highlighting the 'five giants standing in the way of social progress.' These five giants were Want, Squalor, Ignorance, Disease and Idleness. The report specifically focussed on Want which, today, we refer to as poverty. Beveridge believed that it was the government's responsibility to tackle these 'giants' and that a welfare state should be introduced to do so. The founding principles of the **welfare state** were that it should be collectivist (state funded), universal (free at the point of need), comprehensive (available for everyone) and equal (services provided to the same standard regardless of region). This 'from the cradle to the grave', Labour Government welfare state provided a National Health Service, housing, education and employment programmes and benefits, all paid for via taxation and National Insurance in order to tackle poverty and its consequences. Things have changed since the 1940s!

The **Big Society** was a concept introduced by the 2010–15 Coalition Government, whereby a significant amount of responsibility for the running of a society would be devolved to local communities and volunteers instead of ultimately being the responsibility of the state. Policies would be introduced encouraging and enabling people to play a more active part in society.

BENEFITS

The Department of Work and Pensions administers a range of benefits to tackle economic inequalities. Many of them are means-tested, so the amount of each benefit can vary per person/household.

contd

DON'T FORGET

The UK living wage, promoted by the Living Wage Foundation, is currently £7.65, and £8.80 in London. In October 2014, Heart of Midlothian Football Club stated they would implement **the living wage**, becoming the first in Scotland to make such a commitment. This will include staff employed on a part-time and contract basis.

FACT

Work and Families Act 2006 – This sets out statutory rights for leave and pay in connection with the birth and/or adoption of children. Equality Act 2010 – This law makes it illegal for anyone to be discriminated against on the basis of gender, race, age, disability, sexuality, especially in employment.

ONLINE

Follow the link at www.brightredbooks.net to read more about the launch of the 'Big Society'.

The Claimant Commitment (Jobseekers Allowance)	Temporary payment paid to those actively seeking employment. Financial penalties imposed on those who break the terms of their commitment to seek employment.
Income Support	Top-up payment for those on a low income.
Child Benefit (No longer universal)	Paid to parents earning less than £50 000 per year for each child they have. 2014 Child Benefit rates were £20.30 per week for the eldest or only child and £13.40 for each additional child.
Personal Independence Payment (Replaced Disability Living Allowance)	Paid to those who cannot work due to a disability or long term illness.
Working Tax Credits	Paid to those on a low income based on their hours of work per week.
Child Tax Credits	Paid to those on a low income who have children.
Housing Benefit	Payment towards housing costs for those on low or no incomes.

A pilot scheme in some areas is replacing these individual benefits with one Universal Credit payment which will be paid directly to eligble recipients each month.

WELFARE-TO-WORK

The **Work Programme** aims to help the long-term unemployed back to work and if they do not succeed within two years they will be enrolled in the **Help to Work** scheme.

Work experience has come under fire as it has been labelled 'slave labour' and against human rights by some. As a result, many companies have withdrawn their participation.

THE SCOTTISH GOVERNMENT

The SNP Government works alongside private businesses and a range of agencies to tackle Scotland's youth unemployment problem as part of the **More Choices, More Chances** initiative.

Modern apprenticeships are programmes run by Skills Development Scotland providing individuals with the opportunity to secure industry-recognised qualifications while earning a wage.

Educational Maintenance Allowance (EMA) is paid to Scottish students between the ages of 16 and 19 undertaking a range of educational opportunities. There are various eligibility criteria such as family income, numbers of dependent children, age and residency. EMA is also provided in Northern Ireland and Wales, but not in England.

Curriculum for Excellence is the overall development of the school curriculum in Scotland. To improve educational attainment there are now reduced primary 1 class sizes and financial education is provided in secondary schools as well as Skills for Work courses. Free school meals are provided for all primary 1–3 pupils.

VOLUNTARY ORGANISATIONS

The Glasgow Foodbank is one of 185 foodbanks across the UK that can provide up to 3 days of emergency food for families in poverty.

Shelter, Save the Children, Barnardos and Oxfam also work across the UK to tackle poverty.

ONLINE

Explore this further by exploring the link at www.brightredbooks.net

ONLINE

Read more about the welfare-to-work programme at www.brightredbooks.net

ONLINE

Learn more about this topic by following the links at www.brightredbooks.net

THINGS TO DO AND THINK ABOUT

1 Analyse different government policies in tackling inequalities in wealth.
2 Evaluate current UK Government policies to get people out of poverty and in work.
3 Using the internet and local media, research local projects in your area that tackle poverty. Create a leaflet/presentation to outline one of the projects, how it works and what it does.

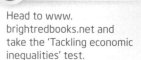
ONLINE TEST

Head to www.brightredbooks.net and take the 'Tackling economic inequalities' test.

ECONOMIC INEQUALITIES IN GENDER AND RACE

ONLINE

Learn more about this at
www.brightredbooks.net

EVIDENCE OF ECONOMIC INEQUALITIES IN GENDER

Despite the fact that women make up around 51% of the UK population, the 2013 **Sex and Power Report** found that Britain is a country run largely by men. 49% of the UK's workforce are women, but there remains a 19.5% median hourly gender pay gap and imbalanced representation at senior management and board level. Women are more likely to live in poverty than men as shown by the fact that low-paid women are paid around 10% less than low-paid men. This is known as the **gender pay gap**. In October 2014, the World Economic Forum ranked the United Kingdom 26th out of 142 when measuring the gender pay gap. The UK was ranked 9th back in 2006.

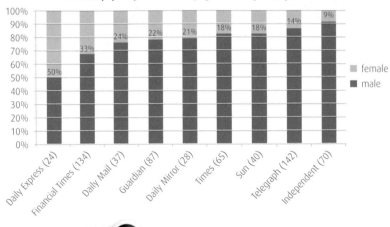

UK newspaper bylines of front-page stories April–May 2012

The Equality and Human Rights Commission (EHRC) has stated that women in full-time employment will on average earn 14.5% less than men over their lifetime.

The **Women and Journalism** study by Professor Suzanne Franks for the Reuters Institute for the Study of Journalism found that female journalists are less likely than men to achieve the more senior and well-paid positions. Franks also reported that women who do secure jobs at a senior level in journalism are more likely than men to be childless. As of 2013, there were only two female national newspaper editors, Dawn Neesom of the *Daily Star* and Lisa Markwell of *The Independent on Sunday*.

FACT ✓

Actress Emma Watson was appointed the Women Goodwill Ambassador for the United Nations in 2014 and has spoken of the need for 'political, economic and social equality of the sexes', and actively calls on the support of men to tackle gender inequality.

FACT ✓

There were only 45 female MSPs elected in 2011 (34.9%) and only 29% of MPs elected in the General Election of 2015 were female. There are examples of female UK Prime and Scottish First Ministers (Margaret Thatcher and Nicola Sturgeon), but they remain in the minority.

DON'T FORGET ✚

Some women have become very successful and are now independently wealthy as a result. Michelle Mone OBE, for example, founded the very successful Ultimo Company.

CAUSES OF ECONOMIC INEQUALITIES IN GENDER

Cause of gender inequality	Description
Interrupted employment/ education/training	Women often have to take time out of their careers or education to have and care for children. This can negatively impact their opportunities, experience and progress.
Presenteeism	Women often struggle to balance career and family making it difficult to exist in corporate culture where male executives spend time together outside of the workplace and outwith normal working hours. Women may even be viewed with suspicion if they do try to compete!
Stereotyping/discrimination/ sexism	There are still some misconceptions that women are incapable of certain tasks or that a male would do the task better. Women may miss out on work or promotion due to assumptions related to domestic responsibilities. This is often called the **glass ceiling**.
The Glass Ceiling	This is an invisible barrier that appears to prevent women from rising to top positions.
Childcare/lone parenthood/ part-time work	Women often take on the role of primary care giver for children meaning they are responsible for the costs involved. This can also impact their employment and educational opportunities. 9 out of 10 lone parents are women. This is often referred to as the **motherhood penalty**. 74% of all part-time workers are women, which affects their income significantly.
Gender segregation	Certain jobs remain 'female' while others remain 'male'. 'Female' jobs are predominantly within the 5 'C's of caring, cleaning, cashiering, catering and clerical. These are often low-paid and/or temporary jobs. Nearly two-thirds of women work in these roles.
Welfare dependency	Lone parenthood and part-time employment often lead women to become reliant on benefits.
Life expectancy	Women tend to live longer than men which can lead to increased female poverty levels in old age. Low income throughout their lifetimes may result in low pension contributions.
Lack of female role models and intimidation	Male-dominated work places can be threatening and there are few women in positions of authority or power to look up to.

EVIDENCE OF ECONOMIC INEQUALITIES IN RACE

Race for Opportunity finds that only one in 16 top management positions and one in 13 management positions are held by people from ethnic minority groups, despite the fact that one in 10 people in employment belong to an ethnic minority group. The majority of management positions within the energy and water, construction, legal, media and political sectors continue to be held by white people.

People from BME (Black and Minority Ethnic) groups are much more likely to be in poverty than white British people. In 2010, nearly three-quarters of 7-year-old Pakistani and Bangladeshi children, and just over half of black children of the same age, were living in poverty. About one in four white 7-year-olds were classed as living in poverty.

In 2009, the **Wealth and Assets Survey** revealed that the average white household had roughly £221 000 in assets, black Caribbean households had about £76 000, Bangladeshi households £21 000 and black African households £15 000.

Only 1.4% of the Scottish Government workforce are from BME groups according to the **Equality Outcomes and Mainstreaming Report 2013**, and those with an identifiably Asian or African name need to make twice as many job applications.

Following the murder of black teenager Stephen Lawrence in 1993, the **MacPherson Report** highlighted the **institutional racism** within the Metropolitan police. This term refers to racism that is so ingrained within an organisation that it affects daily decision-making and produces regular inequality.

CAUSES OF ECONOMIC INEQUALITIES IN RACE

Cause of race inequality	Description
Stereotyping/discrimination/racism	There are still some misconceptions that people from BME groups are incapable of certain tasks or that whites would do the task better. Ignorance and hatred may cause some BMEs to miss out on opportunities.
Welfare dependency/lone parenthood	Many BMEs find themselves reliant on state benefits and therefore on a low income. There are also high rates of lone parenthood within black African and black Caribbean communities.
Language barriers	Some first-generation immigrants may not speak English as a first language which can limit opportunities.
Educational attainment/skills transfer	Qualifications and certification gained outside the UK may not be recognised in the UK.
Culture and tradition	Many Pakistani and Bangladeshi women are expected to stop education, training or work to have children or look after family members. Some jobs that require uniforms may limit cultural dress.
Lack of role models	There are few BMEs in positions of power or authority to aspire to be like. There were only 2 ethnic minority MSPs elected in the 2011 Scottish Parliament election.
Low pay/unemployment	There are more young black males unemployed than employed and there is more low pay among ethnic minority households.

THINGS TO DO AND THINK ABOUT

1 Analyse the consequences of social inequality on women and/or ethnic minorities.

2 Explain the gender pay gap.

3 Can you think of any other policies that could be introduced to tackle inequalities?

DON'T FORGET

Women often bear the brunt of domestic responsibilities too. For example, they spend an average of 26 hours per week on care and household activities, compared with only 9 hours for men.

ONLINE

Read the report at www.brightredbooks.net for more on this.

ONLINE

New revelations relating to the Met Police and the MacPherson Report can be found at www.brightredbooks.net

ONLINE TEST

Test yourself on this topic at www.brightredbooks.net

TACKLING ECONOMIC INEQUALITIES IN GENDER AND RACE

TACKLING ECONOMIC INEQUALITIES

The UK Parliament introduced the Equality Act in 2010 which merged existing legislation such as the Equal Pay Act 1970, the Sex Discrimination Act 1975 and the Race Relations Act 1976 to make it illegal to discriminate on the basis of:

- gender
- pregnancy
- age
- gender reassignment

- race
- religion or belief
- disability
- sexual orientation.

The Scottish Government introduced the **public sector equality duty** to encourage Scottish local authorities to remove discrimination and harassment, encourage equal opportunities and promote positive relations between different groups.

The **Equality and Human Rights Commission** (EHRC) has a mandate by the UK Parliament to identify and tackle areas where there is still unfair discrimination or where human rights are not being respected.

Positive Action is a UK-wide policy that aims to reduce inequalities and improve opportunities for women and ethnic minorities in the workplace by encouraging employers to have an equal and balanced workforce.

FACT ✓

Women-only shortlists for political representation are permitted until September 2030

FACT ✓

Dumfries and Galloway Council in 2013 and North Lanarkshire Council in 2015 have had to deal with equal pay disputes from female employees.

GENDER

- MSN UK have introduced flexible working hours for all staff and Apple have an equal opportunities policy. The Scottish Parliament follows standard working hours and provides childcare facilities.

- The **2012 Benchmark Trends Report**, conducted jointly by **Opportunity Now** and **Race for Opportunity**, identified actions that have the most impact on gender parity in the workplace such as setting and monitoring targets for female recruitment.

- The **Fawcett Society** campaigns for women's equality and rights and puts pressure on the government to reduce gender inequalities in the UK.

- The **Gender Equality Duty** (GED) requires gender to be considered by all public bodies when deciding policy. It requires more than simply the equal treatment for men and women. Public bodies must promote and take action to bring about gender equality.

- **Think, Act, Report** is a voluntary initiative introduced by the UK Government in 2013 to help improve gender equality in the workforce. There are hundreds of companies and thousands of employees signed up. A recent initiative introduced in November 2014 encourages flexible working to support parents.

Despite these actions and the EU Working Time Directive, until all employers introduce standard working hours men, in general, will find it easier to attend training courses, network after hours and so on. and therefore climb the career ladder.

RACE

- The **Ethnic Minority Employment Stakeholder Group** (EMESG) is a government programme that ensures that initiatives focus on reducing the ethnic minority employment gap and encourages employers to tackle discrimination in the workplace.

- The **NHS Equality and Diversity Council** announced in August 2014 that they intend to ensure that employees from black and ethnic minority backgrounds have equal access to career opportunities and fair treatment across the NHS workplace.

- 21 UK universities have signed up to the Equality Challenge Unit's **Race Charter Mark**. Institutions taking part must work to improve the representation, progression and success of minority ethnic staff and students, and submit an action plan for future progress.

- **Operation Black Vote** aims to ensure greater racial justice and equality throughout the UK.

- **Business in the Community** has a racial equality campaign called **Race for Opportunity** which calls for a government review of racial barriers in the workplace and works to ensure ethnic minorities progress into management positions at the same pace as the general working population.

- The **Joseph Rowntree Foundation** publishes information relating to poverty within social groups in the UK and encourages political debate based on their findings.

- **Age UK** is a charity which works to highlight the specific needs of elderly minority ethnic groups and women.

PROGRESS?

- Since the 2011 election, there are now two BME MSPs in the Scottish Parliament as opposed to only one after the 2007 election.

- Nicola Sturgeon became leader of the SNP and the first female First Minister for Scotland in November 2014.

- The female employment rate across Europe increased slightly for the third year running and reached 63% in 2013.

- In the 2015 UK General Election, 191 women MPs were elected, up from 148 in the 2010 election.

THINGS TO DO AND THINK ABOUT

1 Evaluate the effectiveness of government policies to tackle inequalities.

2 Do you agree with women-only political shortlists? Explain your answer.

3 Analyse the consequences of social inequality on ethnic minorities and/or women.

DON'T FORGET

Despite various legislation, there is evidence to suggest that up to 30 000 women are sacked each year simply for being pregnant, and each year an estimated 440 000 women lose out on pay or promotion as a result of pregnancy.

ONLINE

Head to www. brightredbooks.net for further reading.

ONLINE TEST

Test your knowledge of this topic at www. brightredbooks.net

HEALTH INEQUALITIES: EVIDENCE AND POLICY

EVIDENCE

Audit Scotland: Health Inequalities in Scotland 2012 (Impact Report June 2014)

In June 2014, Audit Scotland published its report Health Inequalities in Scotland 2012. The key findings were:

- Overall health in Scotland has improved over the last 50 years but there remain significant differences owing to deprivation and other factors.

- Deprivation is a major factor in health inequalities, with people in more affluent areas living longer and having significantly better health. The average healthy life expectancy is around **18 years lower** among people in the most deprived areas compared with those in the least deprived areas. People in more deprived areas also have higher rates of coronary heart disease, mental health problems, obesity, alcohol and drug misuse problems, diabetes and some types of cancer. Children in deprived areas have significantly worse health than those in more affluent areas.

- Better access to health services may help to improve outcomes for disadvantaged groups.

- Many initiatives for reducing health inequalities lack a clear focus on cost-effectiveness and outcome measures. This means that assessing value for money is difficult.

The report also outlined a series of recommendations focusing on the regular monitoring and evaluation of Scottish Government and NHS Scotland initiatives to tackle health inequalities. Agencies need to work in cooperation with each other along with communities to address specific issues and ensure cost-effectiveness.

ONLINE

Follow the link to Audit Scotland at www.brightredbooks.net to find out more.

ONLINE

Learn more about the Marmot Review by following the link at www.brightredbooks.net

MARMOT REVIEW OF HEALTH INEQUALITIES IN ENGLAND

The **Marmot Review** into health inequalities in England was published in February 2010. It proposed an evidence-based strategy to address the social factors that influence health, the conditions in which people are born, grow, live, work and age and which can lead to health inequalities. It drew further attention to the evidence that most people in England do not live as long as the wealthiest in society and spend longer in ill-health. Premature illness/death affects everyone below the top.

POLICY

NHS Healthcare Quality Strategy

The NHS Healthcare Quality Strategy highlights the Scottish Government's aim to reduce inequality and deliver the highest quality health care services to people in Scotland.

Christie Commission: the future delivery of public services

Chaired by Dr Campbell Christie, the Christie Commission was set up in 2011 to scrutinise public services in Scotland and identify areas requiring reform. The Commission suggests new duties and responsibilities should be given to all public service bodies to specifically tackle inequalities, and targets the root causes of deprivation and low aspiration.

contd

Equally Well: ministerial task force on health inequalities

Equally Well is the Scottish Government's plan to tackle health inequalities in Scotland, outlining the roles of local and national government, NHS Scotland and the **third (voluntary) sector**.

It recognises that health varies according to people's age, disability, gender, race, religion or belief, sexual orientation and other individual factors, and that health improves with socio-economic status.

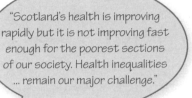

"Scotland's health is improving rapidly but it is not improving fast enough for the poorest sections of our society. Health inequalities ... remain our major challenge."

ONLINE

Read more about Equally Well by following the link at www.brightredbooks.net

Equally Well recognises the need to tackle these individual issues to improve Scotland's health.

The Early Years Framework

The Scottish Government recognises that what happens to children in their earliest years is key to outcomes in adult life. This view is based on a wide range of research evidence from education, health, justice and economic experts. The **Early Years Framework** is about giving all our children the best start in life and highlights the steps the Scottish Government, local partners and practitioners in early years services need to take.

This **early intervention theory** has also been suggested by the former Chief Medical Officer for Scotland, Sir Harry Burns. He has highlighted the biological impact of poverty and the fact that poor social conditions are associated with, and lead to, poor health, and calls this the **biology of poverty**.

He states that the way in which we bring children into the world, and the way in which we look after them in the first years of life is absolutely critical to the creation of physical, mental and social health.

ONLINE

Follow the link to the Glasgow Centre for Population and Health at www.brightredbooks.net

National Parenting Strategy

The National Parenting Strategy champions the importance of parenting, by strengthening the support on offer to parents and by making it easier for them to access this support.

DON'T FORGET

Reducing health inequalities has been a priority for successive governments in Scotland but most indicators show that inequalities are not reducing.

THINGS TO DO AND THINK ABOUT

1. Use http://www.understandingglasgow.com/indicators/health/overview to investigate Glasgow as a health case study. Include aspects such as life expectancy and targets and strategies.

2. Explain the importance of early intervention in tackling poverty.

3. Examine all the findings of the various different government investigations into health inequalities. Summarise the consistent themes and causes.

ONLINE TEST

Head to www.brightredbooks.net and revise this topic by taking the online test.

CAUSES OF HEALTH INEQUALITIES

LIFESTYLE

How people behave and treat their bodies is directly connected to their health. There are clear links between smoking, excessive alcohol intake, drug taking and poor health. Smoking can cause cancer, too much alcohol can severely damage the liver and abusing drugs can result in a number of health problems.

Alcohol misuse costs the NHS between £2.48 and £4.64 billion per year.

Obesity and lack of exercise

Despite repeated advice that regular exercise and a balanced diet can improve health, **obesity** levels are on the increase and two-thirds of people are not doing enough physical activity to benefit their health. Government statistics show that around 2500 people die prematurely per year due to physical inactivity in Scotland.

Dr Andrew Fraser of the Royal College of Physicians in Edinburgh has said: 'obesity is a direct cause of a range of life-limiting and life-reducing illnesses, including a range of cancers, heart disease and diabetes. It means people cannot work, and is also a cause of very significant financial cost to a resource-limited NHS.'

Some doctors have suggested a minimum price per calorie or a tax on chocolate should be introduced to tackle obesity.

FACT

In Scotland, obesity costs the NHS £457 million per year and 61.9% of people aged between 16 and 64 are overweight (2014 figures).

AGE

As people get older, their bodies deteriorate and become more prone to illness and injury. Older people take longer to recover too. Conditions such as Alzheimer's disease, osteoporosis and dementia are more common among the elderly.

GEOGRAPHY

Geography can impact a person's health largely as a result of economic factors and the environment they live in. Health care provision can vary across the UK too. If people live within easy reach of medical services, they are more likely to seek help at an earlier stage, catching problems before they become too serious.

Areas of high unemployment tend to have higher morbidity and mortality rates than other areas, and issues like social exclusion can affect mental health.

Areas with lowest male life expectancy at birth (data is for areas within the UK in 2010–12).

Local area	Country/Region	Life expectancy at birth
Glasgow City	Scotland	72.6
Inverclyde	Scotland	73.7
Blackpool	North-west	74
West Dunbartonshire	Scotland	74.1
Dundee City	Scotland	74.3
Manchester	North-west	74.8
North Lanarkshire	Scotland	74.9
Belfast	Northern Ireland	75.2
Renfrewshire	Scotland	75.3
Burnley	North-west	75.1

Areas with highest male life expectancy at birth (data is for areas within the UK in 2010–12).

Local area	Country/Region	Life expectancy at birth
East Dorset	South-west	82.9
Hart	South-east	82.9
South Cambridgeshire	East	82.8
South Northamptonshire	East Midlands	82.2
Guildford	South-east	82.1
Kensington and Chelsea	London	82.1
Chiltern	South-east	82.1
Harrow	London	82
Christchurch	South-west	82
Epsom and Ewell	South-east	82

Source: Office for National Statistics

contd

There is a clear north–south divide when it comes to health in the UK. The Scots tend to be the unhealthiest population group in the UK, suffering from more long-term illnesses, taking less exercise, having poorer diets and smoking and drinking more than the rest of the UK

Glaswegians from socially deprived communities like Calton have lower life expectancy and poorer health than people from similarly deprived parts of other cities in the UK, especially Manchester, Liverpool and Birmingham. This is known as the **Glasgow effect** and was highlighted in the Three Cities Report 2010.

SOCIOECONOMIC STATUS

Social class and economic status can have an impact on health. Poverty often results in poor health, and the lower down the social class scale the more likely a person is to suffer from health problems. People from deprived communities are more likely to suffer from depression and mental health problems, and statistics for smoking and drug and alcohol consumption are often higher in these areas too.

Attending the gym or participating in sport can be costly and difficult to get to for those on a low income, and transport issues often affect diets too. The inability for those on a low income to travel large distances or pay for delivery often means reliance on local shops for food, which do not always offer the healthiest options.

GENDER

Statistically, women live longer than men, but they often suffer from more health problems than men throughout their lives. Conditions related to pregnancy are obviously specific to women only, but lung cancer is actually the biggest killer of British women. Women have higher death rates from conditions as a result of ageing and mental health, but are more likely to seek medical help than men.

RACE

BME groups are more likely to live in poverty than whites and suffer from poor health as a result. However, evidence shows that BME groups suffer from fewer diseases related to alcohol consumption and often have healthier diets.

THINGS TO DO AND THINK ABOUT

1   Essay Practice: Analyse the different lifestyle choices that can result in poor health.

2   Outline the reasons for the so-called north–south divide in UK health.

3   A chocolate tax has been suggested. Can you suggest any other policies to combat health inequalities?

4   To what extent is poverty the most important factor influencing health?

ONLINE

Follow the link at www.brightredbooks.net to read the WHO article 'Behind the "Glasgow effect"'

FACT

A girl born in Glasgow can expect to live to 78 years, but if she'd been born in the south-west of England she could expect to live to 86 years.

DON'T FORGET

Health is a devolved matter in Scotland.

ONLINE

Read more on this topic at www.brightredbooks.net

ONLINE TEST

Test yourself on the causes of health inequalities at www.brightredbooks.net

TACKLING HEALTH INEQUALITIES

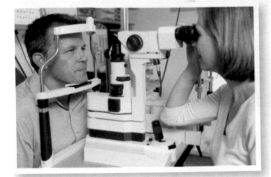

NHS SCOTLAND

Since the National Health Service (Scotland) Act 1947 came into effect in July 1948, the NHS has provided comprehensive, universal and free health care for all. Health is a **devolved matter**, meaning the Scottish Government is in control of health policy in Scotland.

Free prescriptions were introduced in Scotland in 2011, which means everyone can access the medication they need regardless of income. Free eye tests are available for all in Scotland.

NHS Tayside offers specific smoking cessation programmes such as **Quit4U** in Dundee and Angus, which offers pregnant women £12.50 per week in grocery vouchers if they quit smoking. **Give It Up for Baby** is a similar incentive scheme that provides help with buying food and groceries of up to £50 per month to pregnant women who quit smoking. Money is given via an electronic payment card and cannot be used to buy cigarettes or alcohol.

Well Woman and **Well Man** Clinics offer free advice and support related to gender-specific health issues, such as cervical smears for women and prostate cancer checks for men.

Community Planning Partnerships (CPPs) bring key public, private, community and voluntary representatives together with the aim of delivering better, more joined-up public services and focusing on Single Outcome Agreements (SOAs).

SCOTTISH GOVERNMENT POLICY

Smoking, Health and Social Care (Scotland) Act 2005

It has been illegal in Scotland to smoke in the majority of enclosed public places since 2006. England followed suit shortly after in 2007.

Tobacco and Primary Medical Services (Scotland) Act 2010

People must be at least 18 years old to buy tobacco products. Tobacco products cannot be openly displayed in larger shops, and cannot be sold in vending machines. Packs of ten cigarettes and flavours such as menthol will be phased out in accordance with EU regulations from 2016.

The Alcohol (Minimum Pricing) (Scotland) Act 2012

The aim of the Alcohol (Minimum Pricing) Act is to set at a minimum price of 50p per unit of alcohol in an attempt to improve health in Scotland. The Chief Medical Officer has stated that when it is fully implemented, alcohol-related deaths would fall by about 60 in the first year and 318 by year ten of the policy, and hospital admissions would fall by 1600 in year one, and by 6500 per year by year ten of the policy.

The Act was passed in the Scottish Parliament in May 2012, but has been challenged by the Scottish Whisky Association and a number of European wine-producing countries, and in 2015 is still subject to a ruling in the European Court of Justice.

The Schools (Health Promotion and Nutrition) (Scotland) Act 2007

A number of initiatives are aimed specifically at schools and school children. The Schools (Health Promotion and Nutrition) (Scotland) Act combines the work of initiatives such as **Health Promoting Schools** and **Hungry for Success** in Scottish schools.

The Nutritional Requirements for Food and Drink in Schools (Scotland) Regulations 2008 set health standards for school meals.

Health and Wellbeing Outcomes are embedded within the Curriculum for Excellence alongside specific health-promoting programmes such as:

contd

- supervised tooth brushing in primary schools
- substance misuse education
- **Let's make schools more active** initiative increasing PE allocations
- **Active Schools** programmes

- sex and relationships education (SRE)
- HPV vaccinations for girls aged 12–13.
- The Children and Young People (Scotland) Act 2014 – Getting it Right for Every Child, Named Person etc.

Further initiatives

Healthier Scotland policies and initiatives from the Scottish Government help people to improve their health, especially in disadvantaged communities, ensuring better local, and faster access to, health care, such as **Road to Recovery** drug strategy and **ASSIST** peer-education programmes in schools to tackle smoking.

Alcohol Framework for Action works in partnership with the alcohol industry to change attitudes towards alcohol in Scotland and reduce alcohol consumption

Choices for Life is a website aimed at 11–18 years olds, teachers, youth workers and parents to provide health information. Includes information on drugs via **Know the Score**.

FUTURE POLICIES?

80% of people are unaware of the calorific content of alcoholic drinks. Public health doctors would like to see calorie content labelled on alcoholic beverages, as it is on food products, to combat obesity.

The Academy of Medical Royal Colleges have proposed that fizzy drinks should be heavily taxed and junk food adverts banned until after the TV watershed.

In 2015, the UK Government was investigating the introduction of regulations or a ban relating to new psychoactive substances or so-called **legal highs**.

LOCAL GOVERNMENT POLICY

After assessment, local authorities can provide personal care for those over the age of 65. This can include residential care and support to allow the elderly to remain in their own home. This is known as **Community Care**. Personal care is provided free, but non-personal care such as home helps and lunch clubs may be provided for a charge.

Single Outcome Agreements (SOAs) between the Scottish Government and Community Planning Partnerships set out how each will work to improve outcomes for the local people in a way that reflects local circumstances and priorities.

VOLUNTARY ORGANISATIONS AND PRESSURE GROUPS

- **Action on Smoking and Health** (ASH) works to eliminate the harm caused by tobacco by providing information and networking to develop awareness of the **tobacco epidemic** as well as campaign for policy measures to reduce the burden of addiction, disease and premature death attributable to tobacco.
- **Drinkaware** works to reduce alcohol misuse and harm in the UK.
- Other voluntary organisations and pressure groups include the British Heart Foundation, National Obesity Forum and Glasgow Centre for Population Health.

ONLINE

Explore more health services offered by the Scottish Government by following the link at www.brightredbooks.net

DON'T FORGET

Laws and health provisions can vary in different parts of the UK as a result of devolution.

ONLINE

Learn more about this by following the link at www.brightredbooks.net

FACT

The UK is one of the most obese nations in the world with about a quarter of adults classed as obese.

ONLINE TEST

Take the test on tackling health inequalities at www.brightredbooks.net

ONLINE

Head to www.brightredbooks.net for an explanation of how to answer these essay questions.

 ## THINGS TO DO AND THINK ABOUT

1 Essay practice: Explain, in detail, at least **two** causes of health inequalities in the United Kingdom.

2 Essay practice: Analyse a recent government policy used to reduce inequalities in **either** gender **or** race.

CRIME AND THE LAW IN SCOTLAND

THE ROLE OF LAW: RIGHTS AND RESPONSIBILITIES

VIDEO LINK

Watch the clip at www. brightredbooks.net for more on this!

DON'T FORGET

In the UK, laws are made and reviewed by the UK Parliament and by the Scottish Parliament as a result of devolution.

THE ROLE OF LAW: AN OVERVIEW

For society to function in a civilised manner, there have to be boundaries on acceptable behaviour. Rules and laws are developed in order to create structure in society, and to reduce confusion and social and political disorder which might arise from a lack of governmental and societal control.

Rules apply to groups of people, situations or organisations, so they can vary. For example, there may be rules at home and at school about how to behave, as well as on the football pitch. People are encouraged to follow the agreed rules and breaking them can have consequences such as being grounded, sent to detention or sent off the pitch.

Laws apply to a whole country. Laws provide a solution when someone takes unfair advantage of another person. They protect property and allow a person to know the consequences of their behaviour before they act, thus acting as a deterrent. They allow the removal from society of those who are dangerous and protect every person's rights.

LEGAL RIGHTS AND RESPONSIBILITIES

As soon as they are born, people are entitled to have or do certain things. These are known as **rights**. With every right comes a corresponding **responsibility**. The table shows some of the general rights and responsibilities. If responsibilities are not adhered to, then rights may be taken away.

Right	Responsibility
Vote	Make an informed choice and use your vote
Free speech	Do not abuse or offend others
Protest and assembly	Do not damage people or property
Freedom of the press	Not to defame or slander

The **United Nations Convention on the Rights of the Child** (UNCRC) is an international human rights treaty that grants all children and young people (aged 17 and under) a comprehensive set of rights.

In most cases, parents have responsibility for their children until the child is 16 years old. There are, however, occasions where the courts will take action and make decisions that ensure the wellbeing of a child, such as when parents fail to take responsibility.

In Scotland, the policy of **Getting it Right for Every Child** (GIRFEC) which focuses on the rights of children is based on the UNCRC.

AGE LIMITS IN SCOTLAND

As we get older, the law gives us more responsibility for our own lives.

Buy tobacco products	18
Buy alcohol	18
Have your own bank account	From birth
Adopt a child	21
Make a will	12
Give blood	17
Buy fireworks	18
Stand as an MP or Councillor	18
Vote in elections	18 (set to become 16 in Scotland)
Leave school	16
Get a tattoo	18
Get married	16
Get a job	14 (limited hours) 16 (full-time)
Age of consent	16
Get a piercing (with consent)	16

LAWS IN SCOTLAND

Devolution allows the Scottish Government to make and amend laws on a range of devolved matters, including health and crime.

Smoking, Health and Social Care (Scotland) Act 2005	It is illegal to smoke in the majority of enclosed public places.
Tobacco and Primary Medical Services Act 2010	Tobacco products cannot be openly displayed in large shops or sold in vending machines. People must be 18 to purchase tobacco products.
The Road Traffic Act 1988 (Prescribed Limit) (Scotland) Regulations 2014	Series of laws relating to driving: • limit of 50mg of alcohol per 100ml of blood for drivers • speed limits on public roads • all occupants of a car must wear seatbelts • drivers cannot use hand held devices while driving.
Alcohol and Minimum Pricing Act 2012	Has not been officially implemented yet but will ensure that each unit of alcohol costs at least 50p.
Licensing (Scotland) Act 2005	Series of laws to tackle underage and binge drinking: • happy hours no longer permitted • social responsibility fees • no proof, no sale.

UK Drug Classification 2014

Class A	Cocaine, Heroin, Ecstacy
Class B	Cannabis, Ketamine, Speed
Class C	Anabolic Steroids, GHB, Khat

FACT

The 2014 Scottish Independence Referendum gave 16- and 17-year olds the right to vote in the referendum, and it is intended that the legal age to vote in Scotland will be lowered to 16.

ONLINE

For more information about drugs, head to www.brightredbooks.net

FACT

Ketamine was reclassified in June 2014 from a Class C to a Class B drug. Cannabis was briefly classified as a Class C, but is currently a Class B drug.

ONLINE TEST

Test yourself on this topic at www.brightredbooks.net

THINGS TO DO AND THINK ABOUT

1   Create a table of at least three arguments for and three arguments against the voting age being lowered to 16.

2   Describe the current government classification of drugs. Cannabis and Ketamine are drugs that have been reclassified recently. Does this make the classification system flawed?

3   Should cannabis be legalised? Provide arguments for and against.

4   Describe current Scottish government policy relating to alcohol.

THE ROLE OF LAW: THE LEGAL SYSTEM IN SCOTLAND

Law has a role is every aspect of society from registering the birth of a child to dealing with property after death.

There are many different areas of law:

- **civil law** covers private matters between individuals
- **criminal law** covers crime or offences (minor acts of law breaking)
- **employment law** covers the relationships between employers and employees
- **family law** covers family-related matters.

CIVIL LAW

Civil law covers private matters between individuals. Although there are many different types of cases dealt with under civil law, examples would include:

- defamation of character
- legal disputes relating to property ownership
- disagreement in relation to a divorce.

FACT

There were 77 453 civil law cases initiated in 2012–13.

CRIMINAL LAW

Criminal law refers to any acts that are offences or crimes, such as exceeding the speed limit while driving, burglary or murder. The age of criminal responsibility in England and Wales is 10 years old, but because of devolution it is different in Scotland. The age of criminal responsibility in Scotland is 8 years old, but no one can be prosecuted for a crime until they are at least 12. Some people believe that this should change.

> Anne Houston, the chief executive of Children 1st, said: 'It's the Scottish Government's ambition to make Scotland the best place for children to grow up: a country where they are protected, their rights are respected and support given where needed. Our organisations view raising the age of criminal responsibility for children as one of the key actions needed to help make this vision reality.'
>
> *Source: BBC News 2013*

ONLINE

Read more about this at www.brightredbooks.net

The Scottish **Children's Reporter Administration** (SCRA) deals with any criminal cases relating to children in Scotland and the **Crown Office and Procurator Fiscal Service** (COPFS) deals with adult cases.

THE CROWN OFFICE AND PROCURATOR FISCAL SERVICE

The Crown Office and Procurator Fiscal Service is Scotland's criminal prosecution service and is an important part of the justice system. The Crown Office is headed by the **Lord Advocate** and the **Solicitor General** for Scotland. They receive reports from the police and other agencies related to criminal acts and decide what action to take, which may be **prosecution**.

Prosecution involves the legal proceedings against the person or persons accused of a crime. COPFS also investigate deaths that need further explanation and allegations of criminal conduct against police officers.

FACT

The police and other reporting agencies submit more than 250 000 cases a year to COPFS.

TYPES OF CRIME

The **Scottish Crime and Justice Survey** (SCJS) surveys peoples' experiences of crime in Scotland annually. The survey findings show that young males are the most likely social group to be both victims and offenders, and that the crime rate is higher in areas of social deprivation, particularly in Glasgow with 1019 crimes committed in 2011–12 per 10 000 of the population. The information published by the SCJS does not necessarily reflect official statistics.

These figures are not a true reflection of crime rates as many crimes go unreported. For example, nearly 70% of violent crimes went unreported in 2012.

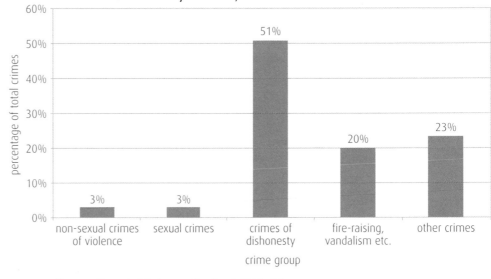

Source: Recorded Crime in Scotland 2013–14

Detective Chief Superintendent John Carnochan of the Violence Reduction Unit, believes there are three main reasons victims do not contact the Police. 'The first one is that they will fix it themselves and that means more violence. The second is that they are too afraid. And the third is that they don't think we can do anything about it.'

Source: Daily Record Feb, 2012

THINGS TO DO AND THINK ABOUT

1 Evaluate the current Scottish legal age of responsibility. Explain your answer in detail and if you believe it should change, what should it be?

2 Both civil and criminal laws have to be regularly updated. Why might this be? Provide examples in your answer. (Hint – think about new technology.)

3 Aside from the three reasons stated by John Carnochan of the VRU, describe the reasons there may be for a crime not being reported?

ONLINE TEST

Head to www. brightredbooks.net to test yourself on this topic.

THEORIES AND CAUSES OF CRIME

To tackle and prevent crime, it is important to examine why crimes are committed. There are a number of social and individual theories. Social theories suggest that crimes are committed due to the community a person lives in and is exposed to, which influences their behaviour. It suggests that the behaviour of others and societal structures create criminals. Individual theorists believe in a more innate biological cause. The overall discussion is known as the **nature vs nurture** debate.

THE THEORIES

The born criminal

Cesare Lombroso was an Italian physician who noted that some physical features such as receding hairlines, forehead wrinkles, broad noses and fleshy lips were shared among criminals. He associated these characteristics with primitive man and labelled this condition **atavism** – the born criminal. Lombroso said the born criminal was pre-destined for criminal behaviour due to their physical configuration. His theories have been discredited but provided a starting point for research into innate biological reasons for crime.

Eysenck's personality theory of offending

Psychologist Hans Eysenck used a series of personality tests to measure the connection between personality and crime. He viewed offending as natural and even rational, on the assumption that human beings were hedonistic, sought pleasure, and avoided pain. He assumed that delinquent acts such as theft, violence, and vandalism were essentially pleasurable or beneficial to the offender.

Strain theory

Most people aspire to similar levels of success and material wealth, but not everyone has the same opportunities or access to employment which can deliver the lifestyle they want. Some people will try to achieve such success through criminal activities.

Labelling theory

The labelling theory suggests that the very act of calling someone a criminal will determine their behaviour and make them more likely to act in a criminal way. Society is less accepting of criminals in terms of social opportunities and employment, so labelling someone a criminal may lead to more criminal behaviour. There are two consequences of labelling – the creation of stigma and the modification of self-image.

In 1973, criminologist William Chambliss conducted a study into the labelling theory where he followed two groups of high school males for two years. Both groups were regularly involved in deviant behaviour and committed crimes, but only one group appeared to face any punishment. He found that because one group came from respectable families, were high achievers and politely spoken, people labelled them as 'good' whereas the other group, who came from poorer family backgrounds and underachieved in comparison, were labelled as 'bad' and faced punishment for their behaviour. This labelling resulted in different consequences for the same behaviour for each group.

Social control theory

Travis Hirschi's social control theory suggests that society places controls on the behaviour of individuals which prevent them committing crime. The controls are imposed through institutions such as schools, workplaces, churches and families.

Social learning theory

Albert Bandura's social learning theory suggests that people learn criminal behaviour – the motivation and the skills – from people they associate with and the behaviour they observe.

Rational choice theory

Theorists such as Daniel Kahneman believe that people take rational decisions about

contd

committing crime by comparing the potential risks of being caught and punished against the benefits of the crime.

Social disorganisation theory

The environment in which a person lives can have an influence on the choices a person makes. In particular, areas of deprivation with poor social structures are more likely to have high crime rates.

CAUSES OF CRIME

It is difficult to state simply one cause of crime. There is usually a combination of factors.

Poverty and social exclusion

Large cities and urban areas tend to have higher crime rates than more rural areas. Many of these areas are considered deprived and Glasgow City Council has more areas of deprivation than any other local authority in Scotland, and has the highest crime rate of all council areas.

In some areas a lack of facilities, especially for young people, can lead to boredom, which can lead to crime.

Drugs and alcohol

In 2011–12, 103 people were accused of homicide (murder) in Scotland. 82% were reported to have been drunk and/or under the influence of drugs at the time.

Greed

Not all crimes are committed by those in poverty. Some crimes are committed by those from affluent backgrounds who want more money and think they can get away with it. This is known as **white collar crime**, and includes crimes such as fraud and tax evasion.

Lack of positive role models and poor family background

Some people may come from poor family backgrounds and have no positive role models in their lives. In some areas, the people who are viewed as successful and influential are those who deal drugs or run gangs.

Case Study - 2011 English riots

Mark Duggan was shot and killed by police on 4 August 2011 in London. The police thought he was armed and planning an attack. This event sparked a series of riots across several English cities, causing an estimated £200 million worth of property damage. Five people died, there were at least 16 injured as well as around 3000 arrests for crimes related to violence, criminal damage and theft.

VIDEO LINK

Watch 'The Peer Pressure Experiment' at www.brightredbooks.net

ONLINE

Read more about Chambliss at www.brightredbooks.net

THINGS TO DO AND THINK ABOUT

1 What is the difference between social and biological theories of crime?
   List the above theories under the appropriate headings 'Biological Theories' and 'Social Theories'. Briefly summarise each theory.
2 Watch the 'Peer Pressure Experiment' on YouTube. How would you react?
3 Carry out your own research into the 2011 riots.
   What were the main causes of the 2011 riots? What theories of crime could be attributed to the riots? Why were the riots nicknamed the 'Blackberry Riots'?
4 To what extent is poverty the main cause of crime?

THE IMPACT OF CRIME

PERSONAL IMPACT

Crime can have a physical, social, emotional and economic impact on individuals. The extent of the impact can vary according to a number of factors such as the type of crime, if the offender was known to the victim and the support the victim receives.

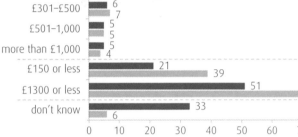

percentage of SCJS property crime where property was damaged/stolen

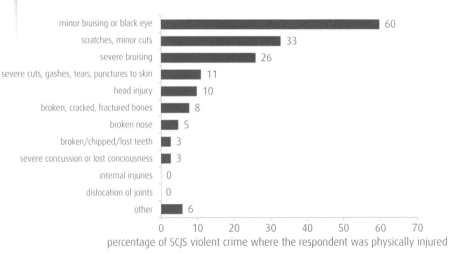

percentage of SCJS violent crime where the respondent was physically injured

Physical impacts

Victims of crime may require medical attention and suffer long-term injury or scarring. People can develop anxiety disorders (PTSD), become depressed and have trouble sleeping.

Social and emotional impacts

Crime can cause people to feel unsafe and, in some cases, struggle to leave their homes. This can affect their employment and education. If someone is the victim of a burglary, for example, they may feel unsafe and anxious even in their own home.

There is also an emotional impact when personal items are stolen or damaged. Across all SCJS crimes, the most common emotions experienced by the victims were annoyance (53%) and anger (52%). Other than annoyance and anger, victims of violent crime were more likely to experience other strong negative emotions than victims of property crime.

Offenders can also be emotionally affected by crime with feelings of guilt or fear of revenge.

Economic impacts

Some crimes have an immediate economic impact such as theft of a handbag where it costs to replace the stolen items. This type of crime can lead on to less obvious and long-term problems such as identity theft or fraud, which can take months to resolve.

Offenders may be economically affected by having to pay fines or compensation. Their employment, education and earning potential can be limited if they are given a criminal record.

	Violent crime	Property crime
Shock	38%	16%
Fear	22%	6%
Loss of confidence	13%	4%
Anxiety	13%	5%
Depression	9%	3%

Strong negative emotions felt by victims of crime

COMMUNITY IMPACT

Unemployment and lack of opportunities

Communities can become run-down if crime is a regular occurrence, so people do not want to live or work there. The value of homes and businesses in those areas depreciates and there can be a lack of investment, so unemployment rises and prospects for individuals fall.

Areas with high crime rates can receive negative reputations, and people from these communities become stereotyped, especially young people.

Social exclusion

In crime blackspots, people may feel unsafe and avoid socialising, meaning there is no sense of community. Gangs and antisocial behaviour may instil fear of public spaces.

Drug and alcohol abuse

Lack of opportunities can lead to people looking for distractions to combat depression and social exclusion. This can mean increased alcohol or substance abuse.

Increased police and CCTV presence

Areas of high crime tend to have more police on the beat and high numbers of CCTV cameras in an attempt to prevent and tackle community problems.

ECONOMIC IMPACT

As businesses try to combat crime, they inevitably increase security, which means increased prices for the consumer. Some businesses cannot cope with these increased costs so shut down or downsize, impacting jobs in certain areas. Companies are also less likely to invest in areas of high crime.

Areas of high or regular crime may face high insurance premiums and low house values. People may have to spend more money on individual security measures such as house alarms.

POLITICAL IMPACT

The Scottish Government may introduce or amend laws to tackle crime. Sometimes these laws can be viewed as controversial such as the Offensive Behaviour at Football and Threatening Communications (Scotland) Act 2012. The government may also make changes to the powers of Police Scotland, which may reduce civil liberties.

Crime means the government has to spend valuable time and money (tax revenue) dealing with its consequences and prevention, which could perhaps be better spent elsewhere. For example, vandalism costs the City of Glasgow local authority around £8 million annually. This figure is actually conservative as many crimes of vandalism go unreported.

If a country has a high crime rate, it can affect its international reputation too.

 ONLINE TEST

Revise your knowledge of the impact of crime by taking the test at www. brightredbooks.net

THINGS TO DO AND THINK ABOUT

1   Analyse the ways in which victims of crime are affected.
2   Explain how civil liberties are affected if police powers and tighter laws are introduced to combat crime.
3   Carry out a local crime survey in your area. You should aim to find out:
    * what types of crime occur
    * why people think these types of crime occur
    * who is blamed for these crimes
    * what people think can be done to tackle crime.
Think very carefully about who and what you'll ask and be prepared to present your findings.

TACKLING CRIME IN SCOTLAND

Various organisations and groups, including the government, are focused on tackling and ultimately reducing crime in Scotland.

POLICE SCOTLAND: PROTECT, PRESERVE AND PREVENT

In April 2013, eight regional police forces merged with the specialist services of the Scottish Police Services Authority, including the Scottish Crime and Drug Enforcement Agency, to create one Scottish police service. This is now the second largest police force in the UK after the Metropolitan Police and it is headed by a Chief Constable. There are many civilian roles within Police Scotland and full-time officers are supported by many part-time voluntary Special Constables.

> Police Scotland aims to protect people and property, preserve order at public events such as sporting events and protests, and prevent crime in general by visiting schools and working with communities.

FACT ✓

Stephen House was appointed Chief Constable of Police Scotland on its creation in 2013. He had previously been the Chief Constable of Strathclyde Police. He resigned in 2015.

DON'T FORGET ✚

Law and order is a devolved matter, meaning that there are differences between Scottish and English police forces and Police Scotland only has authority in Scotland.

ONLINE ➡

Follow the Police Scotland link at www.brightredbooks.net

FACT ✓

Police Scotland introduced 101 calls, which provides a single number for the public to contact police if they don't need an emergency response. 999 remains the emergency number to call.

Alongside the local policing divisions, there are a number of national specialist divisions. The **Specialist Crime Division** (SCD) provides specialist investigative and intelligence functions such as major crime investigation, public protection, organised crime, counter terrorism, intelligence and safer communities. It also incorporates the **National Human Trafficking Unit**, the **Border Policing Command** and the **National Trunk Roads Unit**.

Community policing and initiatives

Within each police division there are community teams which set priorities based on specific community issues such as anti-social behaviour and protecting vulnerable people. Community-based officers work alongside community groups to gain trust and build relationships based on respect and local needs.

Some recent Police Scotland initiatives include:

- specific taskforces focusing on national child abuse, domestic abuse, national rape, hate crime
- knife amnesties
- anti-sectarianism and unacceptable behaviour
- Smartwater – use of a marking solution only visible under UV light to safeguard residential belongings
- Keep Safe Paisley
- Campaign Against Violence (CAV) Aberdeen

Violence Reduction Unit

The **Violence Reduction Unit** (VRU) works alongside Police Scotland and the Scottish Government to tackle violent crime in Scotland. They have introduced initiatives such as **Braveheart Industries** which is based on an American social enterprise project to reduce gang crime and allow former members to access education and employment.

CLOSED-CIRCUIT TELEVISION

Closed-circuit television (CCTV) is used extensively in Scottish towns and cities. There are considerable arguments for and against the widespread use of CCTV.

For	Against
Costs are decreasing, and have fallen by £500 000 since 2013.	Costs around £8.2 million of public money each year. This money could be better spent on street lighting, proper policing and punishing criminals.
Provides around 300 jobs in Scotland.	There are too many cameras – approximately 4114 cameras monitor Scotland's towns and cities.
Invaluable in fighting crime. There were 1806 camera-assisted arrests in Edinburgh in 2014. A Scottish Government spokesperson stated 'CCTV has played an important role in making our streets safer by helping our police and prosecuting authorities catch criminals and tackle antisocial behaviour'.	Invasion of privacy.
CCTV can be in areas where police cannot be, making people feel safer and the fear of crime is reduced.	Images are often too blurry to be used as evidence in court.

SCOTTISH GOVERNMENT INITIATIVES: SAFER SCOTLAND

The Scottish Government has introduced and supported a number of projects to reduce crime in Scotland:

- **Community Safety Units** focus on reducing antisocial behaviour and violence.
- **Cashback for Communities** allows the proceeds of crime to be used to fund community projects to tackle crime.
- Reducing reoffending programme in Scottish prisons.
- Increasing mandatory sentencing from four to five years for carrying a knife.
- Early intervention schemes such as **Kick-it Kick-off** in Dundee.
- The Criminal Justice and Licensing (Scotland) Act 2010 strengthened the law in terms of hate crimes.
- Specialist drug courts.
- Tackling misuse of firearms and air weapons.

DON'T FORGET

Other funding, such as that provided by the National Lottery, can also help support anti-crime projects.

COMMUNITY PROJECTS AND CHARITIES

Across Scotland, there are a wide range of community projects and charities which deal with crime, such as the following:

- **Medics Against Violence** – volunteer health professionals who visit schools to discuss the consequences of violence.
- **FARE/CIRV** – anti-gang projects in areas such as Easterhouse.
- **Includem** – a mentoring scheme for Glasgow's young offenders.
- **Glasgow City Council Nite Zones** and neighbourhood improvement volunteers.

ONLINE

Read more about armed policing in Scotland at www.brightredbooks.net

ONLINE TEST

Test your knowledge of tackling crime at www.brightredbooks.net

THINGS TO DO AND THINK ABOUT

1. Use a variety of sources (newspaper articles, interviews, documentaries, websites, blogs etc.) to investigate the following topics of discussion and debate:
   - Should all Police Scotland officers be armed?
   - Has the creation of Police Scotland been a success?
   - Why was Police Scotland created?
   - CCTV vs. Community Policing.
   - Does CCTV work?
   - Knife crime in Scotland.
2. Evaluate Scottish Government policies to tackle crime.
3. Explain the different government agencies and organisations responsible for tackling crime.
4. Describe the role of CCTV in tackling crime.

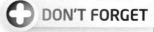

DON'T FORGET

Note your sources and try to make them as recent as possible!

THE LEGAL SYSTEM IN SCOTLAND

The legal system of Scotland involves various agencies and organisations:

- UK Parliament
- Scottish Parliament including the Cabinet Secretary for Justice
- Crown Office Prosecution Service (COPFS)
- Scottish Courts Service
- Children's Reporter Administration
- Police Scotland
- The Scottish Prison Service including Young Offenders Institutions

All courts in Scotland are organised by the **Scottish Court Service** (SCS) led by the Scottish Government. They can deal with criminal and civil cases. If someone is tried under criminal law, the Scottish Government accuses them of breaking a law of Scotland, whereas if a case is civil, it involves a dispute between individuals or organisations.

THE PROSECUTION OF A CRIME IN SCOTLAND

When someone is accused of a crime, the police submit the evidence to the Crown Office and Procurator Fiscal Service (COPFS), who decide whether or not to prosecute.

There are two types of criminal court procedure, **solemn** and **summary**. In solemn procedure, a jury of 15 members of the public listen to the evidence and decide on the **verdict**. A judge is also present, who decides on any sentence that may be issued. Summary procedure is used for less serious cases and does not use a jury.

There are three main criminal courts in Scotland, the **High Court of Justiciary**, the **Sheriff Court** and **Justice of the Peace Courts**.

SCOTLAND'S COURTS

The High Court of Justiciary

The High Court of Justiciary is the supreme criminal court in Scotland and deals with the most serious crimes such as murder (homicide), **culpable homicide** (killing without intention), rape, armed robbery, treason and serious sexual offences, particularly those involving children.

The High Court has unlimited sentencing powers such as life imprisonment (between 15 and 35 years) or an unlimited fine. Prior to 1965, the High Court had the power to issue the death penalty (capital punishment) where those found guilty of murder would be hanged. The death penalty was officially abolished for murder in 1965 but it wasn't until 1998 that it was officially abolished for the crime of treason.

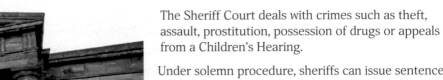

The Sheriff Court

The Sheriff Court deals with crimes such as theft, assault, prostitution, possession of drugs or appeals from a Children's Hearing.

Under solemn procedure, sheriffs can issue sentences of up to five years in prison or an unlimited fine. Under summary procedure, which can also be heard in a Sheriff Court, a sheriff can issue fines up to £10 000 or prison sentences up to 12 months in prison.

The Sheriff Court also deals with civil cases such as separation, divorce or dissolution of a civil partnership, adoption or custody of children.

contd

Justice of the Peace Courts

Justice of the Peace Courts replaced the District Court in 2007 and are lay courts (business can be carried out anywhere) where a Justice of the Peace (JP) presides with the support of a legally qualified clerk. These courts deal with offences such as breach of the peace, drunk and disorderly, assault of a police officer and traffic offences.

A JP can issue a maximum custodial sentence of up to 60 days and a fine of up to £2500.

The Court of Session

The Court of Session is Scotland's supreme civil court and sits in Edinburgh. The Court of Session can be used as a court of appeal and is headed by a Lord President. This court recently rejected an appeal brought by the Scottish Whiskey Association and other wine and spirits producers against the Scottish Government's new alcohol minimum pricing legislation.

YOUTH CRIME IN SCOTLAND

The age of criminal responsibility in Scotland is 8. Children under 16 committed more than 40 000 offences in Scotland in the years 2013–14, including 25 three- and four-year olds recorded for offences such as shoplifting and vandalism. Police also recorded more than 5000 violent crimes by under-16s from 2013–14. However, a study by Edinburgh University published in October 2014 showed that youth crime appears to be decreasing.

ONLINE

Read about the decrease in youth crime at www.brightredbooks.net

THE SCOTTISH JUVENILE JUSTICE SYSTEM

Under the **Children (Scotland) Act 1995** Scotland has a separate juvenile justice system and the Procurator Fiscal decides whether or not to prosecute and refer a case to the **Children's Reporter**.

ONLINE

Follow the link at www.brightredbooks.net for more on the Children's Reporter.

The Children's Reporter

The Children's Reporter receives referrals regarding children and decides if action is necessary, such as a hearing. Referrals can be made by the police, social workers, health and education professionals, members of the public and even children themselves.

Referrals have declined in recent years, from 46 899 children and young people being referred in 2008–09 to 19 077 children and young people in 2013–14.

The Children's Hearing system

The **Children's Hearings (Scotland) Act 2011** outlines the powers and proceedings of the Children's Hearing system. The aim of hearings is to target both offending behaviour and welfare concerns and to provide a safe environment for the child or children involved.

Meetings take place in the child's local area with the child present. There will also be a panel of three adult Children's Hearing members as well as the child's parents or guardians. The child can also bring another person of their choosing. The panel is made up of impartial male and female volunteers who have special training.

Compulsory Supervision Orders (CSOs) put children under the care of a social worker, a relative or foster carers.

CSOs can also limit who the child can associate with and place them into rehabilitation programmes. They can also issue electronic tags.

DON'T FORGET

The Children and Young People (Scotland) Act 2014 came into force in April 2015 and affects the rights of children and young people in Scotland.

ONLINE TEST

Head to www.brightredbooks.net and test yourself on the legal system in Scotland.

THINGS TO DO AND THINK ABOUT

1 Describe all the courts in Scotland, including types of crimes and sentencing powers.
2 Explain why there is a separate justice system for children.
3 Discuss the strengths and weaknesses of the Children's Hearing system.

CRIMINAL VERDICTS

There are currently three **criminal verdicts** available in Scottish courts. Eight out of fifteen jurors must agree to a verdict.

Verdict	Definition
Not guilty	Based on evidence, the accused did not commit any crime and is free to go.
Guilty	Based on the evidence, the accused committed a crime **beyond any reasonable doubt**.
Not proven	There is suspicion of guilt but not enough evidence to convict. The accused is free to go.

DON'T FORGET

The 'not proven' verdict only exists in Scotland.

NOT-PROVEN VERDICTS

Case Study: Murder of Amanda Duffy

In May 1992, 19-year-old drama student Amanda Duffy from Hamilton was found mutilated and murdered after a night out with friends. Francis Auld, whom she had known since school, was accused of her murder when his dental records matched a bite mark on her body and he admitted he had been with her that night. He went on trial that same year defended by Donald Findlay QC, but the jury returned a not-proven verdict. The shocking details of her murder and clear connections to Auld put the not-proven verdict under intense scrutiny and shattered many people's faith in it.

In 1994, Auld was convicted of making threatening phone calls to former friends, telling them: 'You thought Amanda was the last – you're next' and, in 1995, Amanda's parents launched a civil suit against Auld. A judge found him responsible for her death and ordered him to pay £50 000 in damages.

To date, the family claim they have received no payment and Auld has gone on to commit a series of minor offences in England where he now lives.

Arguments for and against the not-proven verdict

Arguments for not proven	Arguments against not proven
Allows judges and juries to express reasonable doubt.	Evidence suggests guilt.
Continues to be used in Scottish courts.	May leave a permanent mark on the character of innocent people.
It may be more satisfactory for victims and witnesses by reflecting the absence of necessary proof without casting doubt on their evidence.	Traumatic for victims and families of victims, and some victims of particular crimes may become more reluctant to come forward and there may not be a definitive result. In 2011 to 2012, Scottish figures for those not found 'guilty' showed 82% were 'not guilty' while 18% received 'not proven' verdicts. However, for rape or attempted rape, 44% were 'not proven' and 21% were 'not proven' for sexual assault.
Juries can be unfairly influenced, particularly by the media.	Confusing to the public.

contd

In 2012, Labour MSP Michael McMahon launched a public consultation into the not-proven verdict after it was announced that Lord Carloway was reviewing Scots law. He said that reform would make the justice system simpler. '[Not proven] exists purely by accident of history and it seems to me illogical, inconsistent and confusing,' he said. However, the Law Society of Scotland were sceptical, and said that removal of the third verdict would mean the remaining two would be 'proven' and 'not proven'.

Mr McMahon and Lord Carloway recognised that removal of not-proven verdicts would lead to further changes within the justice system, perhaps requiring an increased majority within juries, increased from eight out of fifteen to ten. Ultimately, no changes were made on the basis of this consultation.

THE DOUBLE JEOPARDY (SCOTLAND) ACT 2011

In March 2011, the **Double Jeopardy (Scotland) Act** was introduced allowing a person to be re-tried for the same crime if there is 'compelling new evidence'. Angus Sinclair became the first person to be retried and convicted under the new rules in November 2014. He was found guilty of murdering Christine Eadie and Helen Scott, both 17, following a night out at the World's End pub in Edinburgh in 1977. A previous prosecution against Sinclair had collapsed in 2007.

The re-trial of Ronnie Coulter for the murder of waiter Surjit Singh Chhokar in Lanarkshire in 1998 will also now go ahead and there is a possibility of Francis Auld facing re-trial for the murder of Amanda Duffy in 1992.

THINGS TO DO AND THINK ABOUT

1   Should the not-proven verdict be abolished in Scotland? Provide detailed reasons for your answer.

2   Why might some people disagree with the Double Jeopardy (Scotland) Act 2011?

VIDEO LINK

Head to www. brightredbooks.net to watch a clip on this.

ONLINE TEST

Want to revise your knowledge of this topic? Take the test at www. brightredbooks.net

SENTENCING IN SCOTLAND

HMP Polmont Young Offenders' Institution (YOI) near Falkirk is Scotland's national holding facility for young male offenders aged between 16 and 21. HMP Cornton Vale YOI in Stirling is the equivalent for young female offenders. Sentences range from 6 months to life, with the average being between 2 and 4 years.

CUSTODIAL SENTENCES: PUNITIVE SOLUTIONS

Prisons and **Young Offenders Institutions** in Scotland are managed by the **Scottish Prison Service** (SPS) under the jurisdiction of the Scottish Government and the Minister for Justice. There are 16 penal establishments in Scotland and the SPS aim to reduce reoffending and protect the public. Currently, Scotland locks up more of its people than most other countries in Europe and the prison population has increased in every year of this century. It is projected to rise from 8100 in 2009–10 to 9600 inmates by 2018–19.

Young offenders

Young offenders can be sent to a young offender's institution if they have been found guilty of crimes or while they are on remand awaiting trial.

Young offenders are kept separate from adult prisoners and can take part in educational programmes and gain skills and qualifications to help them gain employment on release.

Case Study: HMP and YOI Grampian

At a cost of around £150 million to build, HMP and YOI Grampian in Peterhead began admitting its first prisoners in March 2014. The establishment, with a capacity of about 500 prisoners, including men, women and young offenders, replaced the previous HMPs Aberdeen and Peterhead and is the first community prison in the UK, so most of the prisoners will be from the Grampian area. In a move away from the traditional style of a Scottish prison, it will focus on rehabilitation and providing skills. However, former Peterhead inmate Johnny Steele says: 'at the end of the day a jail is still a jail regardless of what is available to the prisoners inside, whether that be TVs, swimming pools or whatever. It is still a prison.'

ONLINE

Learn more about Scotland's prison population at www.brightredbooks.net

FACT

57% of the Scottish prison population is made up of low-level offenders serving sentences of three months or less. On average, a minor offender will only serve 15 days after conviction on a very short prison sentence.

DON'T FORGET

Crime and justice are devolved matters in Scotland.

MANDATORY SENTENCING

Mandatory sentencing (sometimes referred to as **Automatic Sentence** or **Required Custodial Sentence**) means that people convicted of certain crimes must be punished with at least a minimum number of years in prison. For example, the crime of murder carries a mandatory life sentence in Scotland. The aim is to act as a deterrent and provide uniformity in sentencing but courts may impose a less severe sanction where it would be unjust to impose the mandatory sentence. In the case of the crime of murder, the terms of the life sentence are set by a judge and the average time spent in prison is around 13 years. There are limits set on some crimes, for example, the maximum custodial sentence for a crime involving a knife is five years.

Automatic Early Release

Prisoners serving four years or more have to be released at the two-thirds point of sentence if they are still in custody in Scotland. Under the **Prisoners (Control of Release) (Scotland) Bill** introduced in August 2014, prisoners sentenced to four years or more for sex offences and ten years or more for other crimes will no longer be entitled to automatic early release from prison at any point in their sentence. Some MSPs would like automatic early release repealed altogether.

NON-CUSTODIAL SENTENCING

Prison (custodial) sentences are only one of the sentencing options available to the courts. The table below shows the other options.

Fine/compensation	Offenders must pay money, either to the victim or to the court.
Fixed Penalty Notice (FPN)	On-the-spot fines issued by the police for low-level crimes such as littering.
Restriction of Liberty Order (RLO - electronic tagging)	The offender is given a curfew and their movements are restricted for up to 12 hours a day. They must wear a transmitter that alerts the police if they violate their agreed conditions.
Drug Treatment and Testing Order (DTTO)	This is a rehabilitation-based sentence. People are subjected to random drug testing and court reviews to monitor their withdrawal from drugs.
Home Detention Curfew	Offenders must be in an agreed address by a certain time each day. If the curfew is broken, they may be sent to prison.
Community Payback Order (CPO)	Introduced in 2011 to combine Supervised Attendance Orders, Probation and Community Service Orders, CPOs can be tailored specifically to offenders based on the nature of their crime and the underlying issues which may have led to it. This may include intensive supervision or unpaid work.
Antisocial Behaviour Order (ASBO)	Bans someone (over the age of 12) from causing disruption with their behaviour. ASBOs can be issued for crimes such as graffiti, noise pollution and littering. They also try to keep people away from certain areas. Broken ASBOs can lead to fines or up to five years in prison.

THINGS TO DO AND THINK ABOUT

1 'HMP Grampian is money well spent.' Do you agree or disagree with this statement? Explain your answer.

2 Debate and research these topics:
   - Automatic early release should be abolished.
   - Life should mean life.
   - The death penalty should be re-introduced.
   - More non-custodial sentencing should replace prisons.
   - More crimes should have mandatory sentencing.

3 Explain mandatory sentencing.

4 Analyse policies which aim to reduce reoffending.

RESTORATIVE JUSTICE AND REDUCING REOFFENDING

ONLINE

Read the Audit Scotland report about reducing reoffending at www.brightredbooks.net

FACT

Men under 21 are the most likely group to reoffend.

REDUCING REOFFENDING

Reoffending is a continuing problem in Scotland. Reconviction rates have remained relatively static over recent years. In 2010–11, more than one in five people convicted (9500) had ten or more previous convictions. The Scottish Government estimates that the total economic and social costs of reoffending are about £3 billion a year.

Of the 44 126 people convicted of a crime in 2010–11, 28.4% were convicted of another offence in the next year. Dundee has the highest imprisonment rate in the country with a reconviction rate of 38.3%. This is higher than any other local authority area. Stirling and Clackmannanshire have the second- and third-highest reoffending rates, 35.9% and 34.1% respectively. Three out of every four (or 74%) of offenders who serve short sentences end up committing another crime within two years, but three out of five (or 60%) of offenders who are instead given community service do not reoffend within two years. Figures show that community orders appear more effective than prison sentences in deterring convicts from reoffending.

Figures also show that offenders are less likely to reoffend if they are given other forms of punishment, rather than a short-term jail sentence. The **Scottish Consortium on Crime and Criminal Justice** agrees and has argued that alternatives to prison, such as community payback, are much more effective in reducing crime. They believe that prison should only be used as an absolute last resort for the most dangerous offenders.

RESTORATIVE JUSTICE: SOCIAL SOLUTIONS TO CRIME

There is a belief that a strong social service negates the need for a justice system intended to punish. Focusing on the crime is reactionary, in many cases unjust and, ultimately, impractical due to costs involved.

The **Safeguarding Communities Reducing Reoffending** (SACRO) programme aims to promote community safety across Scotland by providing high quality services to reduce conflict and offending. It provides services in conflict resolution, criminal justice and restorative justice and reparation.

A **restorative justice process** is a process where all those involved participate actively in addressing or repairing the harm that was caused, with the help of one or two trained facilitators. They discuss the facts, consequences and what needs to be done to repair a situation.

DON'T FORGET

Another social solution to crime is Community Payback Orders.

Restorative justice can be used by prison staff as an alternative, non-punitive way of dealing with the harm caused by misconduct, bullying, a breach of prison rules or violence.

SCOTTISH COMPARED WITH SCANDINAVIAN JUSTICE

The rate of reoffending among prisoners in Norway is just under 16% which is the lowest rate in Europe where rates can be as high as 70%. So what's the secret of success for Norway's prison service? The answer is simply offering a normal life style, which allows reintegration through work, social life and free association.

contd

Case Study: Bastøy Prison, Norway

Bastøy is an institution where people live in a community. It is often referred to as a **human ecological prison**. Six inmates share a six-bedroom wooden cottage. Each person has a room of their own. Inmates wake up early to work every morning and earn the equivalent of £6 a day doing a variety of jobs, from farming to repairing bicycles to working in the laundrette. There is a monthly fee of about £70 for buying goods in a local supermarket. For those who want to study, go to mass or play an instrument, there is a library, a school, a church and a guitar teacher.

Visitors are struck by the air of optimism among inmates and comment on the lack of cynicism among guards, who appear to have a genuine sense of pride in their work. Bastøy is also one of the cheapest prisons in Norway to run.

Psychologists say that offenders need a realistic second chance, which is only possible by giving them respect and dignity. Perhaps this doesn't exist in Scottish prisons? One British prison officer is alleged to have said: 'We have to spend time away from our families to look after these vermin.'

THINGS TO DO AND THINK ABOUT

1 Essay practice: Analyse the consequences for reoffending of a restorative justice process approach to crime in Scotland.

2 Role play – in a small group act out a restorative justice meeting. You will need at least one offender and one victim, or relative of a victim, as well as at least one facilitator.

There will need to be some background to the meeting, for example, what crime has been committed?

Is this appropriate for all crimes?

Why might both victim and offender be happy to participate?

Should anyone else be involved? Explain your answer.

Do you think this would reduce reoffending?

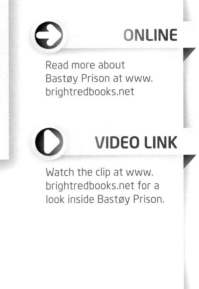

ONLINE

Read more about Bastøy Prison at www. brightredbooks.net

VIDEO LINK

Watch the clip at www. brightredbooks.net for a look inside Bastøy Prison.

ONLINE

Head to www. brightredbooks.net for advice on how to answer an essay question for this topic.

ONLINE TEST

Head to www. brightredbooks.net and test yourself on restorative justice and reducing reoffending.

UNIT ASSESSMENT: DECISION-MAKING

DECISION-MAKING USING SOURCES

Research and use a range of sources of information to make and justify decisions about social issues in the United Kingdom, focusing on either social inequality or crime and the law.

Outcome 1.1: Identify and collect sources of information

You must identify and collect **at least two sources** of information related to the social issue you have chosen. It is a good idea to label your sources and use headings to organise your information.

Suitable sources might include:

* websites

* books, newspapers or journals

* questionnaires, surveys or interviews

* TV documentaries or similar programmes such as podcasts, radio programmes, and online video clips.

Example:

In order to research the issue, I will use the internet to access the Scottish Government website. I will also carry out a survey in my local area to collect the views of the public on the issue. The decision I make will be entirely based on the information I collect.

Outcome 1.2: Synthesise and evaluate information

DON'T FORGET

Synthesis involves making connections and linking related evidence from at least two sources of information.

You must link evidence from at least two sources of information to make a decision about the issue and explain the reasons for your decision. Your explanation must include **at least two developed points**, for example, evidence and reasons.

Example:

I believe that [state decision]. *It is clear from the evidence in the sources that ...... which shows .... This is supported by the evidence in source ...., which clearly shows ....*

Outcome 1.3: Evaluate evidence to support an alternative decision

Use **at least two sources** to make a reasoned judgement about evidence which would support an alternative decision about the social issue you have chosen.

At least two detailed points should be made.

Example:

However, an alternative viewpoint might be .... This is supported by ....

Despite this, I still believe that my original decision is correct because ....

WORKED EXAMPLE

Introduction

I have been asked to make a decision on whether or not to introduce a new law, **Protection Against Second Hand Smoke**. This would make it illegal to smoke in many public places such as outside buildings, as well as parks and beaches.

The decision I make will be entirely based on the information I have collected from the sources I have collected.

Sources

In order to research information on this issue, I have used many sources. These sources are:

1   2011 public opinion survey
2   Cancer UK website
3   statements made by pro- and anti-smokers.

Reasons for my decision

I believe that this new law should be introduced. It is clear from the evidence in the sources that people deserve the right to be in smoke-free environments. Source 3 states everyone should be allowed to be able to enjoy the park or the beach without smoke in their face. This is supported by the evidence in Source 1. This clearly shows that 75% of the 1101 people surveyed, which is a significant amount, support a law that bans smoking in public places like parks and beaches.

Another reason I have decided to support this new law is because Source 3 states that if we can prevent parents from smoking then we can create a new smoke-free society for our young people. The is supported in the same source, as it states that research shows that the less children are exposed to smoking, the less likely they are to take it up.

Criticisms of my decision

Despite the evidence given to support my decision, some people may disagree with it. In Source 3, Nick Matheson from the pro-smoking group claims that most people do not support a further ban on smoking in public places, but insists that annual price increases are the answer. This is supported by Source 1 which shows a majority of the people surveyed (55%) agree with Nick.

However, Source 2 shows that while there is a decrease in the percentage of smokers in social classes A, B and C1 from 20% in 2002 to 13% in 2010, there has been an increase in social classes C2, D and E from 26% in 2009 to 28% in 2010. This is supported by Source 3 which states that deaths linked to smoking are highest in the most deprived areas of Scotland, with people in poor social groups continuing to smoke.

Conclusion

I have decided to introduce this law as smoking is a major life-threatening issue, requiring significant action to be taken to tackle it.

DON'T FORGET

Number your sources to make them easier to refer to in your answer.

THINGS TO DO AND THINK ABOUT

1   Complete your own decision-making exercise. Think about the issues you've discussed and possibly debated in class. Choose a topical issue that has resulted in a few different opinions, such as shopping vouchers being issued to pregnant women to help them quit smoking.

Use three sources to carry out this task. One of them should be a survey that you have carried out yourself.

Carry out a decision-making exercise using the instructions in this section.

Have a classmate or teacher evaluate your work.

2   What other recent social issues could be used for this type of task?

ONLINE

Read more about this at www.brightredbooks.net

CHINA'S POLITICAL SYSTEM AND PROCESSES

Chinese constitution

CHINA'S POLITICAL SYSTEM AND CONSTITUTIONAL ARRANGEMENTS

China is a socialist republic and the political structure is outlined in the Constitution of the People's Republic of China, adopted in 1982. China's people are expected to strictly adhere to the Constitution which states that all citizens 'have the duty to uphold the dignity of the Constitution and ensure its implementation'. China is a single-party state which has been governed by the **Communist Party of China** (CPC) for over 65 years. The CPC permits eight other, non-communist, democratic, political parties to exist in China. However, these parties are small in terms of their membership and are fully controlled by the CPC. Political consultation also involves a number of socially influential mass organisations including the **All-China Federation of Trade Unions** and the **All-China Women's Federation**.

ONLINE

For additional information on China's system of **multi-party cooperation and political consultation** including an overview of the eight political parties which play a very limited role in the way in which China is managed, visit www.brightredbooks.net

POLITICAL PARTIES

The Communist Party of China

The Communist Party of China is by far the largest political party in the world, growing from just 50 members in 1921 to a staggering 87 million members in 2014. The CPC is represented in every corner of Chinese society including both state-owned and private enterprises. The route to CPC membership normally begins by enrolling in the Young Pioneers of China (age 6–14), before advancing to the Communist Youth League (age 14–18) and finally, if selected, becoming a full member (age 18+). Many young Chinese citizens are attracted to CPC membership as they believe it will help them to secure benefits in education or employment, such as gaining a good job with a government agency or state-owned enterprise.

However, the party is often criticised for being largely inaccessible to, and unrepresentative of, much of Chinese society. For example, in 2012, only 23.8% of party members were female, despite the fact that women account for over 48% of the total Chinese population.

CPC membership by occupation is also disproportionate. Industrial workers accounted for approximately 30% of China's labour force in 2012, but industrial CPC membership was below 10%.

Access to the CPC can be difficult for individuals who lack connections. The application process is complex. Prospective members must be proposed by existing CPC members in addition to having to meet strict entry criteria including the successful completion of a one-year probationary period.

Corruption

Concern has been raised about the existence of nepotism within the CPC. A recent internal survey has indicated that many cadres (public officials) believe that they have

DON'T FORGET

Although there are eight other political parties operating in China, they do not act as opposition to the CPC. The CPC dominates all important aspects of Chinese life, including exercising full control of the country's media.

ONLINE

To find out more detailed information about corruption within Chinese politics, view the South China Morning Post's 'Tigers and Flies' report at www.brightredbooks.net

contd

lost out on deserving promotions due to corrupt senior CPC officials who have abused their position and favoured individuals who they are in some way associated with.

Case Study: Xi Jingping's campaign against corruption

Xi Jingping, General Secretary of the CPC and President of China, addressed the Central Commission for Discipline Inspection in January 2014 stating 'the anti-corruption situation remains grim and complicated, the unhealthy influence of the corruption problem is malignant and needs to be solved quickly'.

The statement was made following the release of statistics which indicated that more than 180 000 CPC officials were found guilty of some form of corruption in 2013. By September 2014, over 13 000 officials had been sentenced for a number of crimes including bribery and stealing public money. Xi Jingping was keen to highlight that nobody was safe from graft, not even 'tigers' (high-ranking officials). However, some critics claim that Jingping's corruption campaign is nothing more than an attempt to clear the landscape of potential political rivals, while some economists claim that the anti-corruption campaign is having a damaging effect by reducing public spending. The table highlights some high profile government officials who have fallen from grace.

Image from outside the trial of Bo Xilai

Selected government officials found guilty of bribery and/or corruption

Name	Position	Crime	Punishment
Ji Jianye	Mayor (Nanjing)	Bribery (£1.5 million)	15-year jail sentence (2015)
Su Rong	Vice-Chairman of China's Parliamentary Advisory Body	Corruption and bribery, disclosing national secrets	Life sentence (2015)
Ding Meng	Land Requisition Official (Chongqing)	Bribery	13-year jail sentence (2014)
Jiang Runli	Land Planning Official (Fushun)	Stealing public money, abuse of power	Life sentence (2014)
Bo Xilai	Communist Party Chief (Chongqing)	Corruption, bribery, abuse of power	Life sentence (2013)

The United Front

The table below provides the membership figures for China's other permitted political parties, which make-up the United Front, in 2012.

Party name	Established	Number of members (approx)
China Democratic League	1939	224 000
China Democratic National Construction Association	1945	140 000
Jiusan Society	1946	132 000
China Association for the Promotion of Democracy	1945	128 000
Chinese Peasants' and Workers' Democratic Party	1930	125 600
China Revolutionary Committee of the Kuomintang	1948	101 865
China Zhi Gong Dang	1925	20 000
Taiwan Democratic Self-government League	1947	2100

FACT

The CPC has recently called on local governments to be 'prudent' when enlisting party members in a bid to attract 'quality rather than quantity'. According to a report by the Xinhua News Agency in June 2014, the party is now placing a greater emphasis on recruiting members who are 'enterprising' and can play 'exemplary roles'. The party has also called on its grass-roots organisations to welcome those who 'believe in Marxism, communism and socialism with Chinese characteristics'.

THINGS TO DO AND THINK ABOUT

1 China is described as a 'single-party state'. What does this mean? In what way does this differ from the United Kingdom?

2 Choose either the All-China Federation of Trade Unions or the All-China Women's Federation. Conduct some independent research and create a fact file summarising the role that the organisation plays in China's political process.

ONLINE TEST

Test yourself on China's political system and processes at www.brightredbooks.net

CHINA'S POLITICAL INSTITUTIONS AND PROCESSES

——— Elects/approves   - - - - Exerts influence over

This flow chart gives an overview of the power structure in China

ONLINE

See the 'How China is Ruled: BBC Interactive Flowchart' via www.brightredbooks.net which provides an informative overview of China's main political institutions.

Meeting of National People's Congress.

THE NATIONAL PEOPLE'S CONGRESS

The **National People's Congress** (NPC) is China's legislature, and, according to Article 57 of China's Constitution, is 'the highest organ of state power'.

2987 delegates are elected for a five-year term. The NPC meets once each year for approximately two weeks as one half of the **Two Meetings** (the second meeting being the **Chinese People's Political Consultative Conference**). The vast majority of NPC delegates (approximately 70%) are CPC members.

Article 62 of China's Constitution outlines the NPC's functions and powers which include:

● electing the President of the Supreme People's Court
● enacting and amending basic laws governing criminal offences, civil affairs, the state organs and other matters.

However, according to some commentators, the NPC is nothing more than 'a rubber stamp for party decisions'.

The **National People's Congress Standing Committee** is made up of 150 members who meet about six times per annum. Technically, this committee can change laws, but most of its members are members of the CPC, so the output from the committee is determined by the CPC.

In March 2014, almost 5000 motions proposed by the National People's Congress and Chinese People's Political Consultative Conference representatives were endorsed.

FACT

The revised **Environmental Protection Law** came into effect in January 2015 following changes to the existing law made by the Standing Committee of the NPC in April 2014. The changes include the establishment of an environment and health monitoring survey and risk assessment mechanism, tougher punishments for environmental crimes and the introduction of 'Environment Day' on 5 June.

THE POLITBURO

The **Politburo** is China's 25-member decision-making body elected by the **Central Committee** of the CPC and made up of both military and civic leaders from across China. For the first time in four decades, the current Politburo has two female representatives, Sun Chunlan and Liu Yandong.

In reality, the most important decisions are made by the seven members of the **Politburo Standing Committee** (PSC). This group comprises of China's main political heavyweights including the Party General Secretary (Xi Jingping), the Premier (Li Keqiang) and the Chairman of the NPC (Zhang Dejiang).

The PSC meets regularly to discuss and take decisions on China's most important issues. The meetings are held behind closed doors and once a decision is made, all members of the PSC must stand united.

contd

Politburo Standing Committee: China's most powerful men

Xi Jinping (b. 1953); Party General Secretary; Chairman, Party and State Central Military Commissions; State President (Portfolio: Party, military, foreign affairs)

Li Keqiang (b. 1955); No. 2-ranked PSC member; Premier and Party Secretary of the State Council (Portfolio: government administration and economy)

Zhang Dejiang (b. 1946); No. 3-ranked PSC member; Chairman, Standing Committee of the 12th National People's Congress (Portfolio: legislative affairs)

THE PEOPLE'S LIBERATION ARMY

The **People's Liberation Army** (PLA) is the largest defence force in the world with a well-equipped army, navy and air force.

The PLA is duty bound to defend the CPC. PLA officers are also CPC members. This further consolidates the CPC's unyielding power within China. Mao Zedong once said 'political power grows out the barrel of a gun'. Having control of a powerful army is important both nationally and internationally.

The CPC keeps a close eye on the internal workings of the PLA to ensure that army thinking consistently mirrors party thinking.

The PLA is answerable to the **Central Military Affairs Commission** (CMAC) which is headed up by the General Secretary of the CPC, currently Xi Jingping.

The PLA

 FACT

China's President and Premier are only allowed to serve two consecutive five-year terms in office.

 ## THINGS TO DO AND THINK ABOUT

1 To what extent to you agree with the viewpoint that the NPC is 'nothing more than a rubber stamp for party decisions'?

2 In your own words, explain why the Politburo is such an important and influential body.

DON'T FORGET

Chinese citizens do not get the opportunity to vote directly for senior politicians who make up important groups such as the Politburo. The average citizen only has the opportunity to elect representatives at grassroots levels such as village, town or county elections.

 **ONLINE TEST**

Test yourself on China's political institutions and processes at www. brightredbooks.net

GOVERNANCE, DEMOCRACY AND MEDIA CENSORSHIP

REGIONAL GOVERNMENT

China is broken down into the following regions:

- 22 **provinces**
- five **regions** with increased autonomy and sizeable ethnic minority populations
- four **municipalities**, which are important cities controlled by central government
- two **Special Administrative Regions** (SAR). These regions operate under a capitalist system as opposed to a socialist one. **Hong Kong** returned to China from the UK in 1997 and **Macao** returned to China from Portugal in 1999. China promised not to interfere in each country's established social and economic systems – both countries were handed back to China under the 'one country, two systems' policy.

Administrative divisions of China

HOW DEMOCRATIC IS CHINA?

According to China's Constitution:

- citizens who are 18 years old or above are allowed to vote and stand for election
- citizens can enjoy freedom of speech, freedom of press, freedom of assembly, freedom of association and freedom of procession and demonstration, provided, they abide by the Constitution and they:
  - pay taxes
  - safeguard the unity of China
  - defend China and perform military services
  - safeguard the security and honour of China.

However, in reality, opportunities for political participation in China are limited. Chinese citizens do not get the opportunity to vote for senior CPC leadership. Therefore, they have little say about which individuals get to make the most important decisions for China at a national level. For the vast majority of China's citizens, voting is restricted to electing village committees and local people's congresses. Even at a local level, only candidates endorsed by the CPC are permitted to stand for election, and, access to the party is unachievable for most. In some instances, Chinese citizens are allowed to protest about local matters of public concern such as pollution and poor quality housing, but any criticism of the Chinese government is strictly prohibited.

LOCAL DEMOCRACY

As villages and townships are the only level in Chinese politics where direct and regular elections take place, many believe that they play a vital role in the democratisation of China. However, it is also argued that local elections do nothing more than pay lip service to democracy, due to the behind-the-scenes involvement of the CPC in controlling election committees and selecting the candidates who are allowed to stand.

Village elections were first introduced in 1988 in order to help the Chinese government increase their influence in rural areas, which at that time, they were struggling to control.

Recent debate has looked to build on the successes of local democracy and further extend it to urban areas. For example, deliberative democracy would allow urban citizens to have a direct say in the way in which their communities are governed through attendance at meetings and participation in public consultation exercises.

Village elections take place every three years in approximately 950 000 of China's villages in order to elect the village chief and village committee, who manage all local affairs.

There have also been calls for greater transparency within the CPC and the need for power to be distributed more equally throughout party ranks. A movement towards a tenure system.

Local democracy

ELECTORAL REFORM AND PROTESTS IN HONG KONG

In September 2014, the National People's Congress Standing Committee caused anger and concern when they announced that they were making changes to the process by which the citizens of Hong Kong elect their leader, known as the **Chief Executive**. Although the Hong Kongers will still be able to vote for the territory's leader in 2017, only CPC approved candidates will be permitted to stand for election.

Protest movements such as **Occupy Central with Love and Peace** are actively campaigning against this decision, championing the need for genuine universal suffrage. Domestic and international concern exists about the potential impact that ongoing civil disobedience would have on what is one of Asia's most lucrative economies. Amnesty International reported that 27 people were jailed in February 2015 for supporting the pro-democracy protests in

Hong Kongers protest about parallel trading

Hong Kong. According to the human rights pressure group, the protesters were prevented from enjoying a number of civil liberties including meeting with their lawyers. There were also reports of prisoners being tortured. When Hong Kong transferred from British to Chinese rule in 1997, it was agreed that Hong Kong would be administered with a high degree of local autonomy over a fifty-year period until 2047. Many commentators argue that the current electoral reforms undermine this arrangement, which up until now, has worked effectively.

MEDIA CENSORSHIP

The CPC does not tolerate open dissent from protestors, and media censorship is common. The Chinese government goes to great lengths to try to ensure that social stability is not threatened. However, some people argue that China is 'no longer the journalistic black hole it once was'. Instances of censorship include:

'China is the world's biggest prison for journalists, bloggers and cyber dissidents.'

- state television failing to report large scale protests
- social media sites (such as Facebook, Twitter and Instagram) being blocked
- journalists being targeted by police for publishing negative reports about the CPC
- blogs being closed down for presenting information deemed to be politically sensitive
- limiting foreign news broadcasts by blocking websites and satellite signals
- widespread use of cyber police to monitor web activity.

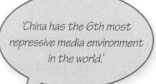
'China has the 6th most repressive media environment in the world.'

Reporters Without Borders

THINGS TO DO AND THINK ABOUT

1 Which SAR was returned to China from Portugal?
2 Name China's four municipalities.
3 To what extent are the views of Chinese citizens represented within the Chinese political system?
4 What decision by the CPC, in September 2014, has led to ongoing protests in Hong Kong?
5 Why might it be problematic for journalists to report accurately when covering stories in China? Provide three reasons.

ONLINE

To read more about human rights violations in China, visit www.brightredbooks.net

FACT

Throughout 2014 and 2015, Hong Kongers have protested angrily about **parallel trading**. This happens when China's mainlanders travel to Hong Kong and purchase goods cheaply which they then take back to the mainland and sell them on to make a profit. This results in higher prices for the Hong Kongers, due to a shortage in supply.

FACT

Chinese police have used pepper spray and tear gas to keep the protestors at bay.

VIDEO LINK

Watch a short video at www.brightredbooks.net that shows how the Chinese media failed to report some of the Hong Kong protests in 2014.

VIDEO LINK

To find out more about the changes to Chinese media, visit www.brightredbooks.net

ONLINE TEST

Test yourself on China's political institutions and processes at www.brightredbooks.net

SOCIO-ECONOMIC ISSUES IN CHINA: ECONOMIC INEQUALITY

CHINA'S WEALTH GAP

China's **Gini coefficient** in 2014 was 0.469. This is above the UN's international warning level of 0.4 which indicates that a severe, possibly dangerous, level of income inequality exists within the country and that there is a possibility of social unrest. The 2014 **China Welfare Development Report** published by Peking University's Institute of Social Science claimed that 1% of Chinese families owned 33% of the country's wealth, while the bottom 25% owned only 1% of the country's wealth. Economic inequality in China is regarded as a serious social issue and, following the nation's rapid economic development of the past forty years, China is now one of the most unequal countries in the world. Many Chinese citizens, such as Ning Shumei, a taxi driver in Beijing, have called for urgent government intervention to address the problem.

China's Gini coefficient from 2004 to 2014

Year	Gini coefficient
2004	0·473
2005	0·485
2006	0·487
2007	0·484
2008	0·491
2009	0·49
2010	0·481
2011	0·477
2012	0·474
2013	0·473
2014	0·469

Source: National Bureau of Statistics

Bar chart of China's Gini coefficient from 2004 to 2014

'Income inequality is a serious issue. People are complaining about it, especially new graduates who are not paid well. They need to change this because I am sure it will affect the health and growth of China. I am not happy with the fact that people are not paid and respected according to what they can do. The rich remain rich, the poor remain poor.'

View of Ning Shumei, 51, taxi driver, Beijing.

DON'T FORGET

The **Gini coefficient** for family income indicates the wealth gap that exists within a country. A Gini coefficient of 0 indicates perfect equality as opposed to a Gini coefficient of 1 which would indicate perfect inequality.

VIDEO LINK

To find out more about income inequality in China, visit www.brightredbooks.net

ONLINE

Visit www.brightredbooks.net to view a picture gallery which illustrates the huge wealth gap that divides China today.

A 2014 joint study between the University of Michigan and Peking University entitled 'Income Inequality in Today's China' highlighted a number of factors which are believed to contribute towards China's wage differentials. These factors include:

- head of household's level of education
- variations across Chinese provinces
- urban/rural gap
- family structure.

THE RICH, THE POOR AND THE MIDDLE CLASS

China is currently suffering from:

- sharp rises in the cost of living
- an ever-increasing income gap (the incomes of the poor are increasing, but the incomes of the rich are increasing at a much faster rate).

The table below gives an indication of the wealth gap that currently exists in China.

China's glaring wealth gap

Number of Chinese billionaires ($)	300+
Number of Chinese millionaires ($)	2.4 million
Average wealth per Chinese citizen ($)	17 126
Median wealth ($)	6327
Number of Chinese people living in poverty	200 million (income of 2300 yuan per annum / approximately $1.25 per day)

contd

The urban elite

The super-rich tend to live in wealthy cities such as Tianjin, Shanghai and Beijing.

Many of China's wealthiest citizens have made their wealth through successful property deals, private enterprise, investing in the stock market and holding senior positions within both domestic and multinational companies.

Many of the Chinese elite are impressed by a Western style of luxury and enjoy spending their money on expensive cars such as Lamborghinis and Ferraris. Many lead ostentatious lifestyles and have a passion for designer labels and vintage wine.

China's top 10 richest people

Position	Name	Source of wealth	Estimated fortune (US $)
1	Jack Ma	Alibaba Group (e-commerce)	19.5bn
2	Robin Li	Baidu (search engine)	14.7bn
3	Ma Huateng	Tencent (internet media)	14.4bn
4	Wang Jianlin	Dalian Wanda Group (real estate)	13.2bn
5	Li Hejun	Hanergy Holdings (renewable energy)	13bn
6	Zong Qinghou	Hangzhou Wahaha Group (beverages)	11bn
7	Wang Wenyin	Amer International Group (metals)	10bn
8	Lei Jun	Kingsoft Gaming (smart phones)	9.1bn
9	He Xiangjian	Midea Group (appliances)	7.5bn
10	Liu Qiangdong	JD.com (e-commerce)	7.1bn

Source: Forbes (October 2014)

Chan Laiwa

Fu Wah International Group logo

The rural poor

Some of the poorest provinces in China are those heavily reliant on agriculture such as Guizhou, Sichuan, Tibet and Yunnan.

Many of China's poorest citizens work on farms. Their work is often carried out by hand as they do not have access to farm machinery. Chinese farmers work long days and, in many cases, work right up until they die.

China's less fortunate are forced to lead very basic lives. Many rural residents do not have access to household commodities such as refrigerators, washing machines and computers which are taken for granted in the bigger cities. In fact, many villages are still deprived of electricity.

The middle class

Almost 70% of Chinese urban households are deemed to be middle class.

China produces over 7 million graduates each year, many of whom are confident that they will achieve the 'Chinese Dream'.

However, soaring property prices make it impossible for many of the emerging middle class to get a foot on the urban property ladder. Real estate in urban and coastal cities is extremely expensive, especially if it is located near to the best schools and universities.

Chinese farmer in Xiaoyi County, Guangxi

THINGS TO DO AND THINK ABOUT

1 According to University of Michigan Sociologist, Yu Xie, 'Income inequality in today's China is among the highest in the world'. What societal problems could this potentially cause?
2 State two reasons why it might be difficult for academics, both Chinese and otherwise, to produce accurate reports relating to socio-economic issues in China?
3 Why might the head of household's level of education be a main cause of wage differentials in China?
4 From the table 'China's Top 10 Richest People' select one company listed and investigate why it has been so successful. You may wish to visit the company homepage or, alternatively, carry out some press scanning.
5 Create a comparison table between Guangdong and Guizhou that includes information about population, economic base, life expectancy, minimum wage (this varies from region to region) and main problems experienced.

VIDEO LINK

Find out more about the 'Chinese Dream' by watching a short BBC report from July 2013 at www.brightredbooks.net

ONLINE TEST

Test yourself on the socio-economic issues in China at www.brightredbooks.net

REDUCING SOCIO-ECONOMIC ISSUES IN CHINA

CHINESE GOVERNMENT POLICIES TO REDUCE ECONOMIC INEQUALITY AND THEIR EFFECTIVENESS

The Chinese government has been highly successful in reducing the number of people living in poverty by approximately 660 million since the late 1970s. Between 2010 and 2012, the living standards of almost one-third of the population (approximately 400 million) improved significantly and in 2011, the national poverty line was increased to 2300 yuan per annum (approximately $1.03 per day). Today, the Chinese government has ambitious goals to double Chinese per capita income between 2010 and 2020. In 2014, Chinese Premier, Li Keqiang, promised to wage a war against poverty which would 'relocate people living in inhospitable areas, nurture small towns, improve transportation infrastructure and give more fair development opportunities to the poor'.

However, over 200 million Chinese citizens are still living in extreme poverty, which is defined by the World Bank, as surviving on less than $1.25 per day.

War on poverty

China's first Poverty Relief Day raised over 5 billion yuan in 2014. This money will help to fund over 125 000 special work teams which provide support and financial assistance in China's 128 000 poorest villages, including the provision of clean drinking water and the upgrading of homes.

Gini coefficient

According to the National Bureau of Statistics, China's Gini coefficient has decreased year on year since 2008, suggesting a reduction in income inequality. Income inequality may be narrowing as a result of measures such as limiting the annual income of company executives, providing tax breaks for small companies and the recent changes to the Chinese social security system including pension reform.

Job creation

In 2014, the Chinese government comfortably surpassed its target of 10 million new jobs by creating over 13 million new jobs. High employment is very important if Beijing is to keep its people happy and remain internationally competitive. Job creation is an important strand of China's 12th Five-Year Plan.

Wage increases

In 2014, civil servants and public employees in a number of Chinese provinces benefited from an increase to the minimum wage. In 2015, some employees of state owned enterprises (SOEs) and other private enterprises are also expected to benefit from an increase in wages. According to researcher Wendy Liu, 'The pay hike indicates Beijing's goal of improving the quality of life for the average Chinese, after having extracted savings by curbing wasteful spending at government branches and SOEs'.

Regional investment

Some provinces have received huge government investment. Guizhou, in the south of the country, has received funding to improve its transport links in order to help the region become a more attractive tourist destination. The local economy has experienced rapid growth which has been supported by the creation of new roads and a new airport. The government has been criticised, however, in some instances, for providing poor quality infrastructure which serves no real purpose.

SOCIAL INEQUALITY

Urbanisation

China now has over 200 million more urban residents in 2015 than it did in 2005. This number will continue to increase with World Bank figures indicating that urban areas are attracting a further 1.8 million migrants each month. Increasing urbanisation presents a number of problems for both rural and urban residents as well as the Chinese government which, in January 2015, was advised by the World Bank that it should attempt to reduce urban sprawl in a bid to make cost savings of almost $1.5 trillion over the next decade. The population in some cities is becoming less dense and this is leading to increased infrastructure development and spiralling maintenance costs.

Urban–rural divide

The table below highlights some notable differences between life in large towns and cities and life in the countryside.

Selected urban and rural disparities

	Urban	Rural
Population	53% of Chinese people now live in towns and cities. The urban population is increasing due to the rapid movement of migrants in search of work. The Chinese government is encouraging urbanisation in order to generate growth.	47% of Chinese people live in the countryside. This figure is decreasing and will continue to do so in the future. Some rural residents benefit from possessing a rural hukou making a decent living from farm rents or selling land to the government.
Poverty	Approximately 50 million people live in poverty.	Approximately 150 million people live in poverty.
Average annual income (2010) *disposable	$10 000 ($2900)* Over 20 million urban residents still qualify to receive the Minimum Living Subsidy, however.	$2000 ($898)*
Financial services	Many people have access to multiple bank accounts and credit cards.	Many people do not have access to a bank account.
Health care	Hospitals are modern. Many residents are covered by both state and private medical insurance. This helps them to feel at ease, knowing that if they were to fall seriously ill, then a significant proportion of the costs would be covered by their insurance. However, there is rising concern over increasing medical costs which often exceed compensation levels.	If residents are fortunate enough to receive medical treatment, they receive it in their home, because hospital stays and operations can cost thousands of pounds and are too expensive for most, with the treatment having to be paid for in advance. Expensive medicine is replaced by alternative herbal remedies.
Education	Schools tend to be well resourced both in terms of equipment and learning materials. Urban schools also attract the top teachers which helps to best prepare their students for the Gaokao. However, the standard of education provision can vary from city to city. Urban pupils are far more likely to gain entry into top Chinese universities and enjoy social mobility.	School buildings are often inadequate and fail to provide environments conducive to learning. Many rural schools lack appropriate learning resources and find it difficult to attract high calibre teaching staff. Pupil dropout rates are high as many rural residents are unable to fund their child's progression through the expensive Chinese education system.
Crime	Due to the wide income gap that exists, low level economic crime, such as pick pocketing, often occurs. According to official Chinese statistics, violent crime rarely occurs. However, crime statistics are not published by the police. Large urban cities have extremely high conviction rates.	According to available Chinese data, more rural children are committing youth crime, in both rural and urban locations. Family feuds leading to assault and domestic violence are common in rural china.

THINGS TO DO AND THINK ABOUT

1 Explain the consequences of rapid urbanisation.

2 What problems do Chinese people living in rural areas experience in comparison with those who live in urban areas?

FACT

China's urban population has grown from roughly 18% of the total population in 1978 to about 53% of the population in 2012 making it one of the fastest growing urban population growth rates in the world. Although the Chinese government see urbanisation as paramount to China's economic growth, they are concerned about its impact on areas such as housing, social security and the environment.

FACT

In 2013, the Chinese government banned all TV and radio advertisements promoting luxury goods in order to reduce the potential risk of a social uprising due to the widening income gap between the rich and the poor.

FACT

China is now home to the world's largest car market, selling an astonishing 2500 cars per hour throughout 2013. Cars are not commonly owned in rural China.

VIDEO LINK

Find out about the push and pull factors driving rural to urban migration by watching a short video clip at www.brightredbooks.net

DON'T FORGET

Improving living standards in rural areas and tackling poverty is a top priority for the Chinese government.

ONLINE TEST

Test yourself on the socio-economic issues in China at www.brightredbooks.net

SOCIAL INEQUALITY: HEALTH AND EDUCATION

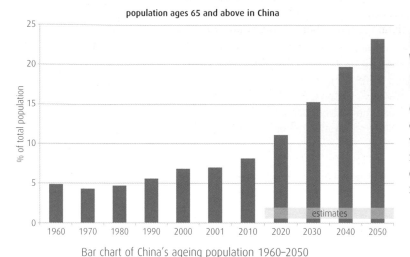

population ages 65 and above in China

Bar chart of China's ageing population 1960–2050

PROBLEMS ASSOCIATED WITH AN AGEING POPULATION

China's population is ageing as a result of the **One-Child Policy** (OCP) which was implemented in the late 1970s. The factsheet provides key details of China's demographic change, and the problems it may cause for future Chinese leaders.

FACTSHEET

- In the 1950s and 1960s China experienced a baby boom. As a result, by the early 1970s, over 50% of the Chinese population were of working age.

- The OCP was introduced in the late 1970s, and, China's birth rate decreased significantly as a result for the next three decades. In 2014, over 70% of China's population were of working age. This has been a key factor in China's unprecedented economic rise.

- The Chinese government recognised that an ageing population would have a negative impact on continued economic growth, and relaxed the OCP in late 2013, stating that couples could have a second child if either parent was an only child. They do not want the population 'getting older before it gets richer'.

- However, the change in policy has not had the effect that was intended. According to an article in the China Daily in January 2015, only 1 million of the 11 million eligible couples have applied to have a second child.

- According to China's National Health and Family Planning Commission, 25% of China's population will be 60 or over by the early 2030s. China will then have one of the oldest populations in the world and a working-age population of just 56%.

- Some experts believe that the **Two-Child Policy** will be fully rolled out by 2020 and that it will be successful in changing China's current population trend. However, Beijing is wary of the costs associated with a young population, including health care and education, and remains cautious about implementing a comprehensive Two-Child Policy. Some population experts, such as Huang Wenzheng, believe that it will provide a limited solution to the problem as some couples don't want children.

DON'T FORGET

Historically, Chinese women who violated the One-Child Policy were punished in a number of ways by the Chinese government. These punishments included forced sterilisation and forced abortion. The families of those breaking the law were also targeted and subjected to beatings, imprisonment and huge fines. Despite recent relaxation of the One-Child Policy, punishments remain severe.

Life expectancy (selected provinces, 2010)

Region	Average	Men	Women
Shanghai	80.26	78.20	82.44
Beijing	80.18	78.28	82.21
Tianjin	78.89	77.42	80.48
Qinghai	69.96	68.11	72.07
Yunnan	69.54	67.06	72.43
Tibet	68.17	66.33	70.07

Source: National Bureau of Statistics 2012, China Statistical Yearbook 2012

HEALTH CARE INEQUALITY

Although approximately 95% of the Chinese population have access to some form of medical insurance, the degree to which they are covered varies significantly. China has three state medical insurance schemes in place, but with a population of 1.36 billion, the Chinese government is unable to provide every Chinese citizen with fully comprehensive medical insurance. Consequently, access to certain specialised health care services is based on the individual's ability to pay. A health care divide therefore exists which has contributed to significant variations in life expectancy between urban and rural regions.

CURRENT HEALTH RISKS IN CHINA

In recent years, China's main health risks have changed from diseases associated with developing nations to those more commonly associated with developed countries. China is now suffering from an increase in deaths relating to a number of **non-communicable diseases** (NCDs) such as heart disease, diabetes, obesity and lung cancer. According to the World Health Organisation (WHO), NCDs are 'driven by forces that include ageing, rapid unplanned urbanisation, and the globalisation of unhealthy lifestyles'. China's ageing population, severe levels of pollution, high tobacco consumption, increasingly unbalanced diets and reduction in exercise have all played a major part in the rise of NCDs within Chinese society. Combatting the rise of NCDs is an important priority for the government of the most populous country in the world.

EDUCATION INEQUALITY

'An applicant from Beijing is 41 times more likely to be admitted to Peking University than a comparable student from the poor and largely rural province of Anhui.'
New York Times, September 2014

China's education system is extremely unequal, with many urban children only gaining access to a high quality education due to the wealth of their parents. Corruption is rife and many families pay exorbitant sums of money to ensure that their child has access to the best schools in a bid to increase their life chances. Some parents also abuse their position within society by exploiting business networks to give their child an unfair advantage. Children who live in rural provinces are at a severe disadvantage due to the poor quality of many rural schools in terms of teachers, equipment and learning resources. Children who follow their parents to the cities are often worse off, as the Hukou system means they are unable to gain entry to urban schools. They are also frequently the victims of societal discrimination.

A disadvantaged group: the educated?

In 2012, the China Household Finance Survey highlighted that the less-educated were more likely to secure employment than those with university degrees. One potential reason for this is China's economic boom driven by the manufacturing and construction industries, both of which do not create an abundance of opportunities for the more academic in society.

Furthermore, in July 2014, the BBC reported that the number of Chinese graduates had increased sevenfold since 1999 to an astonishing 7.26 million. It is estimated that anywhere between 1 million and 2.3 million Chinese graduates could form 'an army of educated unemployed' due to a lack of graduate job opportunities. According to Chinese sociologist Lian Si, the term **ant tribe** describes the high number of unemployed or underpaid graduates who may be unable to realise their potential as a result of failing to secure appropriately satisfying work. The Chinese government are concerned about the potential unrest that may occur from anxious graduates desperate for wealth and success.

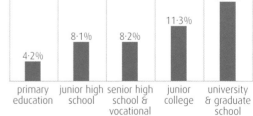

unemployment rate for the 21 to 25 age group breakdown by education level

- primary education: 4·2%
- junior high school: 8·1%
- senior high school & vocational: 8·2%
- junior college: 11·3%
- university & graduate school: 16·4%

Unemployment rate 21–25 age group. Source: 2012 China Household Finance Survey.

THINGS TO DO AND THINK ABOUT

1 Some population experts believe that the Chinese government should 'remove all fines on birth control violations' in order to tackle China's population predicament.
   a In what way would this benefit China?
   b Can you think of any problems it may cause?
2 Why does Shanghai have a 12-year higher life expectancy than Tibet?
3 In your own words, describe two of the education problems currently facing China.

DON'T FORGET

China has three government medical insurance schemes:
- New Rural Cooperative Medical Scheme (NCMS)
- Urban Employee – Basic Medical Insurance (UE–BMI)
- Urban Residents – Basic Medical Insurance (UR–BMI)

ONLINE

To access China's health profile (WHO), visit www.brightredbooks.net

DON'T FORGET

The **Household Registration System** or **Hukou** is a registration record which connects an individual with an area. It acts as a barrier to mobility as individuals are required to remain in their place of birth in order to access various forms of social welfare such as pensions, education and health care.

ONLINE TEST

Test yourself on the socio-economic issues in China at www.brightredbooks.net

SOCIAL INEQUALITY: URBAN HOUSING, WOMEN AND MIGRANT WORKERS

CHINA'S URBAN HOUSING PROBLEM

The past decade or so has witnessed a housing boom which has played an integral part in China's economic growth. According to figures released by the International Monetary Fund (IMF) in 2014, real estate accounted for 15% of China's total GDP in 2012. However, the property market has also presented the Chinese government with a number of serious challenges that they must tackle if this future success is to continue. Some of these challenges are summarised below.

Over-supply of private housing

Although rapid urbanisation has occurred, it has not occurred fast enough to fill the vast number of properties that have been built. Supply is currently outstripping demand partly due to the fact apartment prices are extremely high in comparison to Chinese incomes. This has resulted in the emergence of ghost towns which pose a threat to developers, financial institutions and regional economies.

Lack of affordable urban housing for migrant workers and the urban poor

Accommodation in urban settings is highly sought after but it is also far too expensive for migrants and vulnerable groups such as the elderly or disabled to rent, never mind purchase. The national average house price increased by approximately 250% in the ten-year period between 2000 and 2010. People have suffered as a result of the government's decision to abolish public housing provisions. Many are forced to live in slums and basements and experience health problems as a direct result.

Chenggong, Chinese ghost town

A DISADVANTAGED GROUP: WOMEN

Despite the fact Mao Zedong once exclaimed that 'women hold up half the sky', serious concerns continue to exist about gender inequality in China. Males are viewed as being superior to females and this is clearly reflected in China's birth rate with 118 males being born for every 100 females. Women also experience widespread employment discrimination. According to an article in the South China Morning Post in October 2013, women professionals now feel they experience more sexual discrimination in the workplace than they did in 1993. There is also evidence of a prevailing stereotypical attitude among many men that a woman's place is in the home.

In her book, *Leftover Women: The Resurgence of Gender Inequality in China*, Dr Leta Hong Fincher highlights:

- For some time now, the Chinese government have been aggressively pushing marriage in order to promote social stability. Many women are made to feel inferior and leftover if they do not marry by the time they are 27. This agenda is amplified by the Xinhua News Agency who paint a rather negative image of women who do not marry.
- 70% of women help to buy their home, but only 30% of them have their name on the deeds for the property. It is claimed that many of the women are so desperate to marry, that they are prepared to compromise their independence and financial security in order to ensure that they find a husband.
- Urban women are less likely to be employed than men. The current employment rate for urban women is approximately 61%. This has dropped from approximately 77% in 1994.
- Chinese woman are less likely to own their own homes compared to Chinese men. One reason for this is that Chinese parents are far more likely to help their son buy

ONLINE

For access to more detailed information on China's socio-economic challenges, access the China National Human Development Report 2013 via www.brightredbooks.net

VIDEO LINK

Watch Dr Leta Hong Fincher talk about her book *Leftover Women: The Resurgence of Gender Inequality in China* at www.brightredbooks.net

a home than their daughter. They feel that the responsibility should lie with their daughter's future husband to purchase the marital home.

- A high domestic violence rate exists. According to a 2013 UN study, 50% of all Chinese males surveyed admitted to abusing their partner, either sexually or physically.

A DISADVANTAGED GROUP: MIGRANT WORKERS

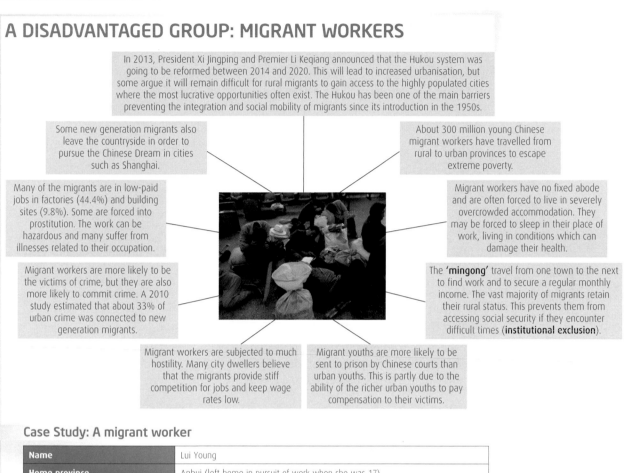

In 2013, President Xi Jingping and Premier Li Keqiang announced that the Hukou system was going to be reformed between 2014 and 2020. This will lead to increased urbanisation, but some argue it will remain difficult for rural migrants to gain access to the highly populated cities where the most lucrative opportunities often exist. The Hukou has been one of the main barriers preventing the integration and social mobility of migrants since its introduction in the 1950s.

Some new generation migrants also leave the countryside in order to pursue the Chinese Dream in cities such as Shanghai.

Many of the migrants are in low-paid jobs in factories (44.4%) and building sites (9.8%). Some are forced into prostitution. The work can be hazardous and many suffer from illnesses related to their occupation.

Migrant workers are more likely to be the victims of crime, but they are also more likely to commit crime. A 2010 study estimated that about 33% of urban crime was connected to new generation migrants.

About 300 million young Chinese migrant workers have travelled from rural to urban provinces to escape extreme poverty.

Migrant workers have no fixed abode and are often forced to live in severely overcrowded accommodation. They may be forced to sleep in their place of work, living in conditions which can damage their health.

The 'mingong' travel from one town to the next to find work and to secure a regular monthly income. The vast majority of migrants retain their rural status. This prevents them from accessing social security if they encounter difficult times (**institutional exclusion**).

Migrant workers are subjected to much hostility. Many city dwellers believe that the migrants provide stiff competition for jobs and keep wage rates low.

Migrant youths are more likely to be sent to prison by Chinese courts than urban youths. This is partly due to the ability of the richer urban youths to pay compensation to their victims.

Case Study: A migrant worker

Name	Lui Young
Home province	Anhui (left home in pursuit of work when she was 17).
Age	20
Employer	Langsha Knitting (world's largest underwear manufacturer). Approximately 4000 employees (mostly migrants). Lui produces 1400 pairs of stockings per day.
Likes	The fact she gets weekends off.
Hates	Standing for 12 hours per day (7am–7pm) Monday–Friday.
Earns	$7 per day – enough to live and send money home to parents.
Accommodation	Lives in a dormitory with 9 of her fellow workmates.
Interesting facts	Lui hasn't seen her parents in 3 years. Langsha Knitting is 'the centre of her life'.

VIDEO LINK

For a detailed videographic on the movement of China's migrant workers, visit www.brightredbooks.net

THINGS TO DO AND THINK ABOUT

1. Describe two of the housing problems that the Chinese government currently face.
2. Chinese men are more likely to own their home than Chinese women. Discuss.
3. Provide a detailed explanation as to why migrant workers are classed as a disadvantaged group.
4. Describe, in detail, two problems many Chinese women face. Do you think the Chinese government is doing enough to tackle these issues?

ONLINE TEST

Test yourself on the socio-economic issues in China at www.brightredbooks.net

GOVERNMENT POLICIES TO REDUCE SOCIAL INEQUALITY AND THEIR EFFECTIVENESS

VIDEO LINK

To find out more about two Chinese government programmes supported by the World Bank which offer free training courses and accommodation for migrant workers, visit www.brightredbooks.net

FACT

In 2015, a Chinese airline provided 160 migrant workers with complimentary return flights home so they could celebrate the Chinese New Year with their families. The airline also provided the migrants with food, drink and gifts.

WELFARE: ACHIEVEMENTS

The implementation of the 2011 National Social Insurance Law has improved the living standards of many Chinese citizens. According to statistics released by the National Bureau of Statistics, by the end of 2012, 340 million people had joined the basic urban pension insurance scheme for employees (an increase of nearly 20 million people since 2011).

HOUSING: ACHIEVEMENTS

The Chinese government is committed to providing housing for those on low incomes. Between 2011 and 2015, as part of the 12th Five-Year Plan, the government aimed to build 36 million affordable homes.

In 2013 alone, over 18 million subsidised homes were built and a further 12 million houses in poverty-stricken areas were refurbished.

The Chinese government has also launched a joint home ownership scheme which has been rolled out across six cities to help disadvantaged young people get a foot on the property ladder.

However, the government has been criticised for cutting corners in order to meet its targets, by using poor quality materials, selecting highly inappropriate building locations and renovating existing properties to a less than acceptable standard.

HEALTH CARE: ACHIEVEMENTS

According to statistics released by the National Bureau of Statistics, by the end of 2012:

- 536 million people had joined the basic urban medical insurance scheme (an increase of 62.5 million since 2011)
- approximately 50 million rural migrant workers had joined the urban basic medical insurance scheme (an increase of 3.6 million since 2011).

The **Healthy China 2020** programme launched in 2008 aims to help China overcome its many health challenges. The Chinese Ministry of Health set a number of targets to ensure that sufficient progress is made. These targets include:

- a life expectancy of 77 by 2020 (currently 75 in 2015)
- an improved health service in terms of access and availability (government reforms have led to a significant improvement in county hospitals)
- an improved medical insurance care system
- a reduction in NCDs (also known as chronic diseases)
- a reduction in child mortality to 13%.

In order to help achieve these targets, the Chinese government has increased its health care spending. Over $125 billion has been spent to roll out public health insurance cover to approximately 95% of the population. In 2013, Beijing increased its health care spending by 27% from 2012, to nearly $42 billion in order to deal with the rising costs of an ageing society.

EDUCATION: ACHIEVEMENTS

China has succeeded in ensuring that over 95% of its total population is literate which has been a main factor in driving its economic success. Many Chinese students perform well in subjects such as science and mathematics and the country is outperforming many Western nations in the OECD's Programme for International Student Assessment (PISA).

Hukou reform has resulted in increased rural access to early, primary and secondary education.

The Chinese government spent over $350 billion on education in 2012. The government has attempted to address inequality in education in a number of ways including:

- providing incentives for teachers to work in rural areas

- providing financial support to poor students to help them complete their compulsory education

- allowing some migrant children to attend urban schools

- introducing admission quotas to allow students from poor provinces access to college and university.

Recently, the Chinese government has invested heavily in improving the educational experience of ethnic minority children in rural locations. In 2014, the Ministry of Education, supported by UNICEF, carried out a pilot in 250 schools across five poor regions to promote social and emotional teaching and learning to better engage the young people. The Chinese government felt the pilot was a success and has now adopted the **National Child Friendly School Standards** which it will further roll out in 2015. This initiative is similar in many ways to the Scottish Curriculum for Excellence in relation to developing the confidence and skills of young people.

GENDER: ACHIEVEMENTS

Gender equality is now an important priority for the Chinese government. Recent developments have included:

- implementation of a law on domestic violence

- increased access to education and the workplace (particularly for poor rural females)

- increasing attention paid to All-China Women's Federation (ACWF) by Chinese government

- Chinese government priority of equal involvement in economy for women.

ONLINE

To read about China's first draft law on domestic violence, visit www.brightredbooks.net

DON'T FORGET

Despite its phenomenal economic growth, China is still officially classified as a developing nation.

ONLINE TEST

Test yourself on this topic at www.brightredbooks.net

THINGS TO DO AND THINK ABOUT

1 To what extent is the Chinese government effectively tackling housing inequality?

2 To what extent is the Chinese government effectively tackling education inequality?

INTERNATIONAL RELATIONS 1

CHINA'S MEMBERSHIP OF INTERNATIONAL ORGANISATIONS

China is the world's largest regional power and holds membership of hundreds of international organisations. Although not always the case in the past, China is currently an active member of a diverse range of organisations of great importance to Asia, and, the world at large. These organisations are concerned with matters such as delivering global security, protecting the environment, promoting human rights and stimulating economic growth. The table below details ten of the key organisations that China is a part of and highlights the year in which it gained entry.

China's membership of selected key international organisations

Name of organisation	Year of entry
African Development Bank (AfDB)	1985 (non-regional member)
Asian Development Bank (ADB)	1986
International Labour Organisation (ILO)	1919
International Monetary Fund (IMF)*	1945 (regained entry 1980)
Shanghai Cooperation Organisation (SCO)*	1996
United Nations (UN) General Assembly and Security Council*	1945 (PRC, 1971)
United Nations Educational, Scientific and Cultural Organisation (UNESCO)	1946
World Bank (WB)*	1945 (regained entry 1980)
World Health Organisation (WHO)	1948
World Trade Organisation (WTO)	2001

denotes China as being a Founding Member

FACT

In 2014, with loans of in excess of $30 billion, China became the Asian Development Bank's largest borrower, closely followed by India.

FACT

Judge Xue Hanqin is China's current representative in the International Court of Justice (ICJ). Judge Hanqin has been a Member of the Court since 2010.

ONLINE

For a detailed and up-to-date overview of China's ongoing contribution to the UN's main bodies, visit www.brightredbooks.net

DON'T FORGET

When exploring an international issue, it is important to refer explicitly to the country in question. Therefore, when writing about China, it is vital to use Chinese examples in your answers.

CHINA AND THE UN

China is a member of the General Assembly of the United Nations and a permanent member of a number of other UN main bodies including the Security Council (UNSC) and the Trusteeship Council.

Throughout 2014, the Chinese Ambassador to the UN, Liu Jieyi, addressed the UNSC on a range of issues of global importance including the situation in the Ukraine, the crisis in the Middle East, the crash of Malaysia Airlines flight MH-17 and combating the rise of Islamic State in Iraq.

Judge Xue Hanqin

In recent years, China has become increasingly active in many of the international organisations that it belongs to, including the UNSC. Since 2011, China has regularly used its veto in relation to the crisis in Syria. One such occasion was in February 2012, when China, along with the Russian Federation, failed to back an Arab Peace Plan which called for the removal of Syrian President Bashar al-Assad. In May 2014, China, again with the support of the Russian Federation, vetoed a draft UN resolution which called for the Syrian crisis to be referred to the International Criminal Court (ICC) for the investigation of war crimes. Both occasions were the subject of widespread international condemnation, with the latter resolution receiving the support of in excess of 60 countries. However, China's deputy UN ambassador, Wang Min, defended its decision to use the veto on the grounds that it would have had a negative impact on resurrecting peace talks.

contd

UN peacekeeping

To date, China has provided over 20 000 peacekeeping personnel to the UN. According to 2015 official UN statistics, China is currently the largest contributor to UN peacekeeping, contributing 2371 peacekeeping personnel to support worldwide operations. These personnel are made up of 176 police, 34 military experts and 2160 troops. Over time, China's increasing commitment to UN peacekeeping is reflective of its increasingly multilateral foreign policy.

Chinese UN Blue Berets

SHANGHAI CO-OPERATION ORGANISATION

Formerly known as the **Shanghai Five**, the **Shanghai Cooperation Organisation** (SCO) was established in April 1996 by the presidents of China, Kazakhstan, Kyrgyzstan, Russia and Tajikistan. Its purpose is to improve security for its member countries of central Asia. This aim continues, and there is now a strong emphasis on fighting international terrorism. A sixth member, Uzbekistan, joined the SCO in 2001. As the biggest members, China and the Russian Federation play a leading role in the SCO. The SCO is notable as an international organisation with no representation from either the European Union or the USA.

THINGS TO DO AND THINK ABOUT

1   From the table **China's membership of selected key international organisations**, identify the organisations which have predominately economic aims.

2   Create a spider diagram or an infographic which illustrates China's involvement in the UN. (You may wish to refer to China's inclusion in the UNSC and its contribution to UN peacekeeping operations.)

INTERNATIONAL RELATIONS 2

DON'T FORGET

Remember, one aim of the G20 is to create global economic stability. Have a quick look at p84 of Bright Red's N5 Modern Studies Study Guide for a brief overview of the G20.

ONLINE

The **BRICS Post** is a news website containing information about China and the other emerging economies of Brazil, Russia, India and South Africa. Why not check it out on Facebook (www.facebook.com/thebricspost) or follow it on Twitter (@TheBricsPost)?

CHINA AND THE G20

China values its status within the G20. According to Xingqiang He, a research fellow and associate professor at the Institute of American Studies at the Chinese Academy of Social Sciences (CASS), 'it remains the only economic institution setting where China can operate on par with major Western powers'.

China has been selected to host the G20 Summit in 2016. Many commentators argue that this is an ideal opportunity for China to become more involved in the G20's leadership, and, as a result, global economic governance.

Contributing to an article in the BRICS Post on in November 2014, He Fan, deputy director of the Institute of World Economics and Politics at CASS writes 'China needs G20 and G20 needs China. China should seek to strike a fine balance between the developed and developing countries granting a credibility to G20 that is badly needed'.

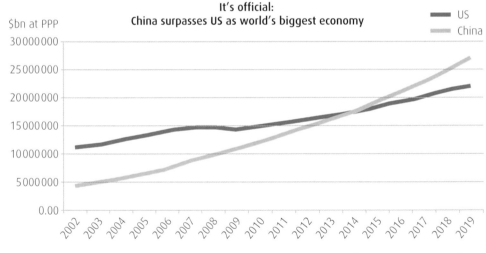

**It's official:
China surpasses US as world's biggest economy**

— US
— China

$bn at PPP

SINO–US RELATIONS

Recent Sino-US tensions

In 2014, it was announced that China had replaced the USA as the world's largest economy. According to official figures from the IMF, and calculated by purchasing power parity (PPP), China's economy is now estimated to be worth $17.6 trillion against the USA's $17.4 trillion. Without question, this announcement will have irritated Washington, who had occupied the top spot for over 140 years.

FACT

There are conflicting reports about the IMF's figures naming China as the world's largest economy.

Many commentators argue that a power struggle exists between China and the USA. In November 2014, **The Diplomat**, an Asia-Pacific current affairs magazine, reported that China was intent on challenging the USA for its position of control within east Asia. China and the USA have had a number of high profile disagreements, many of which centre around China's desire to expand its control of the region. In 2013, the Sino–US relationship was tested when China decided to introduce an **Air Defence Identification Zone** (ADIZ) in the East China Sea following an ongoing dispute with Japan over ownership of the Senkaku Islands.

China has also had disputes with Vietnam and the Philippines, both of whom are American allies. According to an article in the *Washington Post* in July 2014, the USA believes that China is becoming overly aggressive with the threat of military intervention particularly where its perceived sovereignty is concerned. By contrast, China believes that the USA is failing to act in an impartial manner. The USA recently expressed dissatisfaction towards China due to the active role it played in mobilising the introduction of the **Asian Infrastructure Investment Bank** (AIIB) in late 2014. The USA believes that this is an attempt by China to increase its influence as power in Asia at the expense of the USA and other nations such as Japan.

CHINA'S POWER AND INTERNATIONAL INFLUENCE

Economic power

The rise of China's powerhouse economy looks set to continue for some decades as the nation wrestles to increase its economic and political power within the lucrative east Asian market. Experts predict that over the next twenty years or so, China's economy could increase to become double the size of the USA's economy. However, it should also be noted that China is still a developing country with approximately 200 million people living in poverty and it lags way behind many developing countries in relation to per capita income.

Cultural influence

China used the 2008 Olympic Games in Beijing to send a message to the world's global powers that the country was on the rise and that it had matured diplomatically, although China is not as influential culturally as it is economically.

The opening ceremony of the 2008 Olympic Games, Beijing

Military strength

Although conflicting sources of information exist, it is estimated that China's annual defence spending is almost $130 billion, second only to that of the USA. The People's Liberation Army is by far the largest military force in the world and over the past 30 years it has developed highly advanced weaponry, including the Dong Feng-21D Anti-Ship Ballistic Missile and the Chengdu J-20 Fighter. Without question, China is a global military power on the rise and enjoys demonstrating its military strength to the wider world. China is estimated to have over 7500 nuclear warheads. China contributes more peacekeepers to the UN than any other permanent member of the UNSC and plays an active role in maintaining global security.

'Chinese culture is gaining increasing acceptance overseas, which in itself attests to China's progress with burgeoning foreign appetite to know more about China.'

Chinese Ambassador to the UK, Liu Xiaoming

World significance

This quote from the British Ambassador to China, Sir Sebastian Wood, sums up the importance of China to global society.

'The international community now needs China to be actively involved in our collective efforts to address and manage key global challenges – from macroeconomic policy co-ordination in the G20, to maintaining open trade and upholding the WTO, to preventing global warming and preserving the biodiversity of our planet, to combating the spread of anti-microbial resistance, to supporting development in the world's least developed countries, to preventing conflict and combating sources of terrorism in the Middle East.'

Sir Sebastian Wood, British Ambassador to China, October 2014

DON'T FORGET

China is still viewed with suspicion by some G7 nations who are monitoring its relationship with North Korea and the former G8 member, Russia.

THINGS TO DO AND THINK ABOUT

1 Discuss the importance of China occupying a leading position within the SCO.

2 Why do you think losing the status of the world's largest economy will concern the USA?

3 To what extent does China have influence in international relations?

ONLINE TEST

Test yourself on China's role in international relations at www.brightredbooks.net

UNDERDEVELOPMENT IN AFRICA

THE SCALE OF UNDERDEVELOPMENT

Africa's 54 nations

Map showing the division between Africa and Sub-Saharan Africa

Africa is the second largest continent in the world, both in terms of land mass and population. The continent covers an area of over 30 million square kilometres and boasts a population in excess of 1.1 billion people. The demographics are changing dramatically, however, as sub-Saharan Africa is experiencing unprecedented population growth. It is estimated by the Population Reference Bureau that by 2050, the African population will have more than doubled to reach almost 2.5 billion.

The October 2014 edition of *Africa's Pulse*, the World Bank's bi-annual African economic analysis, suggested that Africa's GDP growth was estimated to rise to 5.3% in 2017. This growth potential is fuelled by the successful economic performance of countries such as Kenya and Nigeria which are forecast to enjoy impressive GDP growth rates of 6% and 4.9% respectively in 2015 and feature at position 3 and 6 in Bloomberg's 2015 global poll of the world's fastest growing economies. The poll indicates that the global median GDP growth forecast for 2015 is 3.2%.

However, despite the fact many African economies are now growing faster than the economies of many developed nations, and despite the fact Africa has received over $600 billion in international aid since the 1950s, it continues to remain the world's poorest continent. According to *Africa's Pulse* 'poverty and inequality remain unacceptably high and the pace of reduction unacceptably slow'.

THE POOREST COUNTRIES IN THE WORLD

The following table is based on data obtained from the World Bank and identifies the poorest countries in the world based on GDP per capita. Each is found in Africa.

Rank	Country	GDP per capita($)
1	Malawi	226.50
2	Burundi	267.10
3	Central African Republic	333.20
4	Niger	415.40
5	Liberia	454.30
6	Madagascar	463.00
7	Democratic Republic of Congo	484.20
8	The Gambia	488.60
9	Ethiopia	505.00
10	Guinea	523.10

(World Bank, 2013 Figures)

Children carrying water in Malawi

THE MILLENNIUM DEVELOPMENT GOALS

In 2000, all UN member states and a number of international organisations committed to achieving the following eight Millennium Development Goals (MDGs) by 2015:

1. Eradicate extreme poverty and hunger.
2. Achieve universal primary education.
3. Promote gender equality and empower women.
4. Reduce child mortality.
5. Improve maternal health.
6. Combat HIV/AIDS, malaria and other diseases.
7. Ensure environmental sustainability.
8. Form a global partnership for development.

contd

According to the latest UN MDG Report published in June 2014, although a number of global MDG targets have been met, there is still much work to be done, especially in Sub-Saharan Africa. This list highlights the scale of underdevelopment that still exists in the region:

- In 2010, 48% of the population were still living on less than $1.25 per day. This resulted in well over 400 million Africans living below the poverty line. Currently, only six sub-Saharan African nations (Cameroon, Egypt, Guinea, Senegal, The Gambia, and Tunisia) have achieved the poverty reduction target.
- Between 2011 and 2013, 25% of the population remained undernourished.
- In 2012, 21% of children under the age of five were moderately or severely underweight. Sub-Saharan Africa only managed to reduce its percentage of underweight children by 14.3% over the two decades between 1990 and 2012.
- In 2012, only 78% of children were enrolled for primary education.
- In 2012, only 33% of non-agricultural work was carried out by women.
- In 2014, only 23% of seats in national parliament were occupied by women.
- In 2012, the under-five mortality rate was almost 10% at 98 deaths for every 1000 live births.
- In 2013, in women aged 15–49, the maternal mortality ratio was 510 deaths for every 100 000 live births.
- In 2012, only 53% of child deliveries were attended by qualified health professionals.
- In 2011, out of every 1000 births, 117 of them were to women aged 15–19.
- Between 2006 and 2012, only 28% of women aged 15–24 had a comprehensive knowledge of HIV transmission.
- In 2012, only 64% of the population had access to an improved water source. Many individuals were forced to drink surface water or water that was faecally contaminated.

Factfile: Burundi

President is Pierre Nkurunziza. He has held office since 2005.

Capital city is Bujumbura.

Population is approximately 10.4 million.

Languages spoken are Kirundi, French and Swahili.

The main ethnic groups are Hutu (85%) and Tutsi (14%).

Ranked 180th of 187 countries in the 2013 United Nation's Human Development Index (HDI).

Burundi's development has been heavily restricted by the Hutu–Tutsi civil war. It is estimated that approximately 300 000 civilians have been killed and over one million people have been displaced.

Burundi suffers from a number of infectious diseases including malaria, hepatitis A and typhoid fever.

In 2014, the average life expectancy was 57.94 for males and 61.22 for females.

ONLINE

To read the full UN MDG Report 2014, visit www.brightredbooks.net

VIDEO LINK

Visit www.brightredbooks.net to watch a short video about poverty in the Niger Delta.

VIDEO LINK

To view a short video clip showing how torrential rains devastated Malawi in January 2015, visit www.brightredbooks.net

ONLINE

To access the International Human Development Indicators for Burundi and all other countries, visit www.brightredbooks.net

THINGS TO DO AND THINK ABOUT

1 Explain why the average African birth rate is much greater than that of the UK. Provide two reasons.
2 a Explain why, despite receiving over $600 billion of aid in recent decades, Africa is still the world's poorest continent.
  b Provide two reasons why this might be the case and explain your logic.
3 Which MDGs have the countries of sub-Saharan Africa struggled to meet?
4 In 2012, only 78% of children in Africa were enrolled for primary education. Why is this a problem?
5 Watch the video clip about poverty in the Niger Delta. What is the main cause of the poverty? Why is this ironic?

ONLINE TEST

Head to www.brightredbooks.net and test yourself on the scale of underdevelopment.

CAUSES AND EFFECTS OF UNDERDEVELOPMENT: SOCIAL BARRIERS

There are many social, political and economic factors causing African underdevelopment.

FACT

According to research conducted by a number of influential international organisations in 2013, AIDS-related illnesses were responsible for the deaths of approximately 120 000 young Africans, making them the number one killer of the continent's adolescents.

VIDEO LINK

To watch informative videos produced by the WHO which detail important facts about malaria and TB, visit www.brightredbooks.net

ONLINE

To find out more information about the 2014 Ebola outbreak, visit www.brightredbooks.net to access an 'Ebola Features Map' created by the WHO.

DON'T FORGET

Although the Ebola outbreak dominated the news headlines throughout 2014 and in early 2015, the disease is nowhere near as widespread as other African killer diseases such as malaria and tuberculosis.

SOCIAL BARRIERS TO AFRICAN DEVELOPMENT

Inadequate access to health care

In order to enjoy internationally acceptable living standards and achieve sustainable economic growth, a country's workforce needs to be healthy and must be able to access an appropriate health care system in times of need. Unfortunately, inadequate access to health care severely limits the development of almost all sub-Saharan African nations. These nations are particularly susceptible to a number of serious diseases which have widespread social and economic consequences. The most serious are detailed below.

Main causes of death in sub-Saharan Africa 2012 (excluding AIDS/HIV)

Disease	Number of deaths	Description
Lower respiratory tract infections	1 million + deaths	Examples include pneumonia and influenza.
Diarrhoea	644 000 deaths	Results in death by dehydration. Can be caused by contaminated water supplies.
Malaria	568 000 deaths	Disease is passed to humans via mosquito bites. Common cause of deaths of under-fives. Prominent in countries like Uganda and Tanzania. Mosquito nets and insecticides help to combat the disease.
Stroke	427 000 deaths	Death by stroke is common throughout the world, not just in Africa. Risk of stroke can be increased by smoking and other lifestyle choices such as having a poor diet.
Tuberculosis (TB)	230 000 deaths	TB is commonly linked with poverty. Symptoms include coughing up blood and loss of weight.

HIV/AIDS FACTSHEET

- HIV is the world's leading infectious killer, responsible for around 1.5m deaths in 2013 alone.

- AIDS/HIV is prevalent throughout Africa but especially in countries such as Botswana, Swaziland and Uganda. In 2012, 23% of Botswana's population had HIV.

- HIV can be transmitted in a number of ways including having unprotected sex and sharing contaminated needles.

- In Africa, there are 3 million children with HIV, having contracted the infection from their mother during pregnancy, childbirth or breastfeeding.

- If more African people had access to antiretroviral therapy (ART), the transmission of the disease from the HIV positive partner to the HIV negative partner would be reduced by well over 90%.

Source WHO

contd

Case Study: West African Ebola epidemic 2014

What is Ebola virus disease (EVD)?

The Ebola virus causes an illness, which if left untreated, is potentially fatal. It can be passed to humans from wild animals such as fruit bats or monkeys and apes. It is passed on from human to human via bodily fluids.

What are the symptoms of Ebola?

Initial symptoms include fever, fatigue, muscle pain, headache and sore throat, followed by vomiting, diarrhoea, rash, symptoms of impaired kidney and liver function and internal and external bleeding.

Treatments, vaccines, prevention and control

To date, there is no proven cure for Ebola. However, a number of potential vaccines are currently being tested. Outbreaks can be controlled by quickly identifying individuals who have been in contact with people infected with Ebola and providing appropriate medical care, ensuring medical teams have access to well-equipped laboratories and carrying out safe burials.

Official statement by UN Secretary General, Ban Ki Moon

In August 2014, as EVD continued to spread, Ban Ki Moon announced 'We need to avoid panic and fear. Ebola can be prevented. With resources, knowledge, early action and will, people can survive the disease. Ebola has been successfully brought under control elsewhere, and we can do it here too'.

Affected African countries (2014)

The EVD epidemic affected six of Africa's poorest countries with the most basic health care systems and infrastructure. As of March 2015, the estimated Ebola statistics were as follows:

Country	Identified cases	Deaths
Liberia	9249	4057
Sierra Leone	11 497	3565
Guinea	3237	2141
Nigeria	20	8
Mali	8	1
Senegal	1	0

ELWA3 in Monrovia, Liberia, the largest Ebola treatment unit.

Source: WHO

Inadequate access to education

A high-quality education system and skilled workforce are two essential components of a developed and prosperous economy. Unfortunately, despite a number of measures introduced to improve the learning experience of African children, including a strong focus on achieving MDG #2 (universal primary education), the situation in sub-Saharan Africa remains grim. Many countries have low literacy rates. Problems include lack of finance, lack of resources and large class sizes. According to the **Africa Learning Barometer**, the continent suffers from four major educational problems. These are:

- a high, and increasing number, of non-attenders at school
- a high school drop-out rate
- varying standards of education – many children receive an insufficient quality of education
- educational inequality.

According to UNICEF in June 2015, 'Education saves lives! A child whose mother can read is 50% more likely to live past the age of 5'. In South Sudan, education is a priority because:

- 400 000 children are out of school
- fewer than 10% of children finish primary school
- only 30% of the population is literate.

THINGS TO DO AND THINK ABOUT

1. Choose two of Africa's poorest countries and try to establish some of the main reasons why they are so poor.
2. In developing regions, such as Africa, diseases like pneumonia and influenza can often result in death. Why do you think this is particularly alarming?

ONLINE

To access the Africa Learning Barometer for a closer look at the four indicators which highlight Africa's education problems, visit www.brightredbooks.net

FACT

Eritrea and Liberia have two of the highest school drop-out rates in the world at 66% and 59% respectively.

FACT

Two-thirds of Nigerian children are likely to never attend school.

FACT

According to UNESCO's Institute for Statistics, schools in Cameroon suffer greatly from a lack of materials with a ratio of 1 mathematics textbook to every 13 pupils.

ONLINE

Have a look at the Global Initiative on Out-of-School Children tool, visit www.brightredbooks.net

DON'T FORGET

Absolute poverty is when individuals struggle to access the basic necessities of life such as clean water, food, shelter and access to health care

ONLINE TEST

Test yourself on the causes and effects of underdevelopment at www.brightredbooks.net

CAUSES AND EFFECTS OF UNDERDEVELOPMENT: SOCIAL AND POLITICAL BARRIERS

SOCIAL BARRIERS TO AFRICAN DEVELOPMENT

High youth unemployment

Many African countries, such as Sierra Leone, have high levels of youth unemployment. This is a significant barrier to development. High levels of unemployment may often result in increased instances of crime and conflict due to the inequality it creates. A highly unequal society has the potential to threaten a country's social stability, especially when there is a significant percentage of the population living in absolute poverty. According to an article published in Forbes Magazine in September 2013:

- 70% of Africans are below 30 years old
- 50% of these young Africans are unemployed
- every year 10–12 million new workers need to find work
- the African labour market is unequal and prone to corruption
- working in the informal sector is common. This means that employment may be infrequent, working conditions may be dangerous and poverty is inherent.

In future, many African countries must take urgent action to create sustainable employment opportunities for their young. This is especially true given the fact that by 2040, young Africans will account for 50% of the world's total youth population.

POLITICAL BARRIERS TO AFRICAN DEVELOPMENT

Civil war, conflict and insurgency

For decades, Africa has been plagued by ongoing civil war, conflict and insurgency, all of which have had a devastating effect on the continent's development. Current conflicts include civil war in the Central African Republic and in South Sudan. In January 2015, a report entitled *South Sudan: The Cost of War* was produced by Frontier Economics in collaboration with the Center for Conflict Resolution (CECORE) and the Centre for Peace and Development Studies (CPDS). This report focused mainly on the economic cost of war to Sudan, but also highlighted some of the human costs of war. A selection of the report's main findings are presented in these spider diagrams.

Death:
Tens of thousands of people killed.

Displacement:
Circa 2 million people forced to flee their homes.

Human Costs

Famine:
Approximately 1.5 million people at risk of famine.

Trauma:
Trauma has been experienced by women who were raped, children who were forced to become child soldiers, and families who have lost their livelihoods.

Reduced Economic Activity:
This occurred as a result of the country diverting from 'productive' to 'non-productive' activities. Money was used to buy weapons and ammunition as opposed to being spent on infrastructure projects which promote development. Destruction of key buildings and towns and loss of life have also resulted in a reduction in economic activity. The report asserts that if the current conflict lasts for another 1–5 years, it could cost South Sudan a further US$28bn.

International Impact:
The international community will unquestionably benefit if the conflict is brought to a close within the next year. The report estimates that the international community could save approximately US$30bn as a result of not having to provide humanitarian aid and peacekeeping troops.

Economic Costs

Environmental Degradation:
Large swathes of South Sudan have been destroyed as a result of warfare. Natural resources have been exploited and ecosystems and wildlife have suffered as a result of the continued violence. Costs have also been incurred as a result of polluted water supplies, the destruction of agricultural land and the loss of livestock.

Regional Impact:
The economies of neighbouring countries including Ethiopia, Kenya, Republic of the Sudan, Tanzania and Uganda have suffered as a result of limited trade with South Sudan. According to the report, if the war was to end within the next year, as opposed to lasting for a further five years, South Sudan's neighbouring countries could save up to US$53 billion.

The human and economic cost of the South Sudanese conflict

Case Study: Boko Haram insurgency

Who are Boko Haram?	Boko Haram is Nigeria's largest Islamist extremist group (estimated to have over 9000 members) originally founded by Mohammed Yusuf in 2002. Since 2009, the group has been led by Abubakar Shekau. The US government is offering a reward of £4.6 million for information about Shekau's location.
What does Boko Haram mean?	Boko Haram means 'Western education is forbidden' or 'People committed to the propagation of the Prophet's teachings and jihad'.
Where does Boko Haram operate?	Initially Boko Haram caused havoc in Nigeria, having a strong presence in the north-eastern states of Adamawa, Borno and Yobe. It has also now moved into Cameroon and is attempting to gain territory in Chad and Niger.
Has Boko Haram carried out high profile attacks?	Boko Haram has carried out a number of large scale attacks and abductions of late including: • multiple suicide bombings throughout March 2015 in Maiduguri, Nigeria which collectively killed over 100 people • beheadings (videos posted online in March 2015) • 2000 people massacred in Nigeria in January 2015 • kidnapping of 273 girls from a Nigerian boarding school in April 2014.
In what way has Boko Haram limited development in Africa since 2009?	An estimated 13 000 people have been killed. 3 million people affected by Boko Haram's campaign of terror including the displacement of circa 1.6 million. Vast sums of money have been stolen and extorted by the militants. Government buildings have been destroyed, military bases have been ransacked and homes have burned to the ground. Money has had to be redirected from worthwhile projects to help the Nigerian army combat Boko Haram.
What does Nigeria's newly elected President think about Boko Haram?	In April 2015, following his election as Nigerian President, Muhammadu Buhari claimed 'Boko Haram will soon know the strength of our collective will. We should spare no effort'.

Michelle Obama supporting the Twitter campaign raising awareness of the kidnapping of over 270 Nigerian schoolgirls in May 2014 from their government secondary school in Chibok, Borno State, Nigeria.

THINGS TO DO AND THINK ABOUT

1 'The South Sudanese conflict has had a devastating effect on both the people and the economy of South Sudan'. Discuss.
2 Describe two ways in which the actions of Boko Haram have restricted development in Nigeria.
3 In a similar format to the Boko Haram Case Study, create your own case study for al Shabab. You may wish to include – who they are, where they operate and how their actions have impeded development activity.

DON'T FORGET

An **insurgency** is a rebellion. In the case of Boko Haram, the insurgents are rebelling against the Nigerian government, previously led by Goodluck Jonathan. Recently, Boko Haram pledged allegiance to Islamic State (IS).

Boko Haram logo

VIDEO LINK

For a comprehensive overview of Boko Haram by the Guardian, visit www.brightredbooks.net

FACT

Boko Haram are also linked to the **al-Shabab** Islamist movement who were responsible for killing 148 students at a college in Garissa, Kenya in April 2015. The Somali militants have kidnapped and brainwashed many children to help them fight their opponents, who include the Federal Government of Somalia and the **African Union Mission to Somalia** (AMISOM).

ONLINE TEST

Take the test on the causes and effects of underdevelopment at www.brightredbooks.net

CAUSES AND EFFECTS OF UNDERDEVELOPMENT: POLITICAL BARRIERS

POLITICAL BARRIERS TO AFRICAN DEVELOPMENT

Corruption and ineffective governance

Africa's poorest countries receive billions of pounds of aid from developed nations, international organisations and non-governmental organisations (NGOs). However, according to Transparency International, almost $150 billion per annum fails to reach its intended destination. In reality, corruption costs Africa much more annually than it receives in aid packages. Corruption and ineffective governance are widespread, and, have severely hindered Africa's social, political and economic progress.

The table below shows selected data from the 2013 **Corruption Perceptions Index**. The level of corruption is determined by the country's score, where a high score denotes low levels of corruption and a low score denotes high levels of corruption. As you can see, nations such as Uganda, Burundi and Somalia do not fare well and are perceived as being highly corrupt.

Corruption Perceptions Index 2013 (selected countries)

Rank	Country	Score
1	New Zealand	91
3	Sweden	89
14	United Kingdom	76
19	United States of America	73
30	Botswana	64
83	Burkina Faso	38
119	Sierra Leone	30
140	Uganda	26
157	Burundi	21
175	Somalia	8

Corruption and ineffective governance as a barrier to development

Africa has the potential to generate vast revenues from its abundance of natural resources. However, corruption results in the loss of billions of pounds each year which could otherwise be spent on improving living standards across the continent. Examples of corruption and ineffective governance include:

- The disappearance of billions of pounds of oil revenues over a prolonged period in countries such as Angola and Nigeria. This lost revenue could have been spent on programmes aimed at improving education and agriculture.

- Multiple instances of money laundering and fraud, including the creation of 'phantom firms'. According to the grassroots organisation ONE, 'the DRC lost £880m in just five mining deals from 2010–2012 through mispricing of assets using phantom firms'.

- A lack of consideration when signing important deals. For example, Lansana Conte, Guinea's former president, signed a deal in 2008 to allow BSGR to extract half of the iron ore from the Simandou mine, forgoing $140 billion dollars of income over a 25-year period for the poorest sections of society in Guinea. It has been alleged that the deal was based on bribery. Guinea's current president Alpha Conde is now attempting to revoke the licence, but is meeting resistance from Israeli billionaire Beny Steinmetz, former owner of BSGR.

- The Gambia has witnessed its debt-to-GDP ratio increase significantly in the past five years due to financial mismanagement.

ONLINE

To access Transparency International's Corruption Perceptions Index 2013, which includes an interactive map highlighting the perception of corruption that exists throughout the world, including all African countries, visit www.brightredbooks.net

FACT

According to the Corruption Perceptions Index 2013, Africa's most corrupt countries are Somalia, Sudan, South Sudan, Libya and Chad.

contd

- When people are denied basic human rights, made to feel worthless and are forced to live in absolute poverty, there is an increased chance that they may consider joining militant groups such as Boko Haram. This will lead to conflict and an increase in military expenditure.

- A number of Africa's current leaders have been criticised for corruption and systematic abuse of power, including José Eduardo dos Santos (Angola) and Teodoro Obiang Nguema Mbasogo (Equatorial Guinea).

President José Eduardo dos Santos

President Dos Santos has been criticised for selective distribution of Angola's oil revenues. His daughter Isabel Dos Santos is one of the richest women in Africa. However, it is claimed that she is merely a custodian of the wealth for her father. According to former Angolan Prime Minister, Marcolino Moco, 'It is not possible to justify this wealth, which is shamelessly displayed … there is no doubt that it was the father that generated such a fortune'.

President Dos Santos has been accused by Human Rights Watch of victimising and intimidating journalists who campaigned for a change of leadership in the run up to the 2012 elections. Having ruled for over 25 years, some people argue that it is time for change.

Despite the fact Angola is a top oil and diamond producer, the country has an average life expectancy of 51.46 and an average literacy rate of 70.4%.

José Eduardo Dos Santos,
President of Angola

President Teodoro Obiang Nguema Mbasogo

President Obiang has exploited Equatorial Guinea's oil reserves for personal gain. In late 2014, Obiang's son lost a $30 million Malibu mansion on the grounds it was purchased with stolen cash.

Obiang has been heavily criticised for human rights violations including the use of torture and conducting unfair trials. Serious questions have been raised over the legitimacy of the country's elections.

Many people living in Equatorial Guinea lack access to safe water, electricity and education.

Africa's longest serving leader,
Teodoro Obiang Nguema Mbasogo,
President of Equatorial Guinea

DON'T FORGET

Phantom firms are companies which are extremely difficult to trace and are used by corrupt politicians and businesses to embezzle money.

✔ ONLINE TEST

Test yourself on the causes and effects of underdevelopment at www.brightredbooks.net

💭 THINGS TO DO AND THINK ABOUT

1 Describe, in your own words, what is measured by the Corruption Perception Index.

2 Carry out your own research. Attempt to explain why Somalia is accused of being a corrupt country.

CAUSES AND EFFECTS OF UNDERDEVELOPMENT: ECONOMIC BARRIERS

ECONOMIC BARRIERS TO AFRICAN DEVELOPMENT

Africa's debt boom: key issues

High levels of **borrowing** are a significant issue in African economies. African countries are borrowing more money from private lenders than they are from traditional sources of finance such as the African Development Bank (AfDB), the World Bank (WB) and the International Monetary Fund (IMF). This could create difficulties if the borrower experiences unforeseen financial difficulty and requires an increase to the original loan agreement or requires the repayment period to be extended. In most cases, traditional lenders will be more flexible than private lenders. Many countries are also borrowing much more than they should be based on the size of their country's economy.

An increasing number of African countries including Ghana, Mozambique and Rwanda are now issuing **bonds** as a means of generating income to drive forward development. Many leading economists believe this approach is risky, as the countries are effectively gambling on their ongoing ability to perform well economically when their performance is often determined by external forces. For example, Nigeria has suffered due to the variations in the price of crude oil. According to the IMF, African countries raised approximately $20 billion by issuing bonds in 2014, an increase of 75% since 2009.

The strong performance of the US dollar has recently had a negative impact on the **value of African currencies**, such as the Ghanaian Cedi and the Gambian Dalasi. In 2014, the Dalasi fell by 12% against the dollar. This is problematic as it means that the Gambia is able to purchase fewer goods for its money, including, for example, much needed food supplies. This may lead to more long- and short-term borrowing for the country.

Many African nations are currently struggling to make their debt repayments due to a **drop in the prices of their key commodities or exports**. Examples include copper in Zambia and wood in the Gambia. If prices remain low, then these countries may need to request additional support from key international organisations.

A number of African countries including Eritrea, Ghana, and Malawi spend significant proportions of their government revenue on **repaying debt**. In 2014, Ghana spent 36% of its total revenue on debt repayments.

VIDEO LINK

To watch a short clip which provides an overview of Africa's current debt crisis, visit www.brightredbooks.net:

Burdensome
Sub-Saharan Africa's medium- and long-term debt, $bn

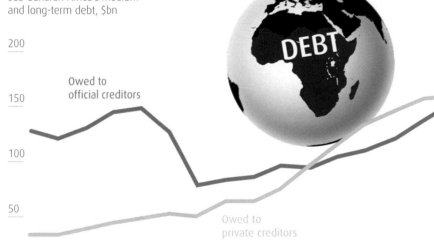

Owed to official creditors

Owed to private creditors

2000 01 02 03 04 05 06 07 08 09 10 11 12 13 14* 15*

* Forecast Source: Economist Intelligence Unit

Sub-Saharan Africa's medium- and long-term debt

'Today's economic environment in sub-Saharan Africa is similar to the boom that preceded the bust in the debt crises in Africa and Asia in the 1990s, when western governments and banks wrote off billions of pounds of debt. Today billions of dollars are again at stake, not to mention the financial stability of the region.'

Judith Tyson, researcher

contd

Barriers to trade

African countries have a strong desire to work their way out of poverty by making the most of their natural resources. However, although the African people appreciate the importance of local, regional and global trade in order to achieve economic growth, there are a number of barriers which prevent sub-Saharan countries from fully capitalising on lucrative trade opportunities. Some of these barriers are described here.

High import tariffs act as a financial barrier to trade by forcing the producer to increase the market price at which their product is sold in order to cover production costs and make an acceptable profit. This can make it extremely difficult for African exports to compete with domestic producers in a foreign market.

African farmers can often struggle to sell their produce in their own country and region due to the availability of **cheap foreign imports**. It is often possible for foreign competitors to produce their goods in a more cost-effective manner as they have access to more advanced production processes and machinery. Many countries also provide subsidies to their own producers in order to give their products a competitive advantage on the international stage.

Some African producers struggle to gain access to **strictly regulated foreign markets** due to very specific **quality requirements**, such as EU licensing regulations.

Some countries in Africa suffer from having to pay **high costs to transport** their goods to the market. In most cases, the countries do not have the **capital** to establish competitive industries.

DON'T FORGET

In the past, many African countries have had huge amounts of debt written off through schemes such as the **Multilateral Debt Relief Initiative** (MDRI).

DON'T FORGET

Africa's highly sought-after exports include oil, diamonds, copper, bauxite, iron ore, coal and timber as well as **cash crops** such as sugar, coffee, tea, maize, cotton, tobacco, bananas and cocoa.

THE EFFECTS OF UNDERDEVELOPMENT

The effects of underdevelopment

Underdevelopment	Effects
Lack of health care/ disease	Lower life expectancy, high number of deaths from avoidable illness, high infant mortality, poor maternal and child health, rapid population growth, high death rate from HIV/AIDS and other serious illnesses, high medical costs.
	Lack of production due to illness (resulting in reduced economic growth), high proportion of child carers, high number of orphans.
Hunger and malnutrition	Lower life expectancy, chronic malnutrition (especially in children under 5), lack of productivity from workforce, low economic development as a result, high infant mortality, high number of deaths.
Lack of education	High illiteracy rate, large class sizes, inability to secure and sustain employment as a result of being poorly educated, low-paid jobs, low living standards, poverty, limited life chances, slow economic growth for the country due to a high proportion of the workforce being uneducated.
Lack of jobs and unemployment	Highly unequal society, a high rate of crime and conflict, a low standard of living for many (extreme poverty), an underperforming economy, increased reliance on international aid.
War and conflict	Government money being redirected from productive to non-productive activities, reduced economic activity, reduced trade, increased reliance on international aid, high number of deaths, denial of human rights, displacement, famine, use of child soldiers, child exploitation, sexual violence, high number of orphans.
Corruption and ineffective governance	Lost government revenue, increased debt, reduced political and economic progress, social instability, increased reliance on international aid.
Debt and barriers to trade	Increased borrowing from a number of sources, higher debt repayments, reduced infrastructure developments and reduced economic growth as a result, lack of international competitiveness, poverty.

DON'T FORGET

The people of many underdeveloped African nations suffer from a range of human rights violations including political oppression, torture, female genital mutilation and lack of religious freedom.

DON'T FORGET

Climate change can result in severe flooding or drought which can lead to crop failure. This can have devastating effects on African countries who rely on the harvest, not only to eat, but also to sell as cash crops.

 THINGS TO DO AND THINK ABOUT

1 Explain two reasons why a number of African countries may see their external debts rise if commodity prices fall or their currency weakens.
2 Provide two reasons why many African producers may struggle to export their goods to the European Union.
3 Complete a spider diagram to show the range of ways underdevelopment impacts on African countries.

ONLINE TEST

Head to www. brightredbooks.net and test yourself on the causes and effects of underdevelopment.

EFFECTIVENESS OF ATTEMPTS TO RESOLVE UNDERDEVELOPMENT

Humza Yousaf, Minister for External Affairs and International Development

ONLINE

For full details of the organisations and programmes funded through the Malawi Development Programme, visit www.brightredbooks.net

DON'T FORGET

The Scottish Government are now funding over 40 projects in Malawi, some of which are helping poor communities deal with the effects of climate change. In the past decade, Scotland has provided £37 million of support to over 100 projects.

VIDEO LINK

To watch the UN's Special Representative for SE4ALL, Dr Kanden Yumkella, speak about the 'Decade of Sustainable Energy', visit www.brightredbooks.net

VIDEO LINK

To watch Humza Yousaf speak about the launch of the Scottish Government's Small Grants Programme for 2015/2016 including an overview of the work of YES Tanzania, visit www.brightredbooks.net

HOW DOES SCOTLAND SUPPORT AFRICAN COUNTRIES?

Despite the fact that Scotland is a small nation, the Scottish Government is determined to play a part in supporting developing countries, particularly those within sub-Saharan Africa. The Scottish Government's International Development Policy 'articulates the vision of Scotland's place in the world as a good global citizen, committed to playing its role in addressing the challenges faced by our world'. The majority of Scottish support is directed towards Malawi.

In January 2015, Humza Yousaf, the Minister for External Affairs and International Development announced 20 projects that will be funded in Malawi between 2015 and 2018 at a cost of £9 245 384. Collectively, these projects focus on a number of areas including civic governance, education, and renewable energy. The financial allocations are documented in the table below.

Projects funded from the Malawi Development Programme (2015–2018)

Project focus	Total recommendations
Health	£2 261 708
Education	£2 651 737
Civic governance	£987 827
Sustainable economic development	£2 146 710
Renewable energy	£1 197 402
Total	**£9 245 384**

Source: Scottish Government website

Specific projects include:

- £600 000 for Oxfam Scotland to help rural farmers and their families increase food production using renewable energy
- £200 000 for Glasgow City Council to improve educational outcomes for children through a project called **Malawi Leaders of Learning** which focuses on improving learning and teaching in addition to educational leadership
- £170 000 for Yorkhill Children's Charity to increase the number of health professionals in order to provide a national eye care service for people with diabetes and reduce unnecessary blindness.

The Scottish Government also allocates smaller sums of money towards a **Small Grants Fund**. Twelve out of the fifteen organisations who received funding in 2015 will operate in African countries including Malawi, Tanzania, and Zambia. A number of these programmes have received project grants, feasibility grants or capacity building grants to tackle the issue of underdevelopment. Some of these are shown in the table below.

Selected beneficiaries of Scottish Government's Small Grants Fund (2015)

Organisation / type of funding	Country	Award detail	Amount
Big First Aid *(Project grant)*	Tanzania	Increasing access to first aid information through mobile devices.	£39 609
YES! Tanzania *(Project grant)*	Tanzania	Using sport to deliver health messages to young people.	£41 333
Grow Volunteer *(Consulting Project grant)*	Malawi	Improve the business skills, and business performance of 250 disadvantaged female entrepreneurs in Malawi.	£59 758
LUV+ *(Feasibility grant)*	Zambia	To conduct a feasibility study and research for support projects for leprosy communities in Zambia.	£8200
Malawi Fruits *(Feasibility study)*	Malawi	To conduct a feasibility study to test growing traditional Malawi fruits as a cash crop for farmers in northern Malawi.	£10 000
Mamie Martin Fund *(Capacity-building grant)*	Malawi	To carry out capacity-building work to develop monitoring and evaluation in Malawi, and printing the impact report in Scotland.	£7 705

Source: Scottish Government Website

Using funds received from the Scottish Government, NGOs, both large and small, have been able to make a considerable difference in Africa by providing voluntary aid. Farming is a good example which illustrates the progress that has been made. Many rural farmers have been educated in effective farming techniques by Oxfam Scotland and, as a result, have managed to increase the productivity of their farms. They have been taught how to maximise their harvest and use the most appropriate irrigation methods to adapt to the

contd

damaging effects of climate change. Many farmers have moved away from subsistence farming and now generate a surplus which allows them to grow and sell cash crops. The producers can feed their families, increase their living standards and help to address Africa's food shortages.

The Scottish Government funds projects which helps African countries to work towards achieving the MDGs and recognise the **Paris Declaration on Aid Effectiveness**.

UK SUPPORT FOR AFRICAN COUNTRIES: BILATERAL AID

The UK Government is keen to ensure that it carefully selects recipient countries so that aid is provided to the people who need it most. The government is also keen to ensure that the money is used for the purpose in which it was intended, and has introduced a **payment by results** system where additional monies are only issued if promised development comes to fruition. It is now widely recognised that money alone will not solve Africa's underdevelopment issues. Despite major cash injections, many African nations are now worse off in 2015 than they were in the 1980s.

The UK Government, through the **Department for International Development** (DFID), will spend £64 567 848 in Sierra Leone, £168 624 324 in Ethiopia and £231 786 340 in Nigeria throughout 2015–16. This money will be mainly spent on improving health and education, helping to protect the environment and deal with the effects of climate change and providing disaster relief in times of crisis. This spider diagram gives an indication of some of the projects which have recently been funded in Sierra Leone.

UK SUPPORT FOR AFRICAN COUNTRIES: VIOLENCE AGAINST WOMEN

In March 2015, DFID, in partnership with the English Premier League and the British Council, launched a programme which aims to reduce violence against women by encouraging men and women to participate in football and develop mutual respect for one another. It is hoped that this initiative will significantly reduce violence against women. 45% of women in the Mount Elgon area of Kenya have reported being the victim of violence from the age of fifteen.

THINGS TO DO AND THINK ABOUT

1. Apart from the Small Grants Funds, describe the range of ways in which Scottish Government aid has helped the people of Malawi.
2. Choose one of the beneficiaries of the Scottish Government's Small Grants Fund. Find out more detail about the project and present your findings in a spider diagram or an infographic.
3. Use the **Aid by Location** development tracker to find out how much aid the UK aims to provide to Libya, DRC and Mozambique throughout 2015–16.
4. Use the **Aid by Location** development tracker (Country Projects) to complete the table.

Country	Population	2015–16 DFID aid allocation	Number of active aid projects	Percentage of budget spent on education	Highest ranking sector by project spend
Ethiopia	87.1 million				
Kenya			29		
Nigeria		£231 786 340			
Somalia					Government
Tanzania				17.56	

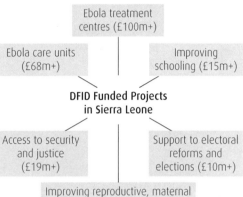

Ebola treatment centres (£100m+)

Ebola care units (£68m+)

Improving schooling (£15m+)

DFID Funded Projects in Sierra Leone

Access to security and justice (£19m+)

Support to electoral reforms and elections (£10m+)

Improving reproductive, maternal and newborn health (£23m+)

ONLINE

For full details of DFID aid spend by country and project, visit www.brightredbooks.net

Since September 2012, the Rt Hon Justine Greening MP has been the Secretary of State for International Development. She is also the co-chair of the Global Partnership for Effective Development Cooperation.

ONLINE TEST

Test yourself on the response to underdevelopment at www.brightredbooks.net

RESPONDING TO UNDERDEVELOPMENT: TIED AID AND AID EFFECTIVENESS

DON'T FORGET

Tied aid is aid that restricts the recipient country to spending financial aid in the donor country. Alternatively, there may be other strict conditions to the aid being granted.

FACT

In 2014, a number of countries including the UK and Denmark reduced funding to Uganda as a direct result of the Anti-Homosexuality Act which was introduced by Ugandan President Yoweri Museveni. The legislation makes it a criminal offence to be gay which can result in life imprisonment.

ONLINE

To access the DFID's Multilateral Aid Review 2011, visit www.brightredbooks.net

ONLINE

Check out the document at www.brightredbooks.net to learn more about the positive impact of UNICEF on Ebola-affected countries.

ONLINE

To access an information sheet on Humanitarian Action for Children in West and Central Africa, visit www.brightredbooks.net

VIDEO LINK

To find out more about the plight of Serengino Nicolette Divine, a 13-year old schoolgirl from Bangui affected by the civil war, visit www.brightredbooks.net to watch a short video clip.

TIED AID

Recent decades have witnessed a significant reduction in the provision of **tied aid**, with increasing international support for a total ban. Countries who often have very little option but to accept tied aid, have greatly reduced purchasing power because they are required to buy goods directly from the donor country. This means that they cannot benefit from the fairest international price for required materials. This can severely limit economic growth as the recipient country has less money available to purchase the materials required for desired infrastructure development. A 2011 report from the **European Network on Debt and Development** (EURODAD) concluded that approximately one-fifth of bilateral aid remains tied.

Many experts argue that the acceptance of tied aid by countries can often result in them becoming worse off. Following the acceptance of a loan from the IMF in 2009, many Ghanaians fell further into poverty as the government was prohibited from granting rice subsidies if they wished to receive future aid. This had a hugely negative impact on Ghana's growing rice industry and led to the Ghanaians having to import rice from countries such as the USA. It is widely argued that poor African nations would be better served by support rather than aid.

International organisations and multilateral aid

The UK provides funds to over 40 international organisations which provide invaluable support to African countries including:

- the Food and Agriculture Organisation (FAO)
- the Global Fund to Fight AIDS, TB and Malaria (GFATM)
- World Food Programme (WFP)
- World Health Organisation (WHO).

Example: UNICEF

The **United Nations Children's Fund** (UNICEF) is a UN **Specialised Agency**. Established in 1946, UNICEF carries out a number of functions including:

- protecting children from violence, exploitation and abuse
- helping children to survive by providing clean water, food and medicine
- helping children overcome barriers to gain access to education
- providing humanitarian support in times of disaster.

Throughout 2014, UNICEF and their partners were responsible for constructing almost 150 **temporary learning spaces** across the Central African Republic, allowing over 20 000 children, who had been displaced by civil war, to gain access to education.

Example: United Nations Development Programme

The **United Nations Development Programme** (UNDP) helps African countries with:

- poverty reduction and achievement of the MDGs
- democratic governance
- crisis prevention and recovery
- environment and energy for sustainable development.

The UNDP helps to develop democracy in order that everyone can share the benefits of economic growth. The UNDP is helping countries like Benin, Sierra Leone and Niger become more democratic in a number of ways including:

- **increasing political awareness** - funding a radio programme in Benin which gives 1 million people the opportunity to listen to live parliamentary debates
- **encouraging political participation** - distributed almost 40 000 ballot boxes throughout Sierra Leone in the run up to the 2012 General Election
- **influencing international funding** – helped Nigeria draw down funding from international organisations to help create effective governance in order to tackle poverty and ill-health.

contd

Case study: Cameroon

In March 2015, the World Bank reported on a successful programme of **Performance-based Funding** (PBF) in Cameroon in which funds are allocated to hospitals based on the standard of care that they provide for their patients. According to the World Bank website, this has resulted in increased patient satisfaction due to a marked increase in the quality of medical provision. Many of Cameroon's poverty-stricken population have benefited from access to appropriate health care and medicines.

The African Union

The **African Union** (AU) was set up in 2002, replacing the Organisation of African Unity (OAU).

The AU's vision is for 'an integrated, prosperous and peaceful Africa, driven by its own citizens and representing a dynamic force in the global arena'. The AU has a number of objectives including promoting unity between African nations, promoting social, economic and cultural sustainability, promoting peace and security across Africa and eradicating preventable diseases through effective international partnerships.

The AU is credited with a number of successes including:

- helping to create strong economies in a number of African countries
- encouraging African countries to allocate 10% of their annual budgets to farming
- helping to reduce political instability in countries such as Madagascar
- devising **Agenda 2063**, a 50-year plan which looks to build on progress which has already been made across the continent.

The AU has been criticised for hindering development by requesting funds from some of its members that they could not afford to part with and for failing to intervene in conflicts quickly enough, such as the civil war in Libya.

AID EFFECTIVENESS

Many African countries have benefited from reconstruction aid which has been provided in times of disaster and emergency. However, 'most independent research suggests that foreign aid has no positive consequences in the long run and that it may come with unintended and unwanted side effects' according to the Institute of Economic Affairs.

Although many would argue against this stance, most would agree that recipients and donors must do more to ensure aid is converted into sustainable development. No matter how good the intention, questions can be raised about whether financial aid is spent in the most appropriate ways. In October 2014, the Guardian newspaper reported that the **Independent Commission for Aid Impact** (ICAI) felt that the DFID was unsuccessful in tackling everyday corruption, claiming that UK aid often made little impact and, on occasion, actually made developing countries worse off. At the inaugural meeting of the **Global Partnership for Effective Development Cooperation** (GPEDC) in April 2014, it was also concluded that there was a greater need for increased partnership working between a number of groups, including donors, recipients, countries with growing economies and private industry. Furthermore, leading NGOs such as Oxfam believe that the way in which aid is delivered is equally as important as the amount of money that is spent.

VIDEO LINK

To find out more about PBF in Cameroon, visit www.brightredbooks.net to watch a short video clip.

FACT

In January 2015, the Zimbabwean President, Robert Mugabe, took over as Chairperson of the AU. Although this is a ceremonial role which only lasts for one year, it has been a controversial decision due to Mugabe's perceived international status as a dictator who has carried out multiple human rights offences.

African Union symbol

ONLINE TEST

Head to www.brightredbooks.net and test yourself on the response to underdevelopment.

ONLINE

Head to www.brightredbooks.net for advice on how to approach these essay questions and sample answers.

THINGS TO DO AND THINK ABOUT

1 'Tied aid can restrict growth within African countries.' Discuss.
2 Describe two ways in which UNICEF helps Africa's children.
3 Describe the role of the African Union in promoting development in Africa.
4 Name three of the main criticisms of foreign aid.
5 Essay practice: Explain, in detail, at least two political barriers to African development.
6 Essay practice: Evaluate the extent to which the international community has been effective in its attempts to promote African development? Provide at least two points for and against in your answer.

USA'S POLITICAL SYSTEM AND PROCESSES

The US Constitution

USA'S POLITICAL SYSTEM AND CONSTITUTIONAL ARRANGEMENTS

The USA's political system is a federal constitutional republic and its structure is outlined in the US Constitution which was written in 1787. The Constitution determines how power should be shared between the federal government's **legislative**, **executive** and **judicial** branches, and also describes the rights and responsibilities of state governments.

The USA is essentially a **two-party system**. Historically, and currently, practically all seats in the legislature are held by Republicans or Democrats. This is largely because, at national level, smaller parties lack both the support and financial resources to challenge the two established parties, and they would find it impossible to win a majority of electoral college votes.

ONLINE

To find out more about the US Constitution, visit www. brightredbooks.net

POLITICAL PARTIES

Although, the US political system is dominated by the Democrats and the Republicans, American citizens have, in theory, a choice of political parties for which they can vote. However, this choice may be more limited depending on the state in which they live.

American political parties can be grouped according to their level of prominence/ popularity throughout the USA.

The **Big Two** – major political parties recognised across **all** US states

The Democrat Party
The Republican Party

Largest third parties, recognised in **10+** US states*

The Libertarian Party (34)
The Green Party (21)
The Constitution Party (12)

Selected other political parties, recognised in **5 or less** US states*

Americans Elect Party (3)
Independence Party (5)
Reform Party (3)
Working Families Party (4)

*Source: Ballotpedia Research – accurate as of April 2015, but figures subject to change as a result of a party failing to meet various 'ballot status' requirements.

DON'T FORGET

Some candidates opt to stand as **independents** at various levels throughout US politics. This means that they are not attached to any political party. The only President ever to be elected as an independent was George Washington in 1789.

contd

The Republican Party

Republicans believe in conservatism (low taxation, less government interference in the economy, etc.) and that traditional marriage is the bedrock of society. Many Republicans are opposed to highly emotive issues such as abortion and same-sex marriage.

George H.W. Bush (1989–1993) and his son, George W. Bush (2001–2009) were Republican Presidents.

The Republican Party is popular in southern and mid-western states such as South Carolina, Texas and Wyoming.

Follow @GOP

The Republican Party enjoys support from much of corporate America and traditionally has a strong following from the wealthier white middle class.

High-profile individuals seeking the Republican nomination for the 2016 presidential election include Senator Rand Paul and billionaire Donald Trump.

Rand Paul believes that the USA should have a fairer and less complex tax system. He believes that **liberal policies** (such as federal or state government spending on employment programmes) have failed to solve the problems faced by inner-cities and believes that areas of high unemployment should benefit from low taxation, through the introduction of **Economic Freedom Zones**.

The Democratic Party

Democrats believe in liberalism (federal and state support to allow individuals to succeed, for example, in employment or education) and that 'America succeeds when everyone gets a fair shot, everyone does their fair share, and everyone plays by the same rules'.

Barack Obama (2009–2016) and Bill Clinton (1993–2001) were Democratic Presidents.

The Democratic Party is popular in north-east and western states such as New York, Illinois and California.

Follow @The Democrats

The Democratic Party attracts greater support from poorer groups in society, especially in urban areas, as well as people from minority ethnic groups.

High-profile individuals seeking the Democratic nomination for the 2016 presidential election include former US Secretary of State Hillary Clinton and US Senator Bernie Sanders.

Bernie Sanders is concerned by a number of issues which currently effect the USA including 'immoral and unsustainable wealth inequality', climate change and the 'horrendous trade policies of the Trans-Pacific Partnership (TPP)'.

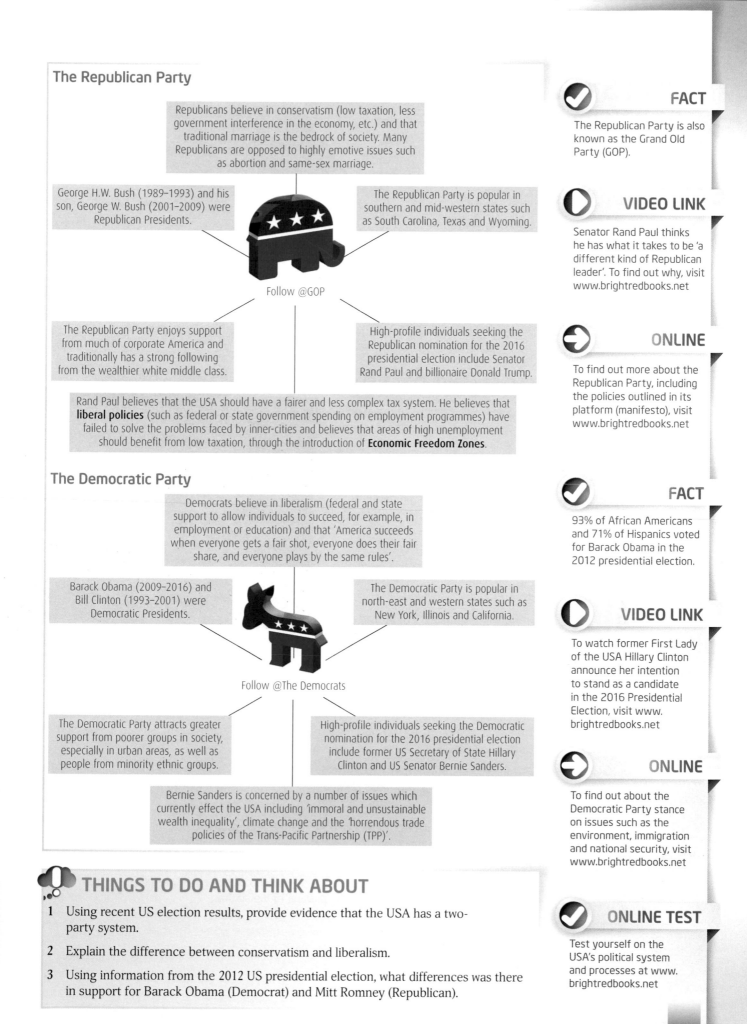

FACT

The Republican Party is also known as the Grand Old Party (GOP).

VIDEO LINK

Senator Rand Paul thinks he has what it takes to be 'a different kind of Republican leader'. To find out why, visit www.brightredbooks.net

ONLINE

To find out more about the Republican Party, including the policies outlined in its platform (manifesto), visit www.brightredbooks.net

FACT

93% of African Americans and 71% of Hispanics voted for Barack Obama in the 2012 presidential election.

VIDEO LINK

To watch former First Lady of the USA Hillary Clinton announce her intention to stand as a candidate in the 2016 Presidential Election, visit www.brightredbooks.net

ONLINE

To find out about the Democratic Party stance on issues such as the environment, immigration and national security, visit www.brightredbooks.net

THINGS TO DO AND THINK ABOUT

1 Using recent US election results, provide evidence that the USA has a two-party system.

2 Explain the difference between conservatism and liberalism.

3 Using information from the 2012 US presidential election, what differences was there in support for Barack Obama (Democrat) and Mitt Romney (Republican).

ONLINE TEST

Test yourself on the USA's political system and processes at www.brightredbooks.net

USA'S POLITICAL INSTITUTIONS AND PROCESSES

The powers of the US government are separated into three branches:

- legislative
- executive
- judicial.

Each branch has its own distinct powers. The US system of government aims to ensure that no one single branch of government has too much power. There are a number of **checks and balances** within the system to ensure that all branches of government must work together to make decisions.

LEGISLATIVE BRANCH

The legislative branch comprises elected senators and representatives who meet in **Congress**. Congress meets in the capital of the USA in Washington D.C.

Congress is known as a **bicameral legislature** and is America's highest law-making body. It is responsible for creating federal legislation that governs the country. Congress also has the responsibility of authorising government spending.

Congress in action

Congress is split into two houses or chambers, the **House of Representatives** and the **Senate**.

The House of Representatives (the lower chamber) is made up of 435 elected members who are elected for a two-year term.

The Senate (the upper chamber) is made up of 100 elected members (two representatives from each state) who are elected for a six-year term. One-third of the Senate are elected every two years.

The legislative branch may limit the power of the executive branch (the President) by impeaching a president or over-riding the presidential veto if two-thirds of each house of Congress agree.

The legislative branch may limit the power of the judicial branch by rejecting presidential nominations to the judiciary.

Congress is an important feature of the US democratic process as it allows the views of everyday Americans to be heard at national level through their elected representatives. These views can help to influence the passing of legislation.

EXECUTIVE BRANCH

The executive branch comprises the **President** of the USA, the **Vice President**, the **Cabinet** and **federal organisations and agencies**. The president's official residence is the White House in Washington D.C.

The President has the responsibility to implement and enforce laws that have been passed by Congress (Article II of the Constitution). The President is also head of state and Commander-in-Chief of the military.

The President appoints a cabinet, which has to be approved by the Senate. The fifteen members of the cabinet each head up an executive department, such as the Department of Commerce or the Department of Justice.

The executive branch exercises influence over the legislative branch, because the President has the power to propose legislation to Congress and can veto acts of Congress that he/she does not agree with.

The executive branch exercises influence over the judicial branch as the President is responsible for nominating Supreme Court and Federal Court judges (which the Senate must approve) and also has the power to 'extend pardons for federal crimes, except in the case of impeachment'.

The President or the Vice President are elected by the Electoral College, and not directly by US citizens.

44th President of the USA, Barack Obama, with Vice President Joe Biden.

DON'T FORGET

The Electoral College is made up of 538 electors – the 435 State Representatives, the 100 State Senators and 3 electors from the District of Columbia.

JUDICIAL BRANCH

The judicial branch comprises the **Supreme Court** of the USA and **lower federal courts**. The Supreme Court meets in the US Supreme Court Building in Washington D.C. The Supreme Court is the highest court in the land.

As of 2015, the Supreme Court is made up of one chief justice and eight associate justices. This is determined by Congress and can change.

US Supreme Court Building

The judicial branch exercises influence over the executive branch through judicial reviews which can deem executive actions to be unconstitutional. Also, as justices remain in post until they choose to leave or they are removed by the Senate, they are unlikely to compromise justice due to political influence.

The judicial branch exercises influence over the legislative branch as it determines if US laws are unconstitutional.

The President is responsible for appointing the justices, but the Senate must approve the President's nominations. Other junior courts also exist. These include districts courts and courts of appeal.

DON'T FORGET

You can keep fully up to speed with all White House developments via social media.

VIDEO LINK

To watch a short video clip which provides an overview of the executive branch, visit www.brightredbooks.net

ONLINE TEST

Test yourself on the USA's political institutions and processes at www.brightredbooks.net

THINGS TO DO AND THINK ABOUT

1   Why is there a system of checks and balances within the US system of government?
2   Describe the powers of the US President. Make at least three points.
3   Describe three powers of the legislative branch of the US system of government.
4   Describe the role of the US Supreme Court in the US system of government.

GOVERNANCE, DEMOCRACY AND MEDIA INFLUENCE

The fifty states of the USA

FEDERAL GOVERNMENT

The US federal government is responsible for dealing with issues that affect all US states. This includes currency, defence, foreign affairs, immigration and civil rights.

The federal government:

- consists of three branches, legislative, executive and judicial
- requires the election of candidates to the executive branch such as the President or Vice President. American citizens do not vote for these individuals directly
- requires the election of senators and representatives (congressional officers) to the legislative branch.

STATE GOVERNMENT

US states are responsible for dealing with domestic criminal matters as well as establishing a state constitution, issuing marriage licences and organising elections.

State governments also consist of the three legislative, executive and judicial branches. Within the executive branch, voters can elect **state governors**. Within the judicial branch, some states hold elections for **court judges**. Within the legislative branch, voters make up **legislative districts** and can vote for both a **senator** and a **representative**

LOCAL GOVERNMENT

Local government is responsible for providing services such as parks and recreation, education and police services. American citizens have the opportunity to vote for public offices such as city council member or mayor.

HOW DEMOCRATIC IS THE USA?

The average US citizen is able to enjoy many freedoms as a result of a series of amendments to the US Constitution. These freedoms include:

- freedom of speech
- freedom of religion
- freedom of assembly
- the right to bear arms
- the right to own private property.

There are also many ways for American citizens to participate in politics. They can:

- vote in federal, state and local elections for a range of elected representatives
- join a political party (remember, there are more than just the big two)
- stand as a candidate in federal, state and local elections
- join an interest group such as American Medical Association (AMA), the National Rifle Association (NRA) or the American Federation of Labour and Congress of Industrial Organisations (AFL–CIO).

However, despite the fact that the USA prides itself on its democratic principles, and boasts that there are many opportunities for political participation, there are also a number of criticisms:

contd

DON'T FORGET

Senior federal posts have strict qualification criteria that an individual must meet in order to run for the post. For example, the president of the USA must be a natural-born citizen of the USA, have lived there for the last 14 years and be at least 35 years old.

DON'T FORGET

Similarly, senators must live in the state they represent, have been a US citizen for 9 years and be at least 30 years old. Entry to the House of Representatives requires an individual to live in the state they represent, have been a US citizen for 7 years, and be at least 25 years old.

FACT

In 2015, the basic salary of a senator or representative is $174 000 + benefits.

- A 2015 study by the **Electoral Integrity Project** concluded that the USA ranked 45th out of 107 countries which have established democracies in terms of electoral integrity. Concerns were raised over 'US electoral laws, the processes of voter registration and the role of money in American politics'. America's poor performance placed it alongside countries such as Bulgaria and Columbia.
- The average American citizen does not get the opportunity to vote directly for the President.
- Many billionaire businessmen are accused of using their vast wealth to influence political decisions. For example, individuals such as Charles and David Koch have spent millions of dollars on TV advertisements to raise awareness of their group 'Americans for Prosperity'. Individuals, such as former US Secretary of Labour, Robert Reich, see this as a move to brainwash the electorate.
- Following the US Supreme Court's **Citizens United** decision in 2010, there is no limit on what individuals like the Koch brothers can spend on media campaigns.
- Minority parties struggle to gain representation as the 'winner takes all'. The two-party system is regarded as one reason for voter apathy and the low voter turnout that goes with it.

Some people question the extent to which average American citizens can influence key decisions.

Social media now plays a vital part in US elections

THE MEDIA

The freedom of the press is an important part of a democratic society. US citizens continue to benefit from access to a wide range of broadcast, print, online and social media which provides them with a vast array of information, some of which is based on facts, to help them form an opinion and make their decision.

Social media

According to a recent poll by the Pew Research Centre, an increased number of voters are now using mobile technology and social media, such as Twitter and Facebook, to obtain political information and follow candidates and other politicians. The table below highlights the increase in usage between 2010 and 2014.

Social media usage in American politics (2010/2014)

	2010	2014
Percentage of those surveyed who used their mobile phones to access political news.	13%	28%
Percentage of those surveyed who used their mobile phones to follow a candidate or another politician.	6%	16%

Source: The Pew Internet Project Survey, Pew Research Centre

US political parties appreciate the important role that social media plays in capturing the imagination of the electorate. In many cases political parties are ruthless, frequently using satire, and attempting to capitalise on any mistake their opponents might make.

THINGS TO DO AND THINK ABOUT

1 Describe the powers of both the federal and state governments.
2 Describe three ways American citizens can participate in US politics.
3 Give two reasons why the US ranks only 45th out of 107 countries in terms of electoral integrity.
4 Use your mobile phone to follow or connect with five political organisations/ politicians in the USA. What important issues are they commenting about? Summarise your findings in a table and report back to the class.

SOCIO-ECONOMIC ISSUES IN THE USA: ECONOMIC INEQUALITY

US cities with the greatest inequality

Rank	Location	Average income bottom 20% ($)	Average income top 5% ($)
1	Bridgeport-Stamford-Norwalk, CT	15 800	782 000
2	Naples-Immokalee-Marco Island, FL	13 900	521 000
3	New York-Newark-Jersey City, NY	12 300	489 000
4	Miami-Fort Lauderdale-West Palm Beach, FL	10 200	375 000
5	Port St Lucie, FL	9800	353 000
6	Santa Maria-Santa Barbara, CA	13 700	478 000
7	Brownsville-Harlingen, TX	6800	242 000
8	New Orleans-Metairire, LA	9000	323 000
9	Durham-Chapel Hill, NC	11 700	383 000
10	Los Angeles-Long Beach-Anaheim, CA	11 700	413 000

Source: 2013 US Census Data

US INCOME AND WEALTH INEQUALITY

As you can see from the table, income inequality varies considerably across US states and is currently a significant issue facing the US government.

The USA's 2014 Gini coefficient was 0.45, above the UN's international warning level of 0.4. This indicates that a severe level of income inequality exists within the country and that there is a possibility of social unrest because of the considerable income disparities that exist between the poorest and wealthiest in American society.

Many American senior citizens are too poor to retire and therefore have no other option but to work well into old age.

There are a number of factors which are believed to contribute towards the USA's income inequality. These factors include:

'After meeting fixed monthly expenses and paying income taxes to the federal and state authorities, there is no – I repeat, no – money left to be able to eat well or do anything in terms of discretionary spending.'

View of Donald, 72, Richmond Virginia.

- **Wealth distribution** Many argue that the US federal government has failed to direct enough money to the poor Americans who need it most and have provided wealthy lobbyists and businessmen with overly-generous tax breaks.

- **Education** The slogan 'skills pay the bills' has never been more true. Changes in the US economy have meant that individuals without college or university educations struggle to find work, and when they do, the work tends to be low paid. Conversely, people with a high level of education are not only more occupationally mobile, but they also command higher salaries.

- **Technology** The number of relatively low-skilled manufacturing jobs has been greatly reduced as a result of technological advancements. In order for the USA to remain internationally competitive, it has outsourced many of its technology-based jobs to countries which command lower wage rates. This has had a serious impact on many middle-income families who can no longer secure permanent, full-time well-paid employment.

FACT

Based on data from the Central Intelligence Agency (CIA), if the congressional district New York-10 was a country, it would rank as the 7th most unequal country in the world, with a Gini coefficient of 0.587.

VIDEO LINK

To find out about the damaging impact of income inequality on global prosperity, have a look at the short video clip from the Organisation for Economic Co-operation and Development (OECD) at www.brightredbooks.net

ONLINE

To find out about the inequality that exists between US cities, visit www.brightredbooks.net

THE RICH, THE POOR AND THE MIDDLE CLASS

The USA is currently suffering from:

- significant rises in the cost of living which is made worse by the fact that wages have fallen or remained static
- a burgeoning wealth gap, where 40% of the wealth is distributed among 1% of the population.

This table further emphasises the wealth gap that currently exists in the USA.

USA's glaring wealth gap

Number of American $ billionaires	537
Number of American $ millionaires	9.6 million
Average wealth per American citizen	$309 000
Median wealth	$45 000
Number of American people living in poverty	50 million (income of $23 550 per annum for a family of 4)

Source: Various

contd

America's super-rich

The super-rich tend to live in wealthy states such as California, New York and Washington.

Many of the USA's wealthiest citizens have amassed their fortunes through innovative entrepreneurship, investing in the stock market, or by making a name for themselves in highly paid professions such as medicine and law.

The American super-rich have a passion for fast cars. For example, Oracle founder Larry Ellison is the proud owner of a $4.1 million McLaren F1 sports car. American billionaire, Donald Trump, on the other hand, prefers to travel by air, and owns a Boeing 757 private jet worth an estimated $100 million.

US-wide protests calling for the minimum wage to be increased from $7.25 to $15 **#Fightfor15** McDonald's agreed to increase its pay to $10 by 2016, but many argue this is still not enough to live on

America's top 10 richest people

Position	Name	Source of wealth	Estimated fortune (US $)
1	Bill Gates	Microsoft (technology)	79.2 billion
2	Warren Buffett	Berkshire Hathaway (multinational conglomerate)	72.7 billion
3	Larry Ellison	Oracle (technology)	54.3 billion
4	Charles Koch	Koch Industries (various)	42.9 billion
5	David Koch	Koch Industries (various)	42.9 billion
6	Christy Walton	Walmart (retail)	41.7 billion
7	Jim Walton	Walmart (retail)	40.6 billion
8	Alice Walton	Walmart (retail)	39.4 billion
9	Samuel Robson Walton	Walmart (retail)	39.1 billion
10	Michael Bloomberg	Bloomberg LP (media)	35.5 billion

Source: Forbes (February 2015)

Walmart is officially the USA's largest retailer

Oprah Winfrey – US billionaire defying the racial wealth divide

US golfing superstar Tiger Woods owns a $60 million Florida mansion; the surrounding estate includes a tennis court, running track and diving pool

America's poor

America's poorest states include Mississippi, Arkansas and Louisiana. Many of the USA's poorest citizens work as cooks, bank tellers, housekeepers, childcare workers or retail sales clerks. These jobs are low paid which makes it extremely difficult for many Americans to escape the poverty trap.

In-work poverty in the USA is high, with almost 75% of working families accessing public benefits such as rent subsidies or food stamps.

America's middle class

In modern day America, what constitutes America's middle class? The median household income in the USA has barely changed in the past 15 years, despite significant increases in the cost of housing, health care and education.

According to a study by the Pew Charitable Trusts, all 50 US states have witnessed a reduction in the number of middle-class families between 2000 and 2013. The Trust defines middle class as having an income between 67% and 200% of the states' median income.

The middle class are credited with being the driving force behind America's great economic success. Many politicians believe that the reduction in the numbers of the middle-class people will result in the disappearance of the American Dream. Winning the middle-class vote will be a top priority for the 2016 presidential election candidates.

 FACT

The Walton family, who own Walmart, are the USA's wealthiest family with an estimated fortune of $160.8 billion.

FACT

The ratio of white-to-black US billionaires is 250:1. In 2015, the USA only had two black billionaires – chat show legend Oprah Winfrey (worth $2.9 billion) and former basketball superstar Michael Jordan (worth $1 billion).

VIDEO LINK

To find out more about the 'Fight for 15' movement, watch the following two short video clips at www.brightredbooks.net

ONLINE TEST

Test yourself on the socio-economic issues in the USA at www.brightredbooks.net

 ## THINGS TO DO AND THINK ABOUT

1. Describe the societal problems that an average Gini coefficient of 0.45 could bring to the USA in the future.
2. Describe two factors associated with the rise of income inequality in the USA.
3. What is the 'Fight for 15' movement? (Watch the recommended video clip to help you.)
4. Explain why a falling number of middle-class Americans would be of concern to American politicians.

REDUCING SOCIO-ECONOMIC ISSUES IN THE USA

US GOVERNMENT POLICIES TO REDUCE ECONOMIC INEQUALITY AND THEIR EFFECTIVENESS

For some time now, income inequality has been a significant economic concern for the US government, and will be a considerable factor in the 2016 Presidential Election. According to official poverty figures, one in seven American citizens currently live in poverty.

Government programs reduce poverty
Supplemental Poverty Rate, with and without targeted government programs (2013)

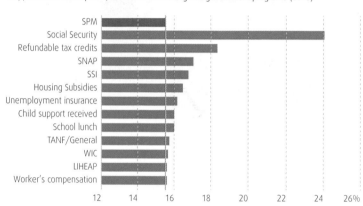

Notes: The red bar shows the actual SPM poverty rate for 2013. The blue bars show what the SPM poverty rate would have been in the absence of the specified program.

Source: Author's analysis of Short, Kathleen. 2014. 'The Research Supplemental Poverty Measure: 2013.' U.S. Census Bureau

US government success

As shown in the diagram, which is based on the **Supplemental Poverty Measure** (SPM), US government intervention has been critical in fighting poverty. The three most effective government poverty-reduction measures have been:

- social security (for example, unemployment benefit)
- refundable tax credits (for example, Earned Income Tax Credit (EITC))
- Supplemental Nutrition Assistance Programme (SNAP, previously known as food stamps).

President Obama has attempted to reduce inequality by increasing the taxes imposed on the more affluent sections of society, and through legislation such as the **Affordable Care Act**, while, at the same time, providing tax credits for those most in need. In January 2015, Obama outlined plans to provide free community college education and reduce mortgage insurance premiums for middle-class Americans. However, this announcement sparked controversy, as this can only be financed by further progressive taxation. This is unlikely to succeed as both chambers of Congress are now controlled by the Republican Party, who do not believe that increasing welfare programmes will solve the nation's inequality problem.

American Recovery and Reinvestment Act (2009)

The **American Recovery and Reinvestment Act (2009)** helped to limit the catastrophic impact of the global recession by providing additional funds for programmes including;

- **SNAP/food banks** (+$20 billion) to combat hunger and prevent ill-health
- **Homelessness Prevention Funds** (+$1.5 billion) to reduce homelessness
- **Weatherisation Assistance Programme** (+$5 billion) to combat fuel poverty
- **Workforce Investment System** (almost $4 billion) to help make work pay.

Temporary Aid to Needy Families

Under the **Temporary Aid to Needy Families** (TANF) programme, individual states receive funding from the federal government to devise initiatives which provide funding and/or support services to needy families, in order to help to create and maintain the traditional family unit, promote self-sufficiency and reduce the need for state assistance. Forms of support include both employability and childcare support. In 2013, the US government spent $17 billion on the TANF programme.

'Based on tax policy alone, Obama has slightly increased the income of the poor, and more significantly reduced the income of the rich.'

Tax Policy Centre, 2014

SOCIAL INEQUALITY

Current health risks in the USA

According to the OECD, the USA currently spends almost $3 trillion on health care each year. However, many American's die from non-communicable diseases (NCDs) such as heart disease, diabetes, obesity and lung cancer which are preventable and are linked with unhealthy lifestyles including excessive alcohol consumption, lack of exercise and unhealthy diets. These diseases have a significant economic cost, not only in terms of the cost of treatment, but also the cost of reduced workforce productivity.

The following diseases are of particular concern to the US government:

- **Heart disease** – Responsible for 25% of all American deaths.
- **Obesity** – According to the Centres for Disease Control and Prevention, over 35% of American adults were defined as being clinically obese between 2009 and 2012. A report by the Trust for America's Health and the Robert Wood Johnson Foundation forecasts that obesity rates will exceed 60% in 25% of US states in the next 15 years.
- **Non-alcoholic fatty liver disease** (NAFLD) – In February 2015, the American Liver Foundation concluded that up to 25% of the US population were suffering from NAFLD, caused by a build-up of excess fat in the liver. NAFLD is closely linked to obesity and will result in increased need for liver transplants.
- **Alzheimer's** – About five million Americans currently suffer from Alzheimer's and it's estimated 0.5 million die from it every year. The cost of caring for people who suffer from Alzheimer's stands at over $200 billion per annum. According to the Alzheimer's Association, over the next 30 years, these costs will explode to over $1.2 trillion.

Health care inequality

The graphic below highlights the variation in life expectancy (in years) by ethnic group. Asian Americans (87.3) and Latinos/Hispanics (83.5) fare particularly well compared to African Americans (74.3) and Native Americans (75.1).

Many African Americans grow up in environments which to do not make securing longevity easy. For example, lack of income, poor living conditions and increased exposure to violence can often result in premature death.

Overall United States	African Americans	Native Americans	Whites	Latinos	Asian Americans
78·6 years	**74·3** years	**75·1** years	**78·7** years	**83·5** years	**87·3** years

American life expectancy 2010–11
Source: American Human Development Project of the Social Science Research Council

According to the report, **Health Insurance Coverage in the United States: 2013**, over 40 million Americans had no access to medical insurance in 2013, including almost 25% of the Hispanic population. Of those that did, many relied on Medicaid, including 27.2% of African Americans and 23.5% of Hispanic Americans. This illustrates the income inequality that exists between different ethnic groups. A key aim of Obama's Affordable Care Act is to reduce the numbers of Americans without access to government and private health care – the so-called Medigap.

THINGS TO DO AND THINK ABOUT

1. Describe three of the US government's most effective poverty reduction measures.
2. Explain how Obama's administration has tried to reduce wealth inequality.
3. Describe two ways in which the American Recovery and Reinvestment Act (2009) helped some of the most vulnerable people in US society?
4. Explain why obesity and Alzheimer's pose a significant risk to the USA.
5. What conclusions can be drawn about life expectancy between each of the different minority ethnic groups in the USA? Provide statistics to support your answer.

FACT

The Obama administration argues that it has successfully supported African Americans. Support has included extending tax credits to help make work pay for over two million families, providing over $1 billion to help the unemployed find work and passing the American Recovery and Investment Act (2009) which has prevented nearly 1.5 African Americans from falling into poverty.

VIDEO LINK

To increase your understanding of the USA's health care system, including problems associated with **Medicare** and **Medicaid**, and the limitations of **Obamacare**, visit www.brightredbooks.net

DON'T FORGET

African Americans tend to have lower life expectancies than all other ethnic groups. They are more likely to suffer from the most common killer diseases such as heart disease, cancer and diabetes. They are also more likely to die young as a result of violence.

ONLINE TEST

Test yourself on reducing socio-economic issues in the USA at www.brightredbooks.net

SOCIO-ECONOMIC ISSUES IN THE USA: SOCIAL INEQUALITY

'To see that young African-American students – or babies, as I call them – are being suspended from pre-kindergarten programmes at such horrendous rates is deeply troubling… It's incredible to think about or fathom what pre-kindergarten students could be doing to get suspended from schools.'

Leticia Smith-Evans, Interim Director of Education Practice at NAACP Legal Defence and Educational Fund

DON'T FORGET

To recap on the general characteristics of suburban and ghetto schools in the USA, see page 103 of BrightRED's National 5 Modern Studies Study Guide.

FACT

Schools located within affluent districts of America tend to have better access to the **3 Ts** – teachers, textbooks and technology. This is because around 88% of school funding is obtained from state and local government.

FACT

With almost 50% of Asian and Pacific Islanders (AAPIs) over 25 having an undergraduate (or bachelors) degree, they are the most educated of all US ethnic groups.

VIDEO LINK

To watch a short BBC news report from March 2015, which highlights the chronic shortage of accommodation which has made 60 000 people homeless in New York, visit www. brightredbooks.net

EDUCATION INEQUALITY

Variations in public school spending and the widening gap in educational attainment

The USA spends about $550 billion per annum on education. However, according to Sheryll Cashin, professor of Law at Georgetown Law School, the quality of education a child receives is 'a lottery of birth'.

Schools in run-down areas are unable to spend enough money on essential resources, whereas schools in more affluent areas have resources in abundance. According to data obtained from the US Census, in 2012, New York City's school district spent $20 226 on each of its one million students, almost double the national average of $10 658, and considerably more than Brevard County, Florida, where the spend was $7 801 per student.

Research indicates that only 10% of students from the poorest American families (the bottom 12.5% of earners) gain entry to the country's top 146 colleges. This clearly indicates that wealth and academic performance are inextricably linked, and that many less affluent schools, are not preparing their students adequately for the college entry **Scholastic Aptitude Test** (SAT).

Racial inequality in education

Data obtained from a 2014 Civil Rights Survey carried out by the US Department for Education, which examined all of America's 97 000 public schools concluded that during the 2011–12 academic year, racial inequality was inherent throughout the US education system. Some key findings were that some ethic groups, particularly those of African American, Native American and Hispanic origin were disadvantaged in relation to:

- **Quality of teacher** – African American, Native American and Hispanic students (3–4%) were more likely to be taught by partially qualified (probationer) teachers who lacked experience, when compared to white students (1%).
- **Access to curriculum** – African American, Native American and Hispanic students were much less likely to be able to study science, technology, engineering and maths (STEM) beyond introductory level than white students. The findings indicated that: 'A third of the schools with the highest percentage of African American and Hispanic students did not offer chemistry'.
- **Discipline** – African American and Native American students were found to be excluded from school at disproportionate rates. This was evident from pre-school stage, where African Americans accounted for nearly 50% of repeat suspensions despite only making up 18% of school enrolment. African American females were excluded from school more than all other ethnic females, and most males.

US schools are under fierce pressure to improve the treatment and attainment of minority Americans, in order to mitigate against the risk of America losing its global competitiveness.

HOUSING INEQUALITY

According to the **National Low Income Housing Coalition** (NLIHC), demand for housing in the USA outstrips supply, with 31 affordable homes available for every 100 families who need them. Renting a home is fast becoming the only option for many American families due to reduced savings and bad debt, partly due to the global recession. African Americans are 45% more likely than white Americans to rent rather than own their homes.

contd

Home ownership

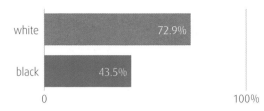

Second quarter 2014 rate, Source U.S. Census Bureau

2014 US home ownership, (Source: US Census Bureau)

There has been a significant decline in homeownership rates among African Americans and Hispanics – Whites and Asians are more likely to be approved for mortgages.

Many Americans are forced to move area in order to reduce their housing spend. There has also been an increase in the number of families who co-habit.

Over 55% of African Americans rent their home, considerably less than America's white population. This problem has been amplified by the particularly damaging effect that the recession had on the wealth of African Americans, reducing their total wealth by almost 50%.

The table on the right illustrates that the recession has had a massive impact on the ability of individuals to secure credit to buy a home, particularly African Americans and Hispanics.

Mortgage data by race (2011)

Race	Application rate	Approval rate
White	63%	73.4%
African American	12.1%	2.0%
Asian	4.6%	7.0%
Hispanic	17.3%	4.5%

Source: Home Mortgage Disclosure Act Data, 2012

ONLINE TEST

Test yourself on the socio-economic issues in the USA at www.brightredbooks.net

FACT

Over 40% of people living in Los Angeles pay out more than 50% of their income in order to meet their housing needs.

INEQUALITY IN THE US CRIMINAL JUSTICE SYSTEM

In August 2013, the **Sentencing Project**, a group that attempts to address racial disparities within the US criminal justice system, submitted a report to the UN Human Rights Committee which asserted that the USA was violating the International Covenant on Civil and Political Rights. The report argued that racial minorities in the USA were more likely than whites to be arrested, convicted and sentenced. The report also stated that:

- According to Justice Department Data, during the period between 1980 and 2010, African American youth were arrested 'at more than twice the rate of white youth for drugs-related crime'. In the six-year period between 1999 and 2005, African Americans accounted for '13% of drug users, but 46% of those convicted for drug offences'.
- '1 in 3 African American males, born in 2013, can expect to go to prison at some point in their life, compared to 1 in 6 Hispanic males, and I in 17 white males.'
- As many more African and Hispanic Americans live on a low income they are less likely to be able to afford expensive private lawyers. Instead they are more often represented by court-appointed lawyers 'from agencies that are underfunded and understaffed'.

Criticism continues to be directed towards white police officers who use unnecessary force on African Americans. One of the most high profile examples of late took place in April 2015, when South Carolina police officer Michael Slager, shot dead African American Walter Scott after pulling him over for a broken brake light. Slager, who fired eight times at defenceless Scott, has been charged with murder. Slager attempted to justify his actions by claiming he was in danger, but this claim was disproven by a mobile phone video captured by a member of the public. Slager has also been accused of using his Taser on another North Charleston African American without sufficient cause to do so.

According to the Sentencing Project, 'since the nature of law enforcement frequently requires police officers to make snap judgements about the danger posed by suspects and the criminal nature of their activity, subconscious racial associations influence the way officers perform their jobs'.

US prison population (sentenced) by gender and race

White male	African American male	Hispanic male	Total male (including other groups and mixed race)
454 100	526 000	314 600	1 412 745

White female	African American female	Hispanic female	Total female
51 500	23 100	17 600	104 134

Source: Bureau of Justice Statistics, National Prisoner Statistics Programme 2013

'The United States now incarcerates more African Americans as a percentage than apartheid South Africa did.'

Nicholas Kristof, *New York Times*.

FACT

The FBI estimate that the USA is home to 33 000 gangs with approximately 1.4 million members.

THINGS TO DO AND THINK ABOUT

1. What evidence is there of a close link between wealth and educational attainment?
2. Explain why many African Americans experience racial inequality in education.
3. Explain why organisations like the Sentencing Project argue that African Americans are treated unfairly by the US criminal justice system. Give at least three reasons.

GOVERNMENT POLICIES TO REDUCE SOCIAL INEQUALITY AND THEIR EFFECTIVENESS

The **Affordable Care Act** (ACA) is President Obama's flagship domestic policy which aims to roll out affordable health insurance across the USA. The policy attempts to achieve this in a number of ways including increased provision of Medicaid, increased provision of tax credits (to both individuals and employers), increased progressive taxation (to ensure the rich contribute more) and a reduction in wasteful health care spending.

Percentage of uninsured Americans (*Source: Gallup-Healthways*)

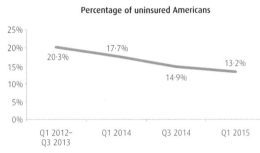

Percentage of uninsured Americans

HEALTH ACHIEVEMENTS: HOW SUCCESSFUL IS THE ACA?

Successes

The graph illustrates the decline of uninsured Americans following the introduction of the ACA.

Between October 2013 and March 2015, the number of US citizens without any form of health care insurance decreased by 16.4 million. This is a reduction of approximately 35%, and is the sharpest decline in four decades.

The ACA is helping to tackle poverty within vulnerable groups including African Americans and Hispanics, with both groups experiencing significant reductions in uninsured rates, of 9.2% and 12.3% respectively.

The Obama administration has invested more money in preventing and treating medical ailments which result in a higher death rate among African Americans. Groups such as Asian American Pacific Islanders (AAPIs) are no longer prevented from joining health care plans due to pre-existing medical conditions such as hepatitis B which is particularly prominent among young AAPIs (19–24). Over 1000 community health centres, where one-third of all patients are Hispanic, have witnessed an increase in funding. According to President Obama, 'this law is saving money for families and businesses. This law is also saving lives'.

Criticisms

- Approximately 63% of Americans wish the law to be abolished.
- The **Congressional Budget Office** (CBO), estimated that by 2023, over 30 million Americans will still be uninsured.
- The CBO estimated that Obamacare, over the next ten years, will drastically exceed the programme's forecast budget of $1 trillion by 0.8 trillion, costing the USA circa $1.8 trillion.

EDUCATION ACHIEVEMENTS

Successes

The Obama administration has invested heavily in the US education system and aims to make education accessible for all. Approximately $40 billion has been invested in **Pell Grants** to help America's less affluent pay for college. Pell Grants have benefited over 60% of African American students and almost 25% of Hispanic and AAPI students. Almost $3 billion has also been invested in **Historically Black Colleges and Universities** (HBCU) to encourage more African Americans to matriculate to higher education.

Within the **American Recovery and Reinvestment Act** (2009), programmes such as **Race to the Top** and **Head Start** have resulted in:

- $4 billion in funding to support 22 million students
- 1.5 million teachers employed to improve the education of 42 000 students in 19 states
- creation of projects to raise student attainment in states such as Tennessee.

DON'T FORGET

Named after US Senator Claiborne Pell, a Pell Grant is financial support provided by the US Federal Government which helps students of low-income families attend college or university.

contd

- $5 billion to fund early learning programmes, such as Head Start, which has had significant enrolments from minority groups including Hispanics (37%). Over 11,000 AAPI children have also enrolled in Head Start.

The current phase of the **Elementary and Secondary Education Act** of 1965 (ESEA), the **No Child Left Behind Act of 2001** (NCLB), has continued to ensure that federal government funds are available for poor school districts in a bid to raise the attainment and educational opportunity of students from low-income families.

NCLB has been commended for:

- attempting to narrow the attainment gap between whites and ethnic minorities
- creating a climate of increased accountability for teachers and schools. Schools, districts and states must report on overall performance and the academic scores of disadvantaged groups such as low-income, disabled and ethnic minority students.

Criticisms

The Race to the Top Programme has received criticism for being inaccessible to a number of states due to strict conditions attached to gaining the grants. This obstacle has affected states such as California, where the Governor considered making changes to the state's education system in order to help improve their chances of securing funding.

No Child Left Behind (NCLB) has received criticism for creating a culture where staff and schools are under pressure to raise attainment or lose funding.

HOUSING ACHIEVEMENTS

Successes

From February–April 2015, the US Department of Housing and Urban Development (HUD) announced funding for projects to assist vulnerable groups, including:

- $1.8 billion for public housing authorities to significantly improve their housing stock
- $150 million to help low-income disabled people pay their rent
- $24 million for the **Jobs-Plus Pilot Programme** to help the residents of nine public housing authorities increase their earning power to become more self-sufficient
- $65 million to help over 9000 homeless veterans find a home.

Criticisms

- **High taxpayer costs** – According to the Cato Institute, in 2014, the cost of HUD was $341 per US household. This is estimated to increase to over $46 billion in 2015.
- **Financial mismanagement** – It has been asserted that HUD has provided some programmes with funding that has been abused.
- **Vouchers** – The value of HUD vouchers does not accurately reflect market conditions, resulting in some landlords refusing to accept them.

CRIMINAL JUSTICE SERVICE ACHIEVEMENTS

Successes

Recent developments have included:

- the 2010 **Fair Sentencing** Act which reduced sentencing disparities between blacks and whites in relation to drug possession
- $263 million to increase police officers' use of body-worn cameras
- a team of researchers funded to look at racial bias in law enforcement and to suggest possible interventions to improve the situation.

Criticisms

Despite efforts from the US government to improve the treatment of minority groups, tensions still run deep, with some US police departments being accused of racism. Consequently, violence has continued to occur in areas like Ferguson, Missouri.

THINGS TO DO AND THINK ABOUT

1 What evidence is there that minority groups are treated less favourably than whites?

DON'T FORGET

HBCUs were established in the early 1960s with the purpose of accommodating African American students. Today, there are still over 100 HBCUs in the USA, although many of them now attract high percentages of non-African American students also.

ONLINE

To find out more detailed information about President Obama's Race to the Top Programme, read 'Setting the Pace: Expanding Opportunity for America's Students under Race to the Top' at www.brightredbooks.net

VIDEO LINK

To watch a short video clip of President Obama in May 2015 announcing $250 billion for e-books for low income students as well as giving 99% of students access to high-speed internet via the ConnectED initiative, visit www.brightredbooks.net

ONLINE

For up to the minute press releases on all HUD activity, visit www.brightredbooks.net

VIDEO LINK

Watch the short video clip which describes the tension that has occurred following shootings of both African American youths and police officers at www.brightredbooks.net

ONLINE TEST

Test yourself on the socio-economic issues in the USA at www.brightredbooks.net

INTERNATIONAL RELATIONS: USA'S INVOLVEMENT IN INTERNATIONAL ORGANISATIONS

US membership of selected key international organisations

Name of organisation	Year of entry
Food and Agriculture Organisation* (FAO)	1945
Asia-Pacific Economic Cooperation* (APEC)	1989
International Monetary Fund* (IMF)	1945
World Bank* (WB)	1945
Nuclear Energy Agency* (NEA)	1976
United Nations (UN) General Assembly and Security Council*	1945
Group of 7* (G7)	1975
International Fund for Agricultural Development* (IFAD)	1977
World Trade Organisation* (WTO)	1995
World Meteorological Organisation (WMO)	1949

*denotes USA as being a founding member

IMF Factfile

Membership	188 member countries
Established	1945
Headquarters	Washington D.C.
Key aims include:	• Promoting international monetary cooperation. • Facilitating the expansion and balanced growth of international trade. • Making resources available to members experiencing balance of payments difficulties.
Key functions include:	• Surveillance – keeping a close eye on the international monetary system and 'financial policies of members' • Lending – providing loans to member countries in times of need. • Technical assistance – providing guidance, support and training to member countries to improve their economic policy and better manage their finances.

Source: IMF

FACT

In March 2014, the USA, supported by Canada, France, Germany, Italy, Japan and the UK decided to suspend Russia from the G8 in retaliation to Vladimir Putin's annexation of Crimea from the Ukraine. As a result, the G8 became the G7.

ONLINE

For up-to-date trade statistics which illustrate the importance of the US-APEC relationship, visit www.brightredbooks.net

USA'S MEMBERSHIP OF INTERNATIONAL ORGANISATIONS

The USA continues to be the most influential country in the world. It has been a founder member of many of the world's leading international organisations and continues to play an active and effective part in these organisations. The USA is at the centre of many of the key global decisions and exercises dominance over matters ranging from international economic policy to global security. The table shows US membership of ten key international organisations and highlights the year in which it gained entry.

USA and IMF

With 16.7% of voting shares, the USA is the IMF's most powerful and influential member and is the only country able to veto changes to the organisation's rules and governance. In recent years there have been attempts to restructure decision-making within the IMF by allowing other nations (such as the so-called BRICS countries) a greater say. However, reform has been blocked by the US Congress leading to allegations that the US is putting its own self-interest before that of the greater global economic good.

Addressing the House of Representatives Financial Services Committee in March 2015, US Treasury Secretary, Jacob Lew, stated 'Our continued failure to approve the IMF quota and governance reforms is causing other countries, including some of our allies, to question our commitment to the IMF and other multinational institutions that we worked to create and that advance important US and global economic and security interests'.

Many senior US figures are concerned that existing IMF members may look towards new institutions for assistance in the future including the BRICS-created **New Development Bank** (NDB) and the China-led **Asian Infrastructure Investment Bank** (AIIB).

USA and the Asia-Pacific Economic Cooperation

The Asia-Pacific Economic Cooperation (APEC) forum was established in 1989 with an initial membership of 12. Its main aim is to have free trade across the Asia-Pacific region by 2020, achieved by trade and investment liberalisation, business facilitation and economic and technical cooperation.

Membership of APEC greatly benefits the USA. It provides trade opportunities in an immense market which accounts for 40% of the world's population and circa 60% of its GDP.

The USA imports more goods from APEC countries than it exports to them. In 2013, the trade deficit was $509.7 billion.

USA and the United Nations

The USA is a founding member of the UN, holds a permanent seat on the United Nations Security Council and plays a full role within the organisation. Today, New York City is home to the UN's official headquarters and five out of the six main UN organs;

contd

the General Assembly, the Security Council, the Economic and Social Council, the Trusteeship Council and the Secretariat.

Case Study: US Support for Syria

In March 2015, the US Permanent Representative to the UN, Ambassador Samantha Power, addressed the Third Humanitarian Pledging Conference for Syria stating 'More than four years after the conflict began, people across Syria are struggling to survive in a state of perpetual siege...No matter what else is going on, addressing the plight of Syrians must remain at the top of our agenda'.

The USA is the largest donor of humanitarian aid to Syria, having provided in excess of $3 billion in assistance since the conflict began.

US Government contributions to the Syria humanitarian response (March 2011-March 2015)

USAID/Office of US Foreign Disaster Assistance (OFDA)	$610 870 250
USAID/Office of Food for Peace (FFP)	$1 421 570 725
USAID/Bureau of Population, Refugees and Migration (PRM)	$1 646 725 086
Total US Government assistance to the Syria humanitarian response	**$3 679 166 061**

Source: The United States Agency for International Development (USAID) 31.03.15

The USA has attempted to address a number of human rights concerns through its participation in the United Nation's **Human Rights Council** (HRC). The USA has been actively involved in renewing mandates and passing and opposing resolutions affecting countries such as Burma and Israel. As a permanent member of the UNSC, the USA has expressed concern about nuclear weapons programmes in countries such as Iran.

US Support to the UN

The USA is the largest financial contributor to the UN, a situation that has been consistent since the organisation was founded in 1945. In line with UN membership rules, the USA is required to pay the maximum assessed contribution to the UN regular budget (22%) which is based on the country's gross national product (GNP). In 2015, the USA is required to contribute $654 778 938. In addition to being the largest contributor to the regular budget, the USA was also the largest financial contributor to UN peacekeeping operations and was required to pay 28.38% between 2013 and 2015.

Ambassador Samantha Power, United States Permanent Representative to the UN

However, despite being a high financial contributor to the aforementioned budgets, the USA is often criticised for making an insufficient human contribution in terms of police, troops and military experts. As of February 2015, the USA provided support which comprised of 77 police, 6 military experts and 36 troops, a modest total of 119 UN peacekeepers. This contribution is miniscule compared to countries like Bangladesh and India, who were contributing 9446 and 8116 peacekeepers respectively by the end of February 2015. Some of this imbalance is due to US public and political opinion which is largely against US soldiers being placed under the command of anyone other than the US military.

THINGS TO DO AND THINK ABOUT

1 How can it be argued that the USA is an influential member of the IMF? Make at least two points.
2 Explain why many nations, including the BRICS countries, are unhappy with the US Congress.
3 Explain why the USA might be concerned with the New Development Bank (NDB) and the Asian Infrastructure Investment Bank (AIIB).
4 What arguments are there for and against the view that the USA contributes too little to the UN in terms of peacekeeping?
5 Why is it important that UN member states pay their contributions on time and in full?

ONLINE

To read more about the removal of Russia from the G8 visit www.brightredbooks.net

VIDEO LINK

Watch US President, Barack Obama addressing the 69th session of the United Nations General Assembly on 24 September 2014 at www.brightredbooks.net

ONLINE

For a detailed and up-to-date overview of USA's ongoing contribution to the UN's main bodies, visit www.brightredbooks.net

FACT

As of July 2015, the USA was responsible for providing almost $190 000 000 of humanitarian assistance to Yemen.

DON'T FORGET

In October 2014, it was reported by the *Guardian* newspaper that the USA owed $800 million to the UN regular budget and $337 million to the UN peacekeeping budget which contributed to a total UN funding gap of $3.5 billion. These claims were refuted by US officials.

ONLINE TEST

Test yourself on USA's role in international relations at www.brightredbooks.net

INTERNATIONAL RELATIONS: USA'S RELATIONSHIPS WITH OTHER COUNTRIES

US–RUSSIA RELATIONS

Recent US–Russia tensions

Selected findings from 2014 and 2015 Gallup polls

Country	2014	2015
Russia	9%	18%
North Korea/Korea	16%	15%
China	20%	12%
Iran	16%	9%
Iraq	7%	8%

Source: Gallup, February 2015

The results of a Gallup poll from February 2015 indicate that the USA's relationship with Russia has deteriorated in recent years. When a sample of Americans were asked the question:

'What one country anywhere in the world do you consider to be the United States' greatest enemy today?'

The top five results were as shown in the table to the left.

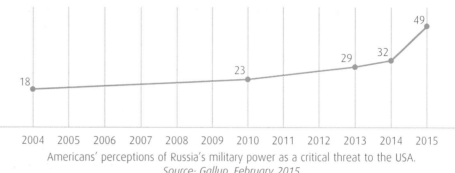

% critical threat

18 · 2004
23 · 2010
29 · 2012
32 · 2013
49 · 2015

2004 2005 2006 2007 2008 2009 2010 2011 2012 2013 2014 2015

Americans' perceptions of Russia's military power as a critical threat to the USA.
Source: Gallup, February 2015

The USA's relationship with Russia has continued to deteriorate throughout 2015, with both countries opting to spend billions on defence. Russia has invested heavily in developing a new cruise missile system, which the USA claims violates the 1987 **Intermediate-range Nuclear Forces** (INF) treaty which aimed to reduce and control nuclear arms. The USA is also concerned by reports that Russia is intending to supply Iran with S-300 missiles. Iran is a lucrative market, and when sanctions are lifted, both Washington and the Kremlin are keen to benefit from access to Iranian oil and other raw materials. Tensions have also surfaced between the USA and Russia as a result of Russia's actions in Ukraine and their support of Bashar al-Assad in Syria.

To find about current US–Sino tensions, turn to the China section of this Study Guide.

USA'S POWER AND INTERNATIONAL INFLUENCE

Economic power

Apple Inc. is currently one of the USA's most successful companies, amassing over $8.5 billion profit in the last quarter of 2014 due to the success of products such as the iPhone 6.

In 2014, the USA was replaced by China as the world's leading economy, a position which the USA has dominated since 1872. However, the USA unquestionably remains an economic force for a number of reasons, including:

- Output and innovation – the USA is responsible for producing about 20% of the world's total output. The USA is home to many entrepreneurs and has created many iconic products which are highly sought after around the world.
- GDP per capita – the USA has one of the highest GDP per capita in the world.
- Natural resources – the USA has access to a multitude of natural resources including farmland, oil and fresh water.
- Political system – the USA has one government and one currency which helps the country maintain a strong economic position.

To find more about China replacing USA as the world's largest economy, turn to the China section of this Study Guide.

contd

Cultural influence

The USA's cultural influence extends across the world, reaching a global audience of about two billion people. American entertainment such as TV sitcoms, films, music and computer games are extremely popular and have resulted in widespread **Americanisation**. American influence is further emphasised around the globe through uptake of American sports such as baseball, basketball and American football, and demand for American food outlets such as Burger King, KFC and Pizza Hut.

Although the vast majority of the two billion people making up the audience for American entertainment will have never visited the USA, they will be aware of most of the personalities and brands shown in this table.

TV shows	Films	Successful American businesses /products	Singers
The Big Bang Theory	Terminator Genisys	Nike	Jay Z
The Walking Dead	Jurassic World	Apple Inc.	Usher
Game of Thrones	Furious 7	McDonald's	Katy Perry
NCIS	The Amazing Spider-Man	Google	Taylor Swift
Gotham	Taken 3	Walt Disney	Eminem

Military strength

Despite recent findings from a new annual report, the **2015 Index of US Military Strength**, which concluded that the USA would be 'ill-equipped to handle two, near simultaneous major regional contingencies', the USA is without question the most powerful military nation on Earth. The USA's 2015 defence spend is estimated to be between $550 and $612 billion, which is more than that of China, Russia, Saudi Arabia, France and the UK put together. The USA has 1.4m active frontline personnel and a reserve force of 1.1m who have access to state-of-the-art weaponry and are highly trained. The US military has a well-stocked arsenal which includes 20 aircraft carriers, almost 14 000 aircraft (including the B-2A Spirit stealth bomber), 72 submarines and approximately 8848 tanks. The US government is constantly developing new technology, for example, the US Navy's new Electromagnetic Railgun, which has the capability to intercept incoming missiles. The USA has allies throughout the world, and is unrivalled in terms of nuclear warheads with over 7 700.

World significance

The USA enjoys enormous political, economic and military strength, and, as a result, has many influential allies throughout the world including the UK, Canada, Japan and Germany. The USA has a dynamic and innovative workforce, excellent infrastructure and access to an abundance of natural resources which help to fuel its successful economy.

However, following the rise to prominence of countries such as China, India and Russia, the extent of the USA's significance is now being increasingly questioned. A 2014 poll by Forbes Magazine ranked Vladimir Putin as the most powerful man in the world, followed by Barack Obama in second place and Xi Jinping in third place.

Controversially, the USA is often regarded as the 'policeman of the world', due to its active involvement, some would say interference, in the domestic matters of other countries. Addressing the UN in September 2014, Barack Obama, spoke about the importance of the USA playing a lead role in combatting militant groups such as Islamic State and helping Ukraine deal with Russian aggression. He stated 'If we lift our eyes beyond our borders – if we think globally and act co-operatively – we can shape the course of this century as our predecessors shaped the post-World War Two age'.

THINGS TO DO AND THINK ABOUT

1 Explain why Russia, China and North Korea were each seen as the USA's greatest enemies in a Gallup Poll of 2015.
2 Explain two factors which have helped the USA to maintain its position as an economic superpower.
3 What evidence is there that the USA remains the world's most powerful military nation?
4 The USA spends disproportionately more on its military than most other developed countries. What consequences might exceptionally high military spending have on domestic spending such as education, health care and housing?
5 For what reasons could it be argued that the USA is not as influential as it was a few years ago? Give at least two explanations.
6 Essay practice: Analyse the causes of wealth inequality in the USA.
7 Essay practice: Evaluate the success of a recent US government policy to reduce poverty in the USA.

B-2A Spirit stealth bomber

ONLINE

If you are interested in this topic, and want to explore it in more detail, access the Heritage Foundation's 2015 Index of US Military Strength at www. brightredbooks.net

VIDEO LINK

Watch the video clip which shows US President Barack Obama speaking about the USA's influence in the world from its historical involvement in Kosovo and Bosnia to current diplomatic efforts in Palestine, Israel and the Ukraine at www. brightredbooks.net.

ONLINE TEST

Test yourself on the USA's role in international relations at www. brightredbooks.net

ONLINE

Head to www. brightredbooks.net for advice on how to approach these essay questions and sample answers

UNIT ASSESSMENT: CONCLUSIONS

DRAWING AND SUPPORTING CONCLUSIONS USING SOURCES

Use a range of sources of information to draw and support conclusions about international issues, focusing on either a major world power or a significant world issue.

ONLINE

A model answer is shown here, make other conclusions using sources online at www.brightredbooks.net

Outcome 1.1: Draw a conclusion

You must draw a conclusion **using between two and four** sources of information.

> **Example:**
>
> *High living standards in China are now increasingly determined by the geographical location in which you are based. If you live in urban China, you are likely to be far healthier and wealthier than those living in rural China.*

Outcome 1.2: Synthesise and evaluate evidence

You must synthesise and evaluate evidence in order to support a conclusion about an international issue **using between two and four** sources of information.

> **Example:**
>
> *I conclude that [state conclusion]. My conclusion is backed up by the evidence in sources ... which show that ... This is further supported by the evidence in source ... which clearly illustrates ...*

WORKED EXAMPLE

Individuals living in urban China are much more likely to be wealthy than those individuals living in rural China. Source 2 indicates that approximately 30% of people in rural provinces such as Guizhou and Sichuan are living in poverty, compared with only 10% in cities such as Shanghai and Beijing. This is supported by the evidence in Source 1, which highlights that urban residents have far greater disposable incomes than their rural counterparts. For example, the average resident in Tianjin has a disposable income of circa $2900, compared to $898, which is the disposable income of someone living in Yunnan. This vast inequality means that urban residents are far more likely to have access to commodities such as cookers and fridges. This is clearly evidenced in the table in Source 3, which shows a 40% differential in cooker ownership between urban and rural residents.

My conclusion is further supported by Source 4, a report entitled 'Income Inequality in Today's China' which indicates that the urban/rural gap is a major factor (>10%) contributing towards China's wage gap. Higher salaries for urban residents mean that they are far more likely to afford private medical insurance. This is illustrated in Source 2, a comparison table which shows that many rural residents rely on herbal remedies and barefoot doctors to cure them as they are unable to afford expensive medication in modern urban hospitals. This means that rural residents are more likely to die from preventable illnesses due to the fact they lack the ability to pay for treatment.

It is based on this evidence, that I conclude, that high living standards in China, namely wealth and health, are now increasingly determined by the geographical location in which you are based.